PRAISE FOR

BALM

"I needed help, but this book wasn't available for me and my family...My story didn't end well; my son died from his addiction. If you or anyone you know has a relative suffering from addiction, this book is for you. ...Bev will give you and your family the best chance to save the life of those with the disease of addiction. This can also bring your family the normalcy and peace that all families deserve."
— **Anthony J. LaGreca**
Bereavement Facilitator for Parents with an Opioid Death
Hope Floats Healing and Wellness Center, Kingston, MA
(www.hopefloatswellness.org)
Activist, FED UP! Coalition to End the Opioid Epidemic

"In her book, *BALM: The Loving Path to Family Recovery*, Beverly Buncher uses our 6 Stages of Change model through the lens of how the process applies to families faced with a loved one's struggles. This book gives families a path to follow through the stages of denial and demoralization, to ambivalence, to planning, to working on the BALM family recovery program, to sticking with it, to completion. Her book helps families to be informed, transformed with love in their approach to their family member with an addiction, and supported along the way."
— **Janice and James Prochaska**
Coauthors of *Changing to Thrive*

"As a Master Certified Coach and Director of Coach Training at the BALM Institute, I have appreciated the privilege of witnessing the transformational power of the BALM approach for families living with loved ones suffering with addiction issues, as well as for the coaches applying these principles in their coaching and their everyday lives. Beverly Buncher is the catalyst of a movement for healing. This book provides inspiring stories and step-by-step practical strategies, principles, and tools. She tells it straight with her vulnerability and transparency. She walks the talk. In the past three years, I have witnessed her apply the BALM approach in her personal life, her professional life, and her relationships, including in her marriage. The fundamental healing BALM for every issue has been this path of *Be A Loving Mirror.*

"Let this book be your call to action.
The time for change is now."

— **Fran Fisher**
Master Certified Coach
Lifetime Achievement Award 2012, ICF Washington State
Deepening the Transformational Zone
Author of *Calling Forth Greatness: Seven Coaching Wisdoms for Transforming Your Life*

The BALM is an empowering tool for my recovery. I would love for everyone hurting because of a loved one's addiction to experience this program. It works."
— **Betty Kreider, BFRC**

The BALM is more than comprehensive learning - it's fast-track learning, which is vital when you have a using loved one."
— **Lisa Costa, CBFRLC, CRLC**

BALM

BEVERLY A. BUNCHER

BALM

THE LOVING PATH TO FAMILY RECOVERY

PEACH ELEPHANT PRESS

This book is designed to provide information that the author believes to be accurate on the subject matter it covers, and is written from the author's personal experience. In the text that follows, many people's and company's names and identifying characteristics have been changed, so that any resemblance to actual persons, living or dead, events, companies or locales is entirely coincidental.

Any references to resources and materials produced by other entities are purely the author's own interpretation. The author does not imply an endorsement from any of the sources cited within this book.

ISBN 978-0-473-43357-4 (PAPERBACK)
ISBN 978-0-473-43362-8 (EBOOK)

First Printing, 2018
Peach Elephant Press
CreateNonFiction.com

This book is dedicated to my cousin Alex Schachter, who was killed at the Parkland, FL shooting at Marjory Stoneman Douglas High School on February 14, 2018.

ALEX SCHACHTER

Though the shooter stole Alex and the other 17 souls from all of us physically, they live on in our hearts.

Alex was a gentle, light-filled soul who taught us all how to live in love throughout his life and left us a legacy of having a moment by moment appreciation of life in this poem he wrote a few weeks before his passing. First introduced to Alex's family and friends at his funeral by his brother, Ryan, and then to the world on CNN by his dad, Max, this poem has a profound message for everyone.

Neither Alex nor anyone in his immediate family has or had a use disorder, yet he was not a stranger to trauma or to renewal. He lost his mom, Debbie, at four, yet was blessed several years later with a new mom, Caryn, and two new sisters, Morgan and Avery.

Perhaps this poem, innocently written by a 14-year-old who loved rollercoasters can help us all take hold of our opportunities to live and love fully in each moment without judgment, fear, or malice, being there fully for ourselves and each other, as we are learning to do through our practice of BALM.

Alex's brilliance lives on through the words of his poem. Though we cannot bring him back, we can find comfort in his words, hoping that when his roller coaster stopped, he was renewed and on his way to the next leg of his journey. We can also easily imagine his loving nature living on, guiding him to wish only healing and hope for all left behind.

Thank you Alex. Your sweetness and light shone brightly during your days on this Earth and continue to carry us through our loss of you. May your words of wisdom touch each heart that sees or hears them.

Life is Like a Roller Coaster
by Alex Schachter

Life is like a roller coaster
It has some ups and downs
Sometimes you can take it slow or very fast
It may be hard to breathe at times
But you have to push yourself and keep going
Your bar is your safety
It's like your family and friends
You hold on tight and you don't let go
But sometimes you might throw your hands up
Because your friends and family will always be with you
Just like that bar keeping you safe at all times
It may be too much for you at times:
the twists, the turns, the upside downs
But you get back up
You keep chugging along
Eventually it comes to a stop
You won't know when or how
But you will know that'll be time to get off and start anew
Life is like a roller coaster

"Your only obligation to another adult human being is to be a loving person."
–Dawn C.

To two important people in my life:
My Al-Anon sponsor, Dawn C., and my husband, Alan Buncher.

Dawn C. has worked with me from 1985 to this day. Her wisdom, experience, and inspiration have had a tremendous impact on the woman I have become. She continues to listen to my challenges, give me sage advice, and guide my path as I move though life. We met one month after Alan and I got married. I had been praying for the right sponsor. One day I walked into a meeting, and she and her husband, Peter, were the speakers. Their message was exactly what I needed to hear that day, and I knew she was an answer to my prayers. Dawn and Peter helped Alan and me navigate our jagged pathways over the years, through good times and bad.

When I was deciding which population to serve as a beginning coach in 2008, my husband, Alan, newly sober from a relapse, pleaded with me to help families since there wasn't anyone focusing on them. He felt I had something to share that could make a difference. For that wise counsel, for walking the marriage path with me, and for being a BALM "test case" off and on for the past thirty-two years, I also dedicate this book to Alan. I have always said there are two kinds of couples: those who have challenges and break up and those who have challenges and stay together. So far, we have renewed our vows one year at a time, thus falling into the second category.

Alan, I love you with all my heart, and I thank you and Dawn for being there with me, over time, as the BALM and this book have blossomed.

Contents

PULL IT ALL TOGETHER

Author's Notes: About the BALM and Your Personal Beliefs or Faith

As the BALM has grown, we have welcomed families and coaches from all faith and nonfaith communities. It is not our intention to provide a specific exclusive path for spiritual growth. For some, this process of walking alongside a loved one who is struggling with a use disorder does become a spiritual journey. For others, though, it is an inner journey that involves growing in wisdom unrelated to a faith path. We have written the following statement to outline our approach to the diversity of belief, including faith and nonfaith of BALMers and those who may wish to join our community.

1. This is a program for all faiths that respects all faiths and beliefs. Your faith or beliefs are very personal to you. We always encourage you to seek and find the wise counsel and connection that you believe is true and right for you.

2. You may find that the tenets of your own religion or philosophy offer you the peace you need to help your family with recovery, or you may find yourself looking for additional help. For some, the BALM is a stand-alone family recovery program. For others, the BALM adds additional skills and tools to support their recovery program and/or way of life.

3. We respect everyone's perspective. The same word (such as *meditation*, *God*, or *Higher Power*) may have multiple meanings depending on your faith tradition or belief system. We encourage you to personalize these words to honor your own understanding.

To explore a few examples of the BALM being integrated into different faith-based perspectives, visit our private download page for readers of this book. You'll find the link on page 326.

Foreward

When I met Beverly Buncher, I knew I had met someone on a mission. Beverly is all about saving lives. She is extremely passionate in her quest to help others. And that help is needed more now than ever before. The opioid epidemic is out of control. The government says the United States has over nineteen million now suffering from the disease of addiction to opioids. This equates to nineteen million families who are suffering as well. Families need help if the addicted one has any chance of surviving and reaching sobriety. This book provides a blueprint with a step-by-step method for the family to get their lives back while helping the addict.

Beverly has put together the BALM philosophy, which stands for Be A Loving Mirror. This book will build off that philosophy's principles and teach you an effective approach to deal with a loved one suffering from addiction. I am a father whose son suffered from addiction for over eleven years, and we went through hell. I know from experience that I needed help, but this book wasn't available for me and my family. My story didn't end well; my son died from his addiction. I never thought it would get to that. I now live with a hole in my heart forever.

If you or anyone you know has a relative suffering from addiction, this book is for you. With her experience and the BALM method, Beverly will give you and your family the best chance to save the life of those with the disease of addiction. This can also bring your family the normalcy and peace that all families deserve.

Anthony J. LaGreca
Bereavement Facilitator for Parents with an Opioid Death.
Hope Floats Healing and Wellness Center, Kingston, MA
(www.hopefloatswellness.org)
Activist, FED UP! Coalition to End the Opioid Epidemic

Preface

Over nineteen million individuals suffer with substance use and other use disorders in the United States. For every one of them, there are five to ten family members affected by their use. That's a total of at least 95 to 190 million people affected by their own or someone else's use disorder.

If you're reading this book, you might be one of them.

If you're reading this book, you most likely know just how difficult it can be to cope with the lifestyle and behaviors of an individual with an active use disorder. You might be desperate for a way to help your loved one. Everybody's telling you to get rid of them, to kick them out or cut them off, but it doesn't feel right. Or maybe you're just feeling hopeless; you've tried countless "methods," and nothing so far has made a lick of difference. Maybe you're feeling confused; you've been told, as your loved one is careening out of control, that there's nothing you can do but stand by and watch.

Well folks, that just *isn't true*. I'm calling out that philosophy.

It's a lie to say there's nothing you can do.

Our whole program is based on the fact that there is *a lot* you can do, for your own health and well-being — and for the health and well-being of your loved one. You have the power to change yourself and change the way you interact, which often makes all the difference in the world. When you are in recovery, you are your loved one's *best chance* at recovery.

For a lot of people, the mindset presented in this book will totally realign their priorities, values, and actions and that's why it was written: to change the face of how society views the family's role in a loved one's recovery. Family members can serve as more than examples of how to live a life in recovery. They can also serve as partners actively engaged in potentially bringing their loved one's recovery about.

In one of our BALM family recovery education classes, a woman told us about how she'd been dealing with her daughter's issues for seven years and was getting nowhere. She was just following her around, hopeless and helpless, taking care of her daughter day and night, obsessed with her every move. That's not healthy for either party. She found the BALM and started to shift the way she acted toward her daughter. Within just a couple of weeks, her daughter made a decision to get well.

Another woman called me about a year and a half ago crying. Her son was an individual with use disorder. She was going to kick him out because she couldn't take it anymore. Instead, she joined the BALM program. Within a week, she had already written and held a loving conversation with her son and convinced him to go to treatment. Yes, you read that right: within a *week*.

People call us when they're hopeless. We start working together, and six months, even three months later, their son or daughter is sober, getting a job, living a life, getting ready to go back to school. This happens all the time in our work. Of course, just because someone gets clean doesn't mean it's permanent. But if you learn new ways to relate, you're not going to contribute to their relapse. You're contributing to recovery. You've become their best chance.

IF YOU'RE FEELING SKEPTICAL

You may be feeling skeptical right now. I get it. I understand you've been given a lot of promises. You've had a lot of people tell you they had your answer. I hear you. But this program has helped hundreds of people to come back from the brink, to regain their hope, to regain their relationships, and to see their loved one come back to life. We don't guarantee sobriety — no program can do that. But don't *you* want to be healthy, peaceful, calm, and aware? At the very least, after BALM, you will be in better shape than you're in now. Hopefully, you'll even be able to help your loved one.

I believe in this program fervently because I saw my own husband transform. The only thing that changed before that was me. Now, I've had proof over and over and over again as I've watched other families use these tools in the same way. At first, I just thought I was teaching some coaches how to help families. After all, this program is about being there for others in a powerful, helpful way. Then the coaches started telling me, *this is a movement.* People who use the BALM don't use it just to help their using loved one. They use the BALM every day, in every situation of their lives.

The BALM permeates everything you do, every conversation you have, the more you practice it. All it really involves is you being *your best self.* When you are healing, when you are at peace, when your focus is on loving effectively, that's when your loved one truly has the best chance at recovery. We will show you how.

QUESTIONS TO PONDER:

1. On a scale of 1—10, what is your level of peace, with 1 being, "I have none" and 10 being, "I am completely serene"?
2. Where would you like to be upon completing this book and its activities?

Acknowledgements

"Never doubt that a small group of thoughtful, committed citizens can change the world; indeed, it's the only thing that ever has."
— Margaret Mead

Recovery is a precious gift.

This book couldn't have happened without the gift of recovery, followed by lapses, followed by recovery in my husband's and my lives so that we could see how the process works in a family and what it takes for a family to be their loved one's best chance.

Drs. James Prochaska and James DiClemente changed my and countless other recovering persons' lives the day they came up with their Six Stages of Change Model. Enormous thanks to them and to Dr. Janice Prochaska who co-wrote *Changing to Thrive* with her husband. It is a wonderful book to help people with a variety of challenges use the transtheoretical model to enhance their lives! I'm so grateful to her for editing the BALM adaptations of their model to ensure we are getting it right.

Dr. William Miller and Dr. Stephen Rollnick's revolutionary model of Motivational Interviewing changed the way we speak to people going through great struggle, paving the way for a method such as BALM to take root in the hearts and minds of family members.

Tim Kelley, for his groundbreaking True Purpose® method, through which I found my purpose and began the journey of helping all families blaze the trail to recovery in their homes.

Alida Schuyler, the mother of recovery life coaching.

This book could not have happened without the dedication of the original Al-Anon members who worked diligently to uncover the way of being that is the foundation of the Be A Loving Mirror Method and way of life. Their willingness to learn a whole new way of peacefully relating to themselves and their struggling loved ones inspired generations of spouses and parents to keep the focus on improving themselves, while treating their suffering loved ones with dignity and respect.

Thank you to Lois Wilson and all of the Al-anon writers and members who created a program that has greatly lessened the suffering of families over the years.

My loving sponsor Dawn C. and the wonderful old timers in those meetings way back when, who taught me that a person is not a disease. That a person is always worthy of our love. That my primary spiritual purpose is to be a loving person.

The anonymous author of the Al-Anon book, *The Dilemma of the Alcoholic Marriage,* taught me how to let go of obsessing about another person's struggles, get support, and then lovingly share the facts I saw to that person at a later time. That formula helped me help my husband and morphed into the Be A Loving Mirror method over the years, thus helping over 1200 families in the past ten years, flying in the face of the tough love epidemic that seemed to warp the message of those original loving Al-Anon members.

The many families I have coached and taught over the years, especially those in the early years, who in essence helped me create the program by showing me what would — and would not — work to help them help their loved ones.

The 40+ certified and in-training BALM Coaches that have believed in the BALM and made a commitment to learning how to be BALMers themselves, and how to help family members the world over be and do so as well. Their dedication and determination has resulted in a growing movement of family recovery that is influencing the recovery world and everyone in it.

Those who have questioned the value of this work and the primacy of love and connection in a family's ability to influence a struggling loved one have helped those of us who understand these concepts get better at explaining it for the benefit of others.

Michael DeForbes, Lisa Costa, and Jim Graham all of whom studied in the first coach training cohort and have helped steer the BALM ship over the years, teaching courses, writing curriculum, and sharing the BALM in their own worlds.

Also at the core of the BALM movement: Marissa Arber, Fran Fisher, Jen Fisher, Jill Prevas, Jeff Spikes, Tracy Ward, and all of our wonderful faculty members and staff who inspire me to learn and grow everyday as we work together to fulfill our mission to help *all* families blaze the trail to recovery in their homes. As an old Yiddish quote says, "There are people who will run through fire for you and people will run up to the fire." These folks run through fire every day in order to help families be their loved ones' best chance at recovery.

Tony LaGreca, Zev Lanton, Marcus Benayon, Sue Barton, Austin Allen, your guidance and generosity in helping us get the word out to the world about the BALM method is more appreciated than words could ever say.

Our faculty in the BALM Institute, who field questions, and gently guide coaches and families to the open, non-judgmental path of love to which we all aspire. They inspire me daily as I listen to their lessons, hear their students' feedback and learn from and with them.

Beth Gross, Jean Harper, Lisa McDonald, and Marc Scannell for their teaching, curriculum writing, and piloting of new courses.

Thank you to Esbe van Heerden, Paul Carleton and the wonderful team at createnonfiction.com, who shepherded this project from beginning to end. I couldn't have done it without you!

To my family, the wonderful people who have had the patience over the years to embrace my various ways of being on the way to BALMing and who love me even when I am less than my best self.

To everyone who has walked this path with me, seeing up close my imperfections and what that quote "You teach best that which you most need to learn" really means — thank you for your patience and love.

Finally, to my Higher Power, whom I choose to call God and to whom I wrote the following prayer of surrender. Thank you for the journey, the people, the blessings, and the words along the way.

THE BALM SURRENDER PRAYER

Almighty One
I surrender all to you.
My ideas, my emotions,
my words, my behaviors.
My friends, family,
activities and possessions,
my life in its entirety.
I ask that you guide me
to lovingly accept and respect
the journey of each person whose life crosses my path.
I ask that you empower me to live life on life's terms,
with gratitude in my heart and joy in my step.
with willingness to Be A Loving Mirror to myself and others,
to serve You and those you place in my path,
I thank you in advance
for allowing your calming presence
to permeate my being and all that I think, say and do.
For allowing me to
Be my loved one's best chance at recovery,
And let go of all results,
with love, acceptance, and compassion in my heart.
AMEN.

Introduction

"A person who has mastered peace of mind has gained everything. To obtain peace of mind you need to be at peace with the people in your environment. You need to be at peace with yourself: your emotions and your desires. Furthermore, you need to be at peace with your Creator."
— Alei Shur, Volume 1, as cited in Zelig Pliskin's book *Gateway to Happiness*

Over the years, the quote above has been a guide to me. It summed up what I saw as the point of the Twelve Steps of Al-Anon. It summed up my understanding of how I was to relate to my God, myself, and the people I would come in contact with; it helped me to see the primacy of being at peace and to pursue peace in each of these areas: Spirit, self, and others.

MY SISTER'S SUBSTANCE USE DISORDER

When I was in my twenties, I had an apartment next door to my sister. Every night, I would hear the furniture in her place moving all night long, back and forth, like she couldn't decide where she wanted her bed to go. I honestly thought she was interested in interior decorating — maybe she was considering a new career path? What other explanation could there be for such erratic behavior?

I was obviously oblivious.

One night, she came to my door and told me: "Bev, I just want you to know that I'm an addict. I'm going to meetings every night because I'm an addict." That's when the noises stopped. See — she hadn't been attempting to try a stylish new job; she'd been on speed.

My sister now has thirty-three years in recovery, and I'm so proud of her. Her addiction and bulimia were my first introduction into this world. I probably wouldn't even be writing this book without that firsthand experience. What's more, I almost certainly wouldn't have met my husband.

After my sister's confession, I started going to Al-Anon regularly, a support group for family members.

LOVING AN INDIVIDUAL WITH USE DISORDER

I've always been the type of person who wouldn't touch drugs or alcohol with a ten-foot pole. This is not because I am somehow more chaste or moderate than anyone else; it's actually my *lack* of moderation that so effectively frightens me away from drugs. When my sister was getting sober from speed, I was out of control with food. As it turns out, I'm an individual with a use disorder, too; my substance just isn't illegal. I'm an individual with a food use disorder. That's why I've always avoided drugs; I instinctively knew that if I could get out of control with food, imagine what I'd do with drugs!

I was also too much of a control freak to do drugs. When I was nineteen, my sister introduced me to pot, and I hated it. I hated it because when I tried it I felt totally out of control, and I didn't like that feeling at all. So I avoided it, along with any other substance that seemed like it might take away my control.

And yet, despite my own aversion to drugs, I always seemed to attract people who love them—or at least once did.

I was getting ready to go to an Al-Anon meeting one night when a friend said she wanted to set me up on a date.

"Can't tonight," I said. "I'm going to an Al-Anon meeting."

"That's okay. He'll drive you there!"

Will he now? I wondered curiously.

And he did. He came to the door that night and told me that he, in fact, was an individual with use disorder. He confessed it immediately and openly.

"Really?" I replied. "Are you recovered?"

"Nope, crazy as ever!" he said with a grin. Of course, I figured he meant he just had a ways to go. That sort of joking modesty is common — it just means you're trying.

Unfortunately, that wasn't what he meant at all. He really was a wildly active user.

By the end of our (arguably wonderful) date, I told him that I couldn't go out with him anymore. When he asked me why, I listed my three important reasons: he wasn't religious (although he was Jewish, like me, which was neat); he didn't have a college degree; and he didn't work the Twelve Steps. Those three things were my absolute bottom line for dating a guy and eventually marrying him. So this guy was no longer an option, and I told him so.

Well, he didn't seem perturbed. The next morning, he called me. "I spent all night working," he said. "I went through all Twelve Steps, I read the Torah, I decided to be an Orthodox Jew, and I finished my college degree." I started laughing so hard I couldn't stop.

To be honest, I really haven't stopped since. Laughing, I mean. He's wonderfully funny and incredibly smart, and our marriage has had a lot of laughter — but we've had a lot of tears, too.

MARRYING AN INDIVIDUAL WITH USE DISORDER

Over the years, I've learned a lot from sharing a life with someone who has struggled with substance use disorder and recovery. Of course, my food addiction gave me a head start on understanding his challenges as well.

The main thing I learned from my husband's experience with use disorder is that *love* is the answer. Love is what brings about change, first in yourself, and then potentially in another person. It's love that works — not harshness, not toughness, not unkindness, not disconnection. It's *always* connection and love.

So, we started to date — I really, *really* liked him. True, I knew he had some problems, and I had my doubts about whether it was a good idea to partner with a person with his struggles, but in the end, we got married. I married a person with a substance use disorder. I went in with my eyes wide open, except when they were shut. I think that, in addition to Alan's powers of persuasion, our love, and my denial, the only thing that allowed me to proceed with such a perilous partnership *was* ignorance — ignorance of what it would actually be like to live with such a sick person… I did not grow up in a family with substance use disorder nor had I seen it up close day in and day out in a legally binding union.

When we got engaged, someone at my Al-Anon meeting said to me, "You must have the lowest self-esteem."

My response was something along the lines of, "Tell me something I don't know!"

Then, more thoughtfully, I added, "I've always dated individuals with use disorders — and I love them." A person is a person, and I happened to be attracted to guys who had substance issues. I finally faced it, and I finally met a really nice guy. As I once told a friend way back then, "He's the nicest addict I've ever met." And that still holds true today.

I realize this was incredibly risky of me, and I don't recommend it for everyone. It was a dangerous move, but it was the path I chose, for better or for worse (literally). If I hadn't met my husband and gone through what we've gone through together, I would have missed the opportunity to be with an incredible human being who today I call my best friend. I would also have no book. I would have no company, and I wouldn't be helping families all over the world face the challenges that an individual with a use disorder brings into their lives.

ATTENDING AL-ANON ON MY OWN

There were only a couple of really bad incidents while I was dating my husband. Once, he went to a friend's bachelor party nearby and didn't show up at home afterward. I drove around the neighborhood for about four hours until I found his car parked outside of what I later found out was his friend's house who was having the party. I went inside and picked him up. He stumbled out of the house completely numb and out of it. His lips were swollen, he was slurring, and he spoke as if he had cotton in his mouth. Unsure where he was, he got in the car and went along with me without any argument. He recently told me he had used from the moment he arrived at the party until the moment he left. I mean, let's be honest: he'd been at a bachelor party, and he was an individual with an active use disorder. Of course he was going to be out of it.

At the time, I couldn't believe he would use knowing his challenges. Letting go of the element of surprise — as in, "I can't believe he did that!" — is one of the hallmarks of family recovery. A lesson that took time for me to learn. An active user who is not involved with recovery is most likely going to use, so there is no reason to be surprised.

Aside from that incident, nothing too intense happened while we were dating. Soon after, we got married and moved to the Washington, DC area, where I saw what was really going on. Because he was a salesman in his family's business he didn't lose his job, but there were days on end where he would just lie in bed, incredibly sick. Part of the problem was that he was withdrawing — he was trying to get off drugs, after all. So he would stay in bed, jonesing, being sick, throwing up, day in and day out. He was in bad shape.

I started to go to Al-Anon again. I went every day, and I noticed something peculiar: most of the members in their twenties and thirties were separated, divorced, or widowed. There were very few couples among the people my age. Some older couples, sure, who'd been married to individuals with alcohol use disorder for much or all of their adult lives, but the young couples? Most were choosing to split.

It was clear why. "What are you, an idiot?" they'd say to me. "Why are you staying with an active user?" But I didn't understand that perspective, to be honest. When I was in Al-Anon before I met my husband, I'd been studying the books and going to meetings in my hometown. I saw a lot of people there who had spouses working the program, and it seemed doable. I remember thinking to myself, *I could marry an alcoholic. That would be easy. I have Al-Anon. I know what to do.*

LOVING MY HUSBAND SOBER

After our wedding, in the first few months of our marriage, I saw how sick he was. More vividly, however, I saw how emotionally unavailable he was. That was a very lonely life. As a newlywed, it wasn't fun at all — my husband was always sick. He was living the life of an individual with active use disorder: sick, dishonest, and distant. It was easy to cover up those symptoms when dating; not so much when married and living together.

I'd hear about recovery every day at the meetings, and then I'd go home and see how far my own husband was from that recovery. I remember calling my sister's best friend, her sponsor, and explaining it to her. "I don't know what to do," I said, over and over. "He's not doing well; this is awful. What am I going to do? How do I help him?"

"Look," she said to me, the very voice of the Al-Anon mantra in those days, "You can't help him. He has to hit bottom. He has to decide for himself."

Then she added, "There are only four ends to an addict, you know — jail, institution, recovery...or death — and you really have no control over which end will be his." I stopped speaking to her for two weeks after that, the shock was so great.

For someone who loves an individual with active use disorder, the worst part is this idea that they have to hit rock bottom and that you can't help them. You just have to take care of yourself, and that's their best chance. At least, that's what people tell you.

But the BALM philosophy is different.

Instead of letting them go and saying, "I'm going to watch you crash, and you might die when you crash," you're saying, "We are in this together, and we will stay connected by love."

At first, I thought I did have to let him crash. I went to Al-Anon meetings regularly; I had no idea how to help him, but I was at least helping myself. I brought other AA folks over to try and talk to him, not sure what else to do, but he simply wouldn't hear it. He was getting sicker and sicker, but he still wasn't open. My little parade of visitors had basically zero effect on his lifestyle.

Then I read a book that literally changed my life: *The Dilemma of the Alcoholic Marriage.*

Written in 1950s vernacular, there was a lot in that book that didn't pertain to life in 1986. Yet for me, its message about how to relate to my husband and his use disorder was revolutionary as it emphasized the loving nature of the family's role in a loved one's recovery, rather than the "get out" message I was hearing from other Al-Anons. As I recall, there is a woman in the story whose husband would stay out all night drinking. Every night, she would make dinner for him, but he would never come home in time. The dinner would sit out and get cold, and she would sit at the table and cry.

Eventually, her husband would come home between 11 PM and 1 AM, and she would start screaming at him promptly. You can understand why, of course; she was painfully frustrated. She would scream at him from the minute he came home until the minute they went to bed, and the next morning they would wake up and start the cycle all over again.

Well, eventually this woman made it into Al-Anon, and she got the first lesson: be loving. Just be loving. That's the true Al-Anon message: treat your loved one with dignity and respect. They're sick — they're not evil.

So this woman changed her habits. She still made dinner every night at 6 PM. If her husband wasn't home by 7 PM, she would cover it up, put it in the refrigerator, clean up, and then head out to her Al-Anon meeting. Then she would come home, and if he wasn't home, she would simply go to bed.

Well, when she started this behavior, it baffled her husband. He would get home at midnight, wake her up, and ask, "Are you okay?" He thought something must be wrong.

"Oh, sure, honey," she would reply. "How are you? I had such a nice evening. How was yours?"

When he was sober the next morning, he asked her what was going on. Here's how I remember her response:

"Every night you go out and drink till all hours while your dinner and I are waiting for you," she replied. "You come in at night and you're extremely drunk, and again and again I've yelled at you. What I have learned is that I cannot do that anymore. It doesn't help you and it doesn't help me. I have to understand that you have your life and you are allowed to live it the way you want to live it. Well, I love you anyway, so I'm going to live my life and stop trying to change you."

This was startling for a guy who was used to being yelled at every night. So, he decided to investigate. The next night, he came home a little earlier, and she wasn't there. She was at her meeting. The third night, he came home for dinner. From then on, he stayed home in the evenings. Eventually, he started going to meetings with her, and soon they built a life in recovery together.

Her *love* is what turned him around.

The day after I read that book, my husband walked into the house. Some drugs he was waiting on didn't arrive on time, and he was frantic. He started running around the house on a rampage, trying to find something, anything, for a fix. He normally didn't drink, but he was so desperate that he found a bottle of vodka we'd been given for our wedding and guzzled it.

Now, my normal MO would be to panic, to yell, to try and stop him. "What are you doing?" I might have screamed. "You're going to kill yourself!" This time I didn't. Instead, I just watched. I observed him down the vodka, run in the bedroom, lie down, and pass out. Not much later he got back up, threw up all over the bedroom floor, and went back to sleep for the rest of the night.

I made sure he was safely alive, and then I went into the spare bedroom, got into bed, and went to sleep.

When he woke up in the morning, he came into the room where I was getting dressed for work and asked me what happened. I explained, matter-of-fact, how he'd rampaged, guzzled, passed out, and thrown up.

"Well, why didn't you clean it up?" he asked.

"Well, honey, two reasons," I said. "Number one, I don't think it's my responsibility to clean up a mess like that — a mess you made from drinking, do you? And number two, you wouldn't have believed me. If I had just told you that this happened, you would have thought I made it up. I thought it was important for you to see the result of your need for a drug. So, I let it be so you could see it." And I kissed his cheek and went to work.

He started listening to me that morning.

That's what I did from then on. I resolved to be loving about the whole thing. When he was doing something, something uncomfortable or wild or unhealthy, I just watched. I wasn't mean, I wasn't hovering — just observing. Afterward, I would just describe the facts. I would tell him what happened. And, finally, I'd say, "I love you so much, honey. I have to go to work now." Then I'd give him a kiss, take my purse and my books, and go to work.

That's exactly what we teach our BALM families to do. That's the foundation of the whole BALM movement and the book you're reading now.

WHY THIS BOOK NEEDS TO HAPPEN

In the olden days of Alcoholics Anonymous and its partner group Al-Anon, individuals spent hours and days helping other people get sober. Meanwhile, the spouses (mostly wives in those days) gave each other support at meetings and in between and there was a camaraderie building within and between the AA's and the Al-Anon's. Then the treatment centers came, and the treatment centers could help thousands of people. Today, those treatment centers still do important work, but unfortunately that shift from individuals helping each other to alcoholics going into treatment to get help also meant that our culture diminished — and even lost — the role of the family in recovery. Though treatment centers to this day guide family members to Al-Anon, the family members often feel disconnected from helping their loved one and even from truly learning how to do so.

Along the way some treatment centers instituted something called "tough love" — *in other words, **he has to hit rock bottom**.* That's what AA became all about, even outside of treatment centers. They'd try to help a drunk for two or three days, and if it wasn't working, they'd move on to the next one because there were so many alcoholics who needed help. They couldn't reach them all, so they waited for them to reach bottom.

This meant two philosophies crept into AA and replaced the *original* loving strategy. One: they have to want help, or you can't help them. Two: tough love is the right love.

BALM, or Be A Loving Mirror, is known as Al-Anon Plus because it goes a step further than Al-Anon's focus on self-care. In Al-Anon, people learn how to take care of themselves and see their loved one as ill rather than as bad. On the deepest level, Al-Anon is all about connection and love. It was developed by family members of people with alcohol use disorder who wanted to survive what they were going through and help their loved ones recover. Over time, it became known as more of a self-care program for the family member, though the family members learned that when they took care of themselves it often rubbed off on their struggling loved one as well.

The woman in *The Dilemma of the Alcoholic Marriage* took care of herself and began treating her husband with dignity and respect. I took her lead and stopped freaking out on my husband, too. Both of us began to be loving and found in the end that love wins the day. As stated, Al-Anon's focus has become mainly about how to save oneself from the disaster of a loved one's use. Over time, you do learn how to help your loved one too, but because that's not the focus, the ins and outs of how to truly help a loved one recover are not taught in a structured manner. You have to stick around for a while or have an amazing sponsor like mine to figure out how to help your loved one. Frankly, with the opioid epidemic requiring quick action on the family's part, people just don't have the time to figure it out. That's why I do what I do. I teach people a step-by-step process of how to get their lives back and how to help their loved ones get *their* lives back. It's a dual-focused program.

THE BALM 7 C'S

When a family member is willing to work on their own self-care while learning this new transformative way of communicating lovingly, miracles happen. I saw it in my life. I still see it in the lives of the people I work with. When my husband got sober back in '86, he'd stand up in meetings and say, "See that woman back there? She got me sober." Now, I didn't get him sober — but I did contribute to his recovery. I did things that made it easier rather than harder for him to get to recovery and things that made it harder rather than easier for him to keep using.

Al-Anon has The Four C's of Recovery: You didn't *cause* your loved one's alcoholism. You can't *control* it. You can't *cure* it. But you don't have to *contribute* to it. If you look for that fourth C at Al-Anon meetings or on Al-Anon blogs and websites, you are unlikely to find it. Yet it is what gave me hope way back then and, as you will soon see, it is, in a differently stated way, foundational to the BALM Program. When I first started in Al-Anon, that fourth C was prominent. It was the focus. But slowly, this started to change. I can't categorically describe exactly when or how it happened, but the fourth C started to slip out of the vernacular.

By the late '80s, what many younger Al-Anons started saying was, "I didn't cause it. I can't control it. I can't cure it... and I'm out of here." They didn't care if they contributed to it — they didn't want any part of it. So divorce became rampant among young people who found themselves married to those with an active substance use disorder (SUD).

Honestly, who can blame them? There are certainly times to get yourself out of a toxic relationship.

The problem is, the person affected by SUD used to be just like you and me. But then they got sick. If they had a heart disease, would you be walking out the door? If they had diabetes, would you be putting their face on the ground?

Through the ages, people with SUD have been stigmatized, just as people with other diseases were in times past. There have been many efforts to lessen the stigma, and these continue to this day. Movies such as *The Anonymous People, If Only, Generation Found, My Name Is Bill W.,* and *28 Days* strive to break that stigma, as do groups such as FED UP!, a coalition to end the opioid epidemic, started by parents whose children lost their lives to opioid addiction.

Yet, the stigma persists. Al-Anon was originally the loving path, but then the whole loving path got twisted by tough love, by "I don't need to be here. I can get out."

There's nothing wrong with the freedom of getting out. Everyone has a choice. But sometimes it's our choice to stay, and to make people seem bad or stupid for choosing to be there for a person they love who is afflicted with a brain disorder, which is what addiction is, is, in my opinion, not only discriminatory. It is wrong.

In my program, the BALM, we have the BALM 7 C's. The first three are the same as in Al-Anon: you didn't *cause* it, you can't *control* it, you can't *cure* it. For the fourth C, we made it positive: you *can contribute* to recovery.

The fifth C: you are *connected* to your loved one on a level much deeper than their struggles. This C recognizes the underlying love we all hold for our loved ones whether they are using or not, and it encourages people to nurture this connection in the healthiest way possible.

BALM has a two-pronged approach based on this concept of connection: help yourself, help your loved one. There are programs that are all "help your loved one" and programs that are all "help yourself," but we're both — because if you don't do both, something's missing. There may be heartbreak and tragedy if you do both; there is no guarantee that what we teach will make somebody's loved one get sober. But we teach families how to be their loved one's *best* chance.

The sixth C: you can learn how to *communicate* effectively. Communication is what it's all about. In addition to the BALM 7 C's and the BALM 12 Principles, we have a seven-step process that teaches people how to communicate effectively with God, with themselves, and with their loved one. Don't worry, you don't have to call it "God" if you don't want to. Call it the Universe, call it Nature, call it whatever — the point is the communication is with Spirit, self, and other. It's transformative. It's also essential, because by the time they come to us, most family members aren't communicating. They're screaming, they're yelling, they're crying, they're begging, or they've become totally silent. Learning that you can communicate is part of taking care of yourself and plays an important role in opening your heart to hope.

The seventh C: you are always at *choice*. Let's say you read the first six C's and said to yourself, "But I don't want to stay." That's okay. That's your choice. It's okay to walk away; it's your freedom. Just remember not to make anyone else feel bad for staying, for loving somebody who is struggling. You can have your stigma, but I don't buy it. This is a human being we're talking about. I love my human being.

THE BALM® PROGRAM

The Be A Loving Mirror (BALM) program evolved out of the idea that people who are afflicted with this disease are human beings — deserving of all the love that *any*one deserves. We, as their loved ones, are free to choose how we relate to them and how we relate to their disorder, but it's very important that we know what we're doing, whether we stay or not.

I've taught thousands of people how to do this. I've seen families reunited after everybody said there was no chance. Now, with the opioid crisis, this method is more important than ever — we can't afford to wait for our loved ones to hit rock bottom. Hitting the bottom means death.

This is about wise love. Love that doesn't mean enabling. Love that doesn't mean giving them what they want or giving into manipulation. We teach families a whole new way to look at their lives, and at its core is love.

What won't be in this book is a mindset of tragedy. We don't spend much time saying the situation is sad, pathetic, or tragic. Families affected by SUD are dealing with something very difficult, and yes, it can certainly be tragic. But the recovery is about, in my opinion, living from a place of peace and love. It's about shifting internally so that peace and love are your default. It's a spiritual way of life so that the way in which you speak to your loved one isn't tragic — it's choosing not to use that verbiage or that perspective. It's matter-of-fact, and it's loving. We can see our loved ones as spiritual beings who are having a difficult physical experience. They are still a human being worthy of your respect and your time, so treat them that way. Treat yourself that way, treat other people that way, and you will live a full and rich life regardless of your loved one's choices.

I admit it — this is a life-and-death matter. I talk about it that way all the time. This is how I talk about it to help the families wake up and take care of what they need to do. But then, it becomes a different approach to life: you're doing your best, and you're going to enjoy this person, no matter their choices. After all, there are a lot of things to enjoy about someone, even when they're ill.

We have the **BALM** 7 C's, we have the **BALM** 12 Principles, and we have 7 Steps to **BALM**.

It's a very rich, deep, and broad program, and I'm excited you've decided to explore it with me.

THE BALM® 7 C'S

1. You did not cause your loved one's SUD.
2. You cannot control your loved one's SUD.
3. You cannot cure your loved one's SUD.
4. You can contribute to your loved one's recovery.
5. You are connected to your loved one on a level deeper than their SUD.
6. You can learn to communicate effectively with your loved one and others.
7. You are always at choice.

QUESTIONS TO PONDER:

1. As you look over the **BALM** 7 C's, what is new to you?
2. What is real?
3. What value could you see these concepts and actions bringing to your life and to your family?

Part I:

THE LOVING PATH

1
The Loving Path
What Does It Mean?

THE LOVING PATH FROM CHAOS TO SANITY

If we start with the Loving Path, what does that mean exactly? What does it mean to be loving? What does it mean to walk the path of love?

To walk a path of love is to live from the deepest part of yourself, the part of you that doesn't judge, the part of you that isn't jealous, the part of you that isn't envious, the part of you that isn't afraid, the part of you that doesn't hold resentment or anger. The Loving Path is the path of peace and of joy, even in your darkest hours. This is the path a family facing probably the hardest thing they've ever faced has the opportunity to walk.

Sometimes the walk changes everything for everyone in such a way that the loved one gets sober and stays sober.

Sometimes there are bumps, but they move powerfully in the direction of recovery. Sometimes the person who practices it changes deeply, but their loved one doesn't make it. What we find is that when family members walk this path, everything changes — whether their loved one survives or not. No matter what happens at the end, those times along the way when the struggling person and their family connect with love become more frequent and can be deeply meaningful and powerful, and that's what the BALM can provide.

STARTING IN CHAOS

When people first try to get help, when they come in to any kind of a family recovery program, they're usually living in a chaotic situation. Either they are in chaos, their loved one is in chaos, or their whole family is in chaos. They've probably heard a lot of people saying, "Get rid of her!"

"Get him out!"

"He has to hit bottom!"

"Enough of this!"

I had someone tell me once that her loved one said he couldn't live without her. She told him he was codependent and needed to learn to live without her. I explained to her that interdependence is not the same as codependence, especially as people get older in a relationship. Sometimes, it really does feel like you couldn't live without that other person. When you combine that with the feeling of lost potential because of the use disorder, *everything* feels like life and death.

Yes, we know that the loved one is ill, but the Loving Path is more individualized than it is labeling. It is peaceful, clear, based on fact, aware of reality, and willing to quietly risk all for a better tomorrow — while staying grounded in today. It's the most powerful path to walk with a struggling loved one, and the most promising. This is your way forward: walk a path where you are oriented toward love instead of toward labeling, judgment, embarrassment, or reacting. Every decision you make is based on love. Sometimes it's love for yourself, sometimes it's love for your loved one, and sometimes it's love for the other people in your family. Sometimes it's love of life — but it's always about love.

Every step you take forward, every decision you make about what you're going to do next or what you're going to point yourself toward should always be based on this question: *Which way does love point?*

Why does this matter? Your loved one is involved in a life-or-death struggle. Of course, it is also true that anybody could die at any minute, but those with SUD are engaged in behaviors that up the ante. However, they aren't engaged in those behaviors *willfully*. It isn't that they're making terrible choices because they hate you, or because they hate their life or want you to suffer. It is, in other words, not about you. It's because at some point, they tried a substance, or a behavior, and they thought it was cool or interesting or pleasurable. But then their brain got hijacked, and they couldn't stop.

The drug or the behavior tells them that they can't survive without it. That's the brain disorder part of them, and it's telling them a lie. It's telling them that this drug or behavior is the way to life, and everything else is the way to death. If somebody thinks they need something to live and you hit them with a bunch of rejection, unkindness, judgment, and anger, you're just adding fuel to the lie's fire.

It's not unlike someone joining a cult against all the advice of their loving family. When someone joins a cult, the cults do something called "love bombing." They just give the person total and overwhelming love and affirmation, and it hooks them. While their family insults their intelligence or yells at them for their bad decision, the cult is over there making them feel good about themselves.

If, instead, you take the Loving Path, you can be an alternative — another life choice. You must be a better life choice, because the user's ability to choose is impaired. That's what use disorder does to the brain: it impairs the ability to choose wisely. We all move toward pleasure and away from pain, right? Well, if there are two painful paths and one of them (the drug) is saying, *You need me or you're going to die — oh, and here's a little pleasure for a couple of seconds to remind you,* which painful path is going to win? Perhaps, then, it's not a bad idea to give some pleasure from your end as well.

Now, to be clear, we're not talking about enabling. The Loving Path is not enabling — but it is very peaceful. In other words, it doesn't yell. It doesn't beg. It doesn't threaten. The Loving Path is about factually describing their words and actions to them in a calm way, a way that shows your love, empathy and non-judgment.

Imagine a shield of denial surrounding every person who's struggling with some addictive behavior. The Loving Path allows your words and your feelings to bypass that denial, to go under the shield and to reach their heart from your heart.

FINDING SELFLESS LOVE

You might be reading this and thinking, I've always loved this person. Everything I've done is out of love!

That's a valid reaction, and honestly — that's really what we all feel, isn't it? *That we love them more than life.* That's why we try everything we can. But when that love manifests in things like bailing them out of jail, paying all their bills, and making life easier for them at every step of the way, it actually makes it *harder* for our loved one to escape from the malady because there is no sense of urgency. There is no feeling of lack.

We're not looking for them to hit a bottom, but the truth is, certain kinds of love hurt and certain kinds of love have more potential to help. There's a misunderstanding that when a person gives and gives and gives — or, on the other side of the spectrum, yells and begs and cries — they're declaring love.

But these forms of love are very selfish in that they make us feel better — they don't actually help our loved one recover.

What we're talking about is a whole different level of love. This kind of love is brave, is willing to do the inner work, is able to stay calm in the face of great difficulty; it's willing to look within, to see one's own shortcomings or wrongs or to see the things that are not working and take the brave stance of making change. This kind of love is willing to learn all about substance use disorder or other use disorders and how they affect the loved one. By doing so, the family is willing to act on that knowledge and understanding rather than on their gut.

If you say to yourself, *I love him and so I'll do anything for him,* is that true? Are you doing the things that are truly helpful, that potentially will keep him alive and encourage recovery? Or are you just doing the things that you've always been doing, which have just barely been working and could in the long run kill him?

It's hard for people to read that, I realize. Many times, before really answering these questions, it's important to work through your heart and your feelings. When I speak with a beginner, I talk to them about their peace of mind. Often, it doesn't exist. So I ask, "What's going on? Why are you so upset?" Usually, I hear answers like, "Well, it's all about my loved one. He's this, he's that."

"She's doing this, she's doing that."

"I can't sleep at night. I get woken up in the middle of the night." The list goes on.

Once we work through that together, then I can say: "What if I gave you a solution that would help you completely get your peace of mind back? Get your life back? Give you the best chance of helping him or her get *their* life back? Would you be interested?"

There are words and behaviors that help more than others, and some that don't help at all. But the Loving Path is just as much about helping *you* as it is about helping your loved one — because ultimately, that's the same thing. While there's no guarantee that what you do will save them, there is a guarantee in the Loving Path that you will become more peaceful and that your relationship with your loved one will most likely improve — whether they stop using or not. Of course, this is not to deny how important their getting sober is to you. But this love goes deeper than that.

This love is a transformative love because it has the power to reshape your outlook, your way of life, and your relationship with your loved one.

HOW TO TAKE THAT RISK

For many people, it can feel like a tremendous risk to let go of how they've been doing things. You know what you've been doing isn't working, but to change is to risk, and this risk has painfully high stakes. How do you learn to love this way? How do you develop the capacity to feel and act on this kind of transformative love?

To help you do so, our program has three parts: information, transformation, and support. The first step, information, is all about educating yourself so that you can be ready to make the transformation. There are four particular things you have to understand about making that transition to the Loving Path:

1. **You have a role to play.** It isn't *their* problem — it's *our* problem, theirs and ours together. We, as a family, have a challenge to overcome.

2. **Your loved one can change.** If they're alive, there's hope that they can change. Change happens in stages over time, and you can play a role in how quickly they move from stage to stage on that path of change.

   As a family member, you, too, have stages to go through on your own change path. Learning about how change happens and working to make the changes in yourself is essential. (See the Stages of Change for Families model in Chapter 6.)

3. **Let go of control.** When you have a loved one who's really struggling, oftentimes all you can think about is, *I've got to save them, I've got to fix this, you've got to help me and we've got to do it now!* But one of the most important things that family members can do is let go of their own desperation and obsessive desire to control — because, no matter what you do, there is no guarantee.

   There's a saying in Al-Anon: "Let go and let God." Many people interpret that as "This is up to God. I'm going to go and handle my own life." But we don't say that. We say it's important to let go but not to give up on your loved one or give in to their manipulations. Let go of this obsessive fear that you're going to lose them, to what your brain is telling you must be done. Most brains in this situation are telling you to yell, to beg, to enable, to pull them out of jail, to fight with the treatment professionals, to do whatever your loved one tells you to do. Let go of all that. Let go of the idea that if you just push hard enough, everything will be okay.

   It's an incredibly difficult concept to digest, I know. But please consider this: letting go without giving up or giving in (BALM Principle 3) is to let go of the desperate obsession, without giving up on what you know helps. Love them, but don't give in to their manipulations.

4. **You can be their best chance at recovery** (BALM Principle 4). This attitude is required before a person can walk the Loving Path. It starts with seeing that you have a role to play in their recovery (BALM Principle 1); that change does happen in stages (BALM Principle 2), not all at once; and that your obsession with fixing it is not going to fix it. Rather, your educated work to sanely and rationally get them the help they need, without giving into their manipulations, while treating them with love and respect, will make all the difference. Understanding this mindset is crucial to your ability to walk the Loving Path.

Once you understand all that, you'll understand that you're their best chance — specifically, that you are their best chance when you stay aware. Don't allow yourself to go back into denial and do not enable. Once you get to that place of consistent awareness, you'll be contributing to recovery again, not to their disorder.

CONTRIBUTE TO RECOVERY

A recent speaker on a BALM webinar, with years of BALM recovery experience herself, said, "Enabling is when you are the solution, and empowering is helping *them* be the solution." The Loving Path is one of empowerment, always contributing to their recovery — not to their use disorder. The whole BALM program is about how to contribute to recovery, and this Loving Path provides the framework. Once you understand the attitudes I've just mentioned and shift your perspective, then you are working diligently to *Be A Loving Mirror*, which is the transformative process that our families go through.

Many great religious leaders embody this concept of love. Gandhi, Buddha, Jesus, the Ba'al Shem Tov — they all focus on love. Love is the universal tonic. It's the path of the ages. We've known that love is the answer to our fears and struggles from time immemorial; we've heard from all our great thinkers that love heals all wounds. It's very important to understand that this entire program is predicated on the idea of love. In fact, BALM Principle 6 states that "Your primary task is to *be a loving person.*" Love is all-forgiving, but that doesn't mean there isn't some structure along the way. It's nonjudgmental, it's not angry; it's objective, and it's peaceful. It's not dissimilar to how to make a long-term marriage successful.

Once I started seeing my husband through the eyes of love, I stopped pushing. Once I stopped pushing, he was free to look at his life in a deeper way. As long as I was pushing, there was a natural human tendency to resist. So I realized, If I'm resisting you, you're going to resist me back. But what if I stop resisting and just love you? Might you then begin to look at yourself?

That doesn't mean I don't help you recover; rather, I just don't tell you how bad and wrong you are for your behavior. I don't shame you. I treat you with dignity and respect. That's the Loving Path: treating someone with total dignity and respect even when they seem least "deserving."

When I stopped pushing against my husband one day as a newlywed and began non-judgmentally loving him several months into our marriage in Spring 1986, there was a palpable sense of relief in our home that had simply not been there before. I could feel him go from feeling judged and shamed and horrible about himself, like he had really let me down, like he was a useless human being, to simply loving me back. Something shifted in him because when I got home the next day, he was in treatment. He wrote me a long letter, saying, "I've realized I really have a bad problem and I have to address it." Until that point, I was pushing, pushing, pushing for him to get help — and he was resisting, resisting, resisting.

USING THE CALENDAR

My husband and I married in August 1985. By December, I realized on a much deeper level how truly ill he was. I loved him very much, but this was not the way I wanted to live my life. I wanted to help him get well, but I also knew that I couldn't guarantee it.

A close friend of mine, Frumma Gottlieb, who is now one of our BALM coaches, invited me to open up a calendar, count three months ahead, and in the box for the first day of that month and every third month actually write the words: "how are things now?" And that is what I did, evaluating and writing the answer to that question down on the first day of every third month.

Prior to this practice, every day was chaos. Every day was questioning: *Should I stay? Should I go? What should I do?* But once I settled on the three-month rule, I took that feeling of total confusion, that chaotic inner turmoil, and I let it go. I decided, *Today I'm going to stay and be loving,* and there would be ninety days until I had to ask myself that question again. Every morning I would wake up with that affirmation in mind. I decided to give myself a year before I made a decision on whether to stay, but every three months I would check in.

That window of every three months helped shift my energy. I went from chaos and panic every day to a focused, clear plan. I calmed down because it gave me energetic and mental space to calm down. I took a step in letting go, and I didn't even realize it. Within five months of that calendar's beginning, my husband was in treatment.

During that time, I was going to meetings every day. I was looking into treatment centers, and that's when I read *The Dilemma of the Alcoholic Marriage.* I was living in the moment, taking the big decision of whether I was going to stay or not off the table — I was planted there, for the present. I was able to let go of having to fix the situation and instead simply look for solutions that would be both loving and constructive.

Could this be that time for you?

THE BALM® 12 PRINCIPLES

1. The family has a crucial role to play in a loved one's recovery
2. Change happens in stages
3. It is important to let go without giving up or giving in
4. You can be your loved one's best chance at recovery
5. When you take your focus off of your loved one and put it on yourself, you will both benefit
6. Your primary task is to be a loving person
7. Don't set a boundary unless you are determined to stick to it
8. Getting support will greatly enhance your recovery
9. It is important to explore and/or heal your relationship with your spirituality
10. It is important to heal your relationship with yourself
11. It is important to heal your relationship with others
12. Be A Loving Mirror is the journey and the destination

QUESTIONS TO PONDER:

1. What are you on edge about in your life?
2. How could a time line help you get rooted in each moment?

2

The Power of This Day
to Create a Better Tomorrow

TODAY IS ALL WE HAVE

Whether sober, not sober, rich, poor, healthy, unhealthy, foolish, or wise, all of us are equal in at least one way: today is all we have. This moment is all that's guaranteed, and this day is the only day we have to work with.

The amazing thing about being in relationship with someone who is engaging in life-and-death behaviors is that we are forced to face a truth most people can easily ignore: *we only have today*. When you're faced with that fact, you can choose a different perspective regarding your situation. For many people facing a loved one's SUD, their perspective is terror. They hype themselves up. They get into a hypervigilant, hyperventilating crisis mood when their loved one is using, but, though understandable, it's not helpful to anyone — it's just crazed.

The purpose of this chapter is for you to really discover the value *in this moment*. To help you experience your loved one playing with their own life as their gift to you rather than as the horrible thing that's going to kill you.

First, let's look at what it's like when you see your loved one's using as an unbearable tragedy that only you are comprehending and taking seriously enough. As far as you can see, no one else seems to understand how important this is, and the more you see things this way, the more you find yourself escalating internally when you try to talk to other people about the situation. This is why loved ones who are using and in early sobriety, and the treatment centers and other professionals that work with those loved ones, often think the families are crazy and don't want to have anything to do with them. The old line "if you had a wife/mom like his, you'd use too" comes to mind. Yet what is happening is that the family members are so traumatized by the potential loss of their loved one that they're on overdrive. They're not functioning well. They're not thinking well. Even if they have some clear thoughts, their form of sharing those thoughts is alienating. What they see, though, is not their own turbulence; rather, they see their loved one and/or the treatment center shutting them out.

Family members in this state are living in a future possibility that scares them to death. They're looking in the future and borrowing trouble instead of being in today. Because of this misspent focus, they lose some of the inner power they could better spend being part of the solution.

BEING IN THIS MOMENT

The whole idea behind "being in this moment" starts with understanding. It is crucial to recognize that although it may seem like your loved one is the *only* one who could go at any minute, the reality is actually more universal: you could go at any minute, your neighbor's loved one who doesn't have SUD could go at any minute, the world could go at any minute. We can't control that, though most people willfully ignore it. Once we come to terms with it, however, our perspective becomes very present-moment based. We start to see that there really is no tomorrow — there's just today. It's a different way of looking at things that allows us to make the most of what we have.

The double benefit of the in-the-moment perspective is not only letting go of your future, it's letting go of your past. Let's say for years you've been enabling or shaming your loved one. Or maybe it's simply that your whole life has been centered on someone else. Suddenly, you wake up to the fact that you're fifty years old and you just spent the last thirty years circling your life around someone else's — and you're making zero progress. That wake-up is painful, and most often full of regret.

But the power of being in today is in *letting go of the past.* Accept that whatever happened was what you needed to experience in order to get where you are. Allow its power over you to dissipate so that you can be most powerful *today.*

There's a saying in Al-Anon's Twelve-Step rooms: If you have one foot in tomorrow and one in yesterday, you're peeing on today.

When I was a newcomer to Al-Anon and was working with my beloved sponsor, Dawn, she loved to give me homework.

"Here's what I want you to do," she'd say with every problem I brought to her.

"Okay," I'd reply, waiting for her advice like it was God's word coming down from the mountaintop.

"Stay in present time."

That was it? *Excuse me?* My husband could die, and she's sitting here telling me to stay in present time?

Yep. Exactly. All you have is right now. You don't have tomorrow. Anyone could die.

At that time, I thought that was the most ridiculous thing I'd ever heard — because, honestly, the present time seemed awful! What I learned, however, is that present time is never awful. How I *think* about present time, on the other hand, makes all the difference as to whether it's awful, beautiful, poignant, tender, or challenging. The power of this day is that when we put our attention fully in the present, we have the opportunity to do things in such a way that tomorrow has the potential to be better. That's the power of this day.

Over time, I saw the value of this. At first, of course, I'd call Dawn screaming and crying and she'd say, "Stay in present time," and it would piss me off. I would get so mad, I'd mimic her over the phone in pure frustration. But eventually, I started to say it myself. I started to preface my stories with it. I started to get it, and it made all the difference.

REACHING FOR TOTAL FAMILY RECOVERY

One thing I want to be clear about: I don't underestimate what families have done to get to wherever they are with their loved one. If their loved one is still alive, they've most likely done some things that have helped. But our goal here is much more than just survival. Our goal is total recovery for the whole family. Though we can't guarantee it, we teach families how to give their loved one the best chance, and give themselves a fabulous chance of having a better life for themselves.

Being in this moment means you can focus on love, on seeing that other person as a human being. Then you're getting oriented on a Loving Path. Instead of trying to run, you just start to walk toward the next step, feet on the ground, eyes in front of you, bringing calm wherever you go.

Face it: it's not just their future that you're worried about — it's the future that you want for yourself. And your best chance of having that, of helping yourself and your loved one, is to get your life back.

DEALING WITH NEGATIVE RESPONSES

Once you start on the Loving Path, your loved one may not initially respond well. We teach our families how to handle loving conversations that are grounded in love and in the facts, and that (when necessary) include a boundary. The response to these loving conversations, especially prior to sobriety, is not always positive. Sometimes your loved one just freaks out on you; they might be wildly upset with you. If you, as their family member, aren't grounded in your own sense of peace and calm, that kind of response can be too much to bear. I've had families who have been unable, unwilling, to be on the Loving Path in this way because they couldn't stand their loved one's response.

Our whole transformative process is one of first becoming peaceful. B*e the peace you wish to see in the world.* That's the **first step** to Be A Loving Mirror. We teach families mindfulness and meditation techniques to increase the level of peace in their life. Then we teach them to objectively observe what's happening with their loved one in the moment, so they can see the facts of the situation without injecting their opinions about the facts. That's the **second step**: just observe what's happening. He's walking. He's stumbling across the wooden floor. He just threw up all over the coffee table.

No judgment — just facts.

At that point, the **third step** is to feel what's going on inside you. Become aware of your inner emotional landscape without judgment, just as you watched what your loved one did without judgment. Be aware of what you're feeling, of what's happening inside of you. We have lots of tools and techniques we teach families so that they can deal with and come out on the other side of their emotional turmoil, most of which are incorporated into the 7 Steps to **BALM**.

One tool is the Four-Four-Eight breathing technique. It goes like this: Say you're driving down the road by yourself. Suddenly, you're having that panicked feeling, that "Oh, my God! He could die. What do I do? I can't take it!" feeling. Your heart rate goes up. You're upset. You're obsessing, your mind is racing. At that point, try the Four-Four-Eight breathing technique: breathing in for a count of four, holding it in for a count of four, and breathing out for a count of eight. Do that three or four times, until you are a little bit calmer.

If that doesn't work for you, try what we call Focus on the Task at Hand. First, look at where your hands are. Then, describe out loud what they're doing and, by extension, what you're doing, as in, *"My hands are now on the steering wheel. I'm turning my head left and looking out the rearview mirror. I'm looking in the side mirror; I'm turning my head back and I see that tree to the right."*

Focusing on a combination of Four-Four-Eight technique and Focus on the Task at Hand allows both your breath and your thinking to converge, leaving little attention left for the thoughts swirling around in your head.

The first time you do this, you'll probably have to redo it about thirty to forty times in an hour — at least every other minute. You will find yourself losing focus and having to bring yourself back that often — and sometimes even more than that. The more you practice it, the less often you'll need to reboot; it will become easier to pull yourself back and calm yourself down. Soon that calm, that presence of mind, that attention to what you are doing in the moment, becomes the default perspective.

Millions and millions of people every day try a drink or a drug. Some find they have a use disorder, but not all. The fault

isn't in the trying or in the becoming — it's simply what is.
Children, teens and adults experiment, and some will develop
the brain disorder SUD. It's a disease, and our loved ones who
have it need our love, not our judgment or shame. Stigma and
blame do not help them stop or get well. We need to separate
ourselves from focusing on their faults. The only way you have
control over your future is to live in the right now. Through
this peace, love will radiate out.

QUESTIONS TO PONDER:

1. How often do you find yourself thinking upsetting
thoughts of the past or focusing on fears of the future?
2. What will it take for you to stay in the present time?

3

The Promise of the Loving Path

OBJECTIVE, TRUTH-SEEKING PEACE

The Loving Path is peaceful. As you've heard me say before and will hear me say again, *be the peace you wish to see in the world* (BALM Step One). I've heard many people who run clinics and treatment centers say, "It's never the clients who push you out of the treatment field. It's all the people *around* the clients." And of course, they are referring to the family members — also known as "those who hover."

It's so easy to fall into this panicked chaos when your loved one is using, but who is your panicking helping? Certainly not you. Certainly not your loved one.

Over the years, I have learned that my job as a family member is to be the peace. Do I always do it? No. Do I work on it? Absolutely.

This book is an invitation to join me in the journey of letting go of hovering, controlling, and self-terrorizing.

From a peaceful perspective, you will see things more objectively. You will have inner emotional awareness without judgment. You'll understand what's happening more clearly.

Through practicing the peace of Step One, the objective observation of Step Two and the emotional awareness of Step Three, you'll be able to move to the **Fourth Step** on the loving path to BALM: *Document the facts.*

CLEAR/UNCLEAR

This is one of the many exercises we use to help our BALM family members document the facts. For example, a couple called me one day and said their son was in trouble. They didn't know if he was using and hoped I could help. Rather than my telling them what I saw, I took them through the Clear/Unclear exercise. We each made a chart with two columns: On one side, we wrote down everything they knew for sure, everything that was totally clear. They told me all the facts they knew about their son's behavior. When you're doing something like this, think like a journalist: just the facts, ma'am! Then, anything they weren't totally sure about went on the unclear side.

By the end of the conversation, we had fifty or sixty facts on the clear side that described someone who was using. On the unclear side was only one question: "Is he using?"

It became pretty apparent to the parents, that, in fact, he was and since they figured it out themselves through a view of the facts, they could see through their own denial rather than be stopped by it.

Try filling out the following Clear/Unclear chart to help you discern a challenge you are facing. Observe the words and actions of those around you, become clear about what the facts really are (and what you're not sure of), write them down, and find out what's really going on.

CLEAR/UNCLEAR CHART

This tool is designed to help you get out of a confused state of mind and into clarity. Here is how it works:

1. Write down the problem you are facing.
2. In the clear column, list everything you know for sure about this problem. State all the facts and things and ideas you are absolutely sure of. Add as many rows as you need.
3. Then, in the unclear column, write down everything unclear to you about the situation — whatever you are unsure of, whatever questions you have, whatever you think might be true but don't know for a fact.

Once you have made both lists, read each column and jot down a few notes about any new conclusions you may now have and anything you now know you need to explore.

When people use this tool, they often find themselves feeling much clearer about the challenge, or, at the very least, they know what they still need to find out and can then get to work exploring those things.

If you find you need more help with this, first look again at the things you said you were clear about. Ask yourself if you are absolutely sure you know these things are facts. If you are not sure, put them in the unclear column. If you would prefer to work with a guide as you move through this process, ask your BALM coach to take a look at it. Sometimes a second set of eyes can make all the difference!

CLEAR	UNCLEAR

OFF THE PATH

There are many more people deeply impacted by this illness than are actually getting help. For some families, the maze of treatment centers and support options can be more than they can handle or may just feel inhospitable or unworkable.

Of course, a family's level of chaos doesn't determine their level of care for their loved one. Almost always, they love them more than life. But many families, because of the trauma they've experienced or their lack of information about the family's role, simply don't understand the power they can have to effect positive change for themselves and their loved one. A lot of families haven't even heard of BALM, Al-Anon, SMART Recovery, Learn to Cope, or CRAFT. Or maybe they went once to any one of them, didn't relate immediately, and never went back.

The Loving Path is designed to give you a process to figure out how to navigate your path and potentially, that of your loved one, at the same time, through clarity, self-care, loving relationships, and awareness. The Loving Path doesn't require you to dump your loved one off at a center and leave without giving or getting help, reassurance, or support. This path empowers you to become an advocate for your own recovery and your loved one's recovery as you find and partner with the professionals who are working with them and you.

Many families benefit from having their own professional or volunteer helpers as they navigate their own recovery. Whether a BALM Coach, the BALM Program, Al-Anon, a sponsor, a therapist or other support group, there are people schooled in helping families be there for their loved ones and for themselves in a positive healing way.

You will find me referencing BALM Coaches in this book since I know the work we do is designed to help both the family and their loved one in a loving non-judgmental way.

Our work is designed to help you get your life back while you also focus on how to help them, if that is your choice. Often, people who gravitate to us value their family relationships and their own sanity and want a program which allows them to focus on both.

In terms of helping your loved one, sometimes a treatment center is the best option. If it is, consider using a coach or other guide to help you find the best fit. But whether your loved one goes to inpatient treatment, gets a coach, recovers through an outpatient program, through mutual support meetings, or all of the above, the Loving Path can make a huge difference in how you relate to your loved one, those helping him or her, and your own life.

The power of the Loving Path is in its ability to completely transform your inner and outer relationships. You will find *you can do something*. The promise of the Loving Path is that you *will* get your life back, and you will be your loved one's best chance.

In other words, there is hope.

TRANSFORMATIVE POWER

When you focus on transforming your life from within, it's not just in the context of your loved one's SUD. You transform your life in every way, in every context, because these timeless tools are useful for life itself. Great saints and sages throughout time have focused on the power of love. And their ability to help others grow came from deep within due to their own inner transformation. This is a journey to being the love and peace you wish to see around you. On that basis, you will be able to have a transformative effect first on yourself and then on those you love.

When I first started doing this work, I had been meditating for many years, in addition to working the Twelve Steps of Al-Anon and Overeaters Anonymous. I had achieved a degree of transformation that allowed me to have loving conversations with those I loved, and when I worked with clients, I was able to script loving conversations that they could have effectively with their loved ones. The family would tell me their problem, and I would tell them who they had to talk to and what to say. After the conversation, they'd come back to me, and I'd script another one.

As you can see, that is a limited form of help because these families depended on me for the scripting. Sometimes, however, because they saw how I did it, they got it.

At a certain point, coaches asked me to mentor them in the recovery arena. Later, a group of coaches asked me to start a school so they could do with families what I was doing.

And that's why we're here today.

At first, the BALM Institute had the BALM 12 Principles. These included attitudinal shift principles, action principles, and relationship principles. But then the coaches accurately pointed out that those principles didn't explain specifically *how* to help families have these loving conversations. That's when I wrote down what it took, from the inside out, to have a loving conversation, and what it took to sustain the *ability* to have a loving conversation. I put my transformational process on paper, and that process became the 7 Steps to BALM.

7 STEPS TO BALM®

1. Be the peace you wish to see in the world.
2. Objectively observe what your loved one does and says.
3. Become aware of your inner emotional landscape without judgment.
4. Document what you see and hear (just the facts!).

5. Script a loving conversation, paying particular attention to your tone.
6. Have a loving conversation with your loved one, at the right time and place.
7. If necessary, set a boundary.

The first three steps, covered in the last chapter, were missing in my prior work with my clients, and they alone compose a lifetime of work. Those first three steps are an inner transformation that can continue to expand as you move through your life if you choose to focus on them. The last four are practical interpersonal communication tools, best done when deeply informed by the first three.

If you're being the peace, observing your loved one, staying aware of your inner emotional landscape, and documenting the facts, then at that point you're going to know when you see a pattern. You're going to know how to script the conversation. You're going to know how to have the conversation and when to set a boundary. In the early days, I was the determining factor in the success of those conversations. Once we had those 7 Steps to **BALM** in place, however, things changed. One of my coaches, who is now the lead teacher of the 7 Steps to **BALM**, told me at that time, "What you have here is a transformational process." The hair went up on the back of my arms.

From that point on, we began training families to be their own best chance at family recovery. I didn't want to be the determining factor in their success; I didn't want to be their or their loved one's best chance. This training would make them their *own* best chance. And if you work these 7 Steps to **BALM**, you will become *your* loved one's best chance at recovery.

With their **BALM** inner transformation, people are renewed in ways they've never been renewed before. Often, their relationships with their spouses, their coworkers, their loved ones — with everyone — completely change. Al-Anon teaches the inner transformation, but the reason we're called

Al-Anon Plus is that we also teach this step-by-step process that transforms the relationship with both self and others.

OUTSIDE OF THE "AFFECTED FAMILY" REALM

This step-by-step process ends up being a specific tutorial for how to be a loving person. This means it can be profoundly useful in any area of life, not just in how you relate to a struggling loved one.

At first, my coaches and I really only thought about these 7 Steps to BALM in terms of individuals with use disorder. Then, one of our first BALM coaches, Jim — a very active BALMer and a recovering alcoholic with around two decades of sobriety — told us he'd been using BALM at work. The CEO of a small family business, he started to use it with his business partner, his wife, and all his employees. He noticed that, as a result, the tone at work completely changed. (See Jim Graham's story in Chapter 14, too.)

When he pointed out the value of BALM beyond talking to an individual with use disorder, some of us started to catch on. One of our coaches works with parents of children and teens without SUD, and she started to see the value of the 7 Steps to BALM for those parents. Couldn't BALM help any mom speak with her child or teen? she reasoned. Or talk to the school to advocate for her child?

It only grew from there. Suddenly, we noticed that these principles and steps are useful, period — regardless of whether you're living with SUD in the family or simply trying to live a good life.

We also noticed that this program is most effective if you use it holistically, across all areas of your life. It's tempting to compartmentalize it just to the context of your loved one's SUD, but it's actually much easier to let it into your entire life.

It gives you momentum. It makes you a master practitioner of love because you're practicing it in every aspect of life.

Before long, the principles and steps were being adapted to navigating individual life, coaching development, business development along with family recovery. Finally, a set of the **BALM** 12 Principles and 7 Steps to **BALM** have been adapted for the individuals with use disorder as well.

A DIFFICULT DECISION

A while back, I was coaching Tracy Ward, a single mom, who was training to be a BALM coach. Her son, who was practicing harm reduction (see glossary) without guidance, had just finished treatment, as well as a several-month stay in a sober living facility, and wanted to come home. After a lot of tough deliberation, Tracy decided to let him do so. Everyone told her to say no; all her friends and family advised against it. To be honest, so did I. But she decided to let him come home, and she continued to work her BALM program diligently. It's had its ups and downs, and it has not been easy. But she has walked the Loving Path powerfully over the months.

Along with his struggles, Tracy's son has also displayed growth and a sense of resilience that she noticed when she allowed him to run his life rather than her insisting on controlling it. One day on FaceBook, Tracy's son posted a public statement admitting his problem and apologizing to anyone he had hurt. He also added that if anyone needed support, to please reach out to him — because he wanted others to know that there was hope.

That's a real transformation. Did he say it was all because of his mom? Hardly. He didn't even mention her. But his transformation, his ownership of his actions, his honesty, and his hope for the future — that's what his mom wanted to see, and each day she did the inner work necessary to share the facts in a loving way in order to be a peaceful and helpful presence in his life. It's not about credit; it's about being the best chance for your loved one.

As Tracy shared, "Today, we rarely have conflict. I stick to my boundaries. He talks to me about everything. He comes to me for guidance. I have let him have his journey of figuring out what works and doesn't work to get where he wants to go. He is doing that! He is growing up and becoming a responsible, productive man."

Tracy is an example of someone walking the Loving Path. Before the BALM, she was a "raving lunatic" (her words, not mine). She couldn't figure out what she was doing or how to help her son. With BALM, she has moved healthfully into recovery and he has a better chance to recover as well. To learn more about Tracy's journey, read our interview in Chapter 14.

THE BALM® 7 C'S (REVISITED)

One of the first things BALM families learn are the BALM 7 C's. As mentioned, the first three were borrowed from Al-Anon. The fourth used to be part of Al-Anon but was stated in a different way. The fifth, sixth, and seventh provide BALM's special contribution to understanding the family's role. Here are all seven again as a prelude to a discussion of five, six and seven:

1. You did not cause your loved one's SUD.
2. You cannot control your loved one's SUD.
3. You cannot cure your loved one's SUD.
4. You can contribute to your loved one's recovery.
5. You are connected to your loved one on a level deeper than their SUD.
6. You can learn to communicate effectively with your loved one and others.
7. You are always at choice.

CONNECTION, COMMUNICATION, AND CHOICE

Many, though not all, BALM coaches are like Tracy. They join the BALM to use it in their own life as well as help others. You will find several of their powerful stories in Chapter 14. I credit the powerful urge BALM family members often have to help others to three of the BALM 7 C's: *Connection, Communication,* and *Choice*.

These life-changing C's, uniquely added to Al-Anon's first C's by the BALM, inspire great change in BALM families along with a desire to help other families awaken to recovery.

Knowing that you are connected to your loved one beneath their SUD will help you let go of stigma and will reawaken within you a sense of closeness with your loved one. Another mom and BALM coach, Marissa Arber, shared, "To this day, I refer to the C 'You are connected to your loved one on a level deeper than their SUD.' It reminds me of the deep love for my child that had been covered too long by sorrow, pain, and fear. It allowed me to shamelessly love my son again, only this time in a healthier, stronger, more helpful way." (To learn more about Marissa's story of family recovery, go to Chapter 14.)

After you transform yourself from the inside out, the next part of the program is transforming your communication. You see, relationships are the heart of the BALM program, and at the heart of relationship is communication. The core of our program is about communicating effectively — that is the essence of what "be the peace" means. If you are the peace, you will communicate effectively, and that's when you'll be contributing to recovery.

The seventh C — Choice (you are always at choice) — holds true at the beginning of the journey, the middle, and the end. It is in every part, because even from the very start you can make a choice to not do BALM. It's your choice. You are the chooser. Once you are committed to the program, you get to choose how intensively you will dive into study and practice of the principles and steps. Then, once you really go through the process, you will be at a much deeper level of choice as to how you will use what you have learned and even if you will use it. You will have a profoundly transformed perspective and a profoundly transformed ability to choose. When you release yourself from all the desperation, torture, and suffering, you've given yourself choices. The world has opened for you.

ALWAYS AT CHOICE CHART

Developed by Marissa Arber, Certified **BALM** Coach

People often tell us what we should be doing. Sometimes we tell ourselves we should be doing something other than what we are actually doing. In this chart, we look at the "shoulds" and at our actual choices so that we can take personal responsibility for the choices we make every day. In this sample, the BALM family member was being pressured to do what others in her family felt she 'should' do, though she was neither in need of extra money nor was she using her time poorly. Once you read the sample, try the exercise with a challenge facing you.

What someone else (or a part of me) thinks I should be doing: I can do what someone else tells me to do as in when they say: "You should get a job."

What I am at choice to do: I can make my own decision. "I could get a job and if I am able to pay my bills without it, I can choose not to. It is my choice."

ALWAYS AT CHOICE CHART: STOP SHOULDING ON YOURSELF!

What someone else (or a part of me) thinks I should be doing:	What I am at choice to do:	What I actually chose to do:	Homework to help me actualize my choice:

What I actually chose to do: I made my own decision. "I chose to focus on my recovery and my family and to explore interesting ways to use my free time."

Homework to help me actualize my choice: I will make a list of options that appeal to me and discuss them with my coach. "I've always enjoyed volunteering. Perhaps I could volunteer at my church."

THE PROMISE OF THE LOVING PATH

What does the Loving Path promise? Does it promise that your loved one will stay alive? No. But it does promise hope. It promises a future for you, a present for you and your loved one, and that you can be your loved one's best chance of a future lived in recovery.

So often, family members have difficulty conjuring pleasant memories of a loved one who is struggling. Instead, the family members' minds are consumed with recent heartache and repeated near tragedies. Then, those memories turn into present-day experiences, and everything magnifies. As my former teacher Maharishi Mahesh Yogi used to state again and again, *"That which you put your attention on grows stronger in your life."* If you're focusing on how bitter and awful your recent memories are, that perspective will grow stronger in your present life. If I'm thinking about how horrible my life is, how awful my loved one is, or how bitter I am because "God has cursed me," I'm not on the Loving Path. Rather, I'm on the path of pain, sorrow, anger, and resentment.

With BALM, we invite people to a path of love where they can see every experience with their loved one as an opportunity to be loving, to share sweet memories, and to recall all the good times of the past — even if the present is challenging.

The promise of the Loving Path is that when we see our loved one through the eyes of love, we see deeper than their use disorder and often find opportunities to contribute to their recovery.

You may experience pain, but you don't have to suffer.
That's the promise of the Loving Path.

QUESTIONS TO PONDER:

> What challenge are you facing today with your loved one or in your own recovery that could benefit from greater clarity?
> Pull out a sheet of paper and create your Clear/Unclear chart. Write the challenge at the top and list everything you know about it on the left and questions and things you don't know on the right.
> Use this information to find patterns, gain clarity, and determine your next steps.

4

BALM® Lights the Way

THE THREE PARTS OF BALM®

People often ask me what do I mean by Be A Loving Mirror. Early on, I put together this short definition of the phrase to help people understand this core phrase of our program: Be A Loving Mirror!

PART ONE: **BE**

The first part of Be A Loving Mirror is just to *be*. What is your state of being? Who are you being? Who are you in this moment? You have a choice in this, as in all things. What are you going to be?

PART TWO: **LOVING**

What does it mean to be loving? Being loving is about being nonjudgmental, being present with another person, allowing them to be who they are without your judgment, without your opinions in the middle of it, all while simply being aware of their presence. Being loving means allowing someone to take personal responsibility for their life — not shaming them. Being loving is treating others with dignity and respect.

This is a merciful sort of humanness, where you don't forget that this person is a human being. As soon as you remember that, it enhances your own ability to be a flawed human being and increases your own humanity and humility. This is not about having an excuse to make mistakes. It means recognizing that being flawed is inevitable. Welcome to the human race!

When you're being loving in all this, you develop the attitude that kindness is key, that compassion is crucial, that empowering them to take personal responsibility as much as possible is important, that you're all about helping — not enabling. All of that is packed into being loving, including loving yourself. You care about yourself enough to not damage your own physical, mental and spiritual health. You stay calm for your own benefit as well. (See the Four Aspects of Self-Care Chart on page 58 on how to nurture yourself.)

PART THREE: **MIRROR**

What does it mean to be a mirror?

A mirror reflects back. A BALM mirror shares the facts with the other person in a loving way so they can hear it. The mirror part of this is received from the calmness you're broadcasting. The mirror is about what you reflect to them, what you observe. In other words, you mirror their words and behavior through factually yet calmly sharing them. They can hear the objective facts of what they've said and what they've done. On that basis, they can perhaps make a different decision for their future behavior.

When we stop criticizing, crying, making it about us; when we stop demanding that people change and focus on our own change and growth; when we love our loved ones, however they are — everything changes. Be A Loving Mirror lights the way for change.

THE FOUR ASPECTS OF SELF-CARE CHART

The chart on the next page gives some examples of aspects of self-care in each area of self: physical, mental, emotional, and spiritual. See which aspects you have been attending to and which need more help. Then, think of additional ideas for self-care not listed here and add them to the chart.

MY SOUL IS A LIGHT

Be A Loving Mirror creates a light in the room that wasn't there before. The BALMer is illuminated from the inside out, and when they share that light, when they share the BALM conversation, they are in essence lighting the other person. One soul lights another, and the path is revealed over time.

One of the beautiful things that happens in the BALM conversation is that over time, your loved one will often begin to give you BALM conversations themselves. My relationship with my husband is a perfect example of this.

Over fourteen years ago, he had a five-year relapse, and I made a terrible mistake. I saw things going wrong, but rather than call him out with Be A Loving Mirror like I did thirty-some years ago, I went back into denial.

PHYSICAL SELF-CARE:	MENTAL SELF-CARE:
Exercise Annual physical exam Six-month dental cleanings Healthy nutrition Seven to eight hours of sleep each night Conscious breathing exercises	Attitude of gratitude Focus on the Task at Hand Living one day at a time Conscious breathing exercises Physical exercise Sleep Nutrition Community Education
EMOTIONAL SELF-CARE	**SPIRITUAL SELF-CARE**
Not taking things personally Detachment from obsession Enjoying life Healthy relationships Fun Happiness Practicing breathing exercises Self-love Assertiveness Accepting life on life's terms	Prayer Meditation Fellowship Quiet time Enjoying nature Reading inspiring literature Hearing spiritual music Journaling

The end of that relapse was when I realized this and started to BALM once more.

At that point I explained to him, "Rather than calling you out in a loving way, I just allowed myself to be lulled back into denial. I take responsibility for my part of our family malady. I will never again see you having problems and not say what I see." And then, I called him out in a loving way about what was happening. The calling out of it is so powerful. I've continued to do that for him over the last nine plus years, and what's really remarkable is that he's been doing it for me, too. I attribute him as being my best chance. I was in a food relapse for five years, but my husband was a loving mirror for me, gently, until I could wake up and get my recovery back.

My example became my family's way of life. My daughter has even done it for us! Now, it's not like we're this perfect family. We're not perfect at BALM — we're highly emotional, and occasionally, we still yell. But our level of calm with each other has increased, and so when one of us gets upset, the others are less likely to escalate the situation the way we use to.

No family can be the perfect family. No one can be the perfect human. The point is figuring out, How do you live your life in peace? How do you live your life in a constructive way? And then working at it day by day, using what you learn to Be A Loving Mirror.

WHY BALM®?

The truth is, BALM isn't the only way. We don't have a corner on the market of helping people (and, frankly, that's a good thing — the more help, the better). What BALM provides is a powerful path to spiritual awareness. While other books and programs can provide this, too, BALM is specifically applied to bringing awareness to yourself *and* your struggling loved one.

What BALM recognizes is that the key to peace of mind is to have peace in all your relationships. Peace with your Creator. Peace with yourself. Peace with others. As the quote in the introduction to this book alludes to, when you have peace with the people in your environment, with your emotions and desires and with your Creator, you will have peace of mind. The BALM is a path to that peace.

When I first started writing blogs, I was writing all about this. At first, people didn't get it, and some still don't. "What are you, crazy?" they would write. "Why should I do all that work? It's their problem."

The answer is simple, because it's your work too: the BALM journey can help you, and potentially your loved one, and beyond that it is its own reward.

THE JOURNEY AND THE DESTINATION

The important thing to remember about BALM is it's not just the journey — it's also the destination. Be A Loving Mirror is the Loving Path to family recovery, and the destination of practicing this Loving Path is the ongoing practice of BALM with self, loved ones, family, and friends. That continual practice of loving others is the definition of family recovery itself

There's no guarantee of any specific result of this practice other than that you will Be A Loving Mirror. Often, though, people report a positive shift in the family's challenging situations. As my wise sponsor, Dawn, told me many times:

"Your only obligation to another adult human being is to be a loving person. It is what we are spiritually called to be and to do."

BALM is the result of my interpretation of Dawn's guidance, and the experience of so many of us on this path is that BALM gives us the ability to be loving in a profound and ongoing way, so we can be and do who and what we are called to be and do.

BALM builds connection with your loved one, and that connection is also the journey and the destination. You already are connected; the people we love the most are part of us, and we are part of them. To feel bad that you're related to an individual with use disorder is like feeling bad that you have a broken arm. That arm is still a part of you. The connection is a fact.

What BALM does is grow that connection. When we're not BALMing with our loved ones, we are growing the separation. When we're BALMing, we are growing the connection. A lot of times, even in recovery, a family grows apart because they're so involved in the community of their own recovery. In BALM, we're about saving families who want to be saved and keeping them connected. The work we do as family members, the BALMing that we do, serves to help our loved ones choose to heal. It serves to bring the family closer together, because we learn how to communicate in such a way that the connection continually grows stronger, even in early recovery.

The BALM method is the Loving Path. It is practiced in present-day awareness. When we're practicing BALM, we're in the moment. We are seeing the facts of what is happening. We're aware of facts that have happened. We keep track of them as we go, but not to shame our loved one. Our goal is to recognize any patterns so that we can have their back. We want to be able to see past their blind spots and help them do the same.

HOW TO HAVE A BALM® CONVERSATION

A BALM conversation starts with you scripting it. Before you even meet with your loved one, list the facts you plan to share: that's documenting the facts. Then, make a plan that works for both of you for exactly when and where to speak, and ask your loved one to meet you there and then.

Of course, it is important that your loved one be lucid during the conversation. So if you are meeting to share a using episode, you may need to allow for time between the incident and the conversation.

Additionally, if the incident upset you greatly, you will need time to come down from any flooding you are experiencing. These two reasons are why it is so important to decide when to speak rather than just having a spontaneous conversation.

The BALM conversation is to be a clarifying, calm, and calming event, held with the intention to help your loved one see past their blind side in the most loving way possible.

Another thing it will do is give you a chance to vent in a planned manner. In other words, it provides a process of sharing what is bothering you in a non-defensive and inoffensive way. Without judgment, malice, or anger, you share the facts of what you see and hear with your loved one.

The power of such a loving interchange cannot be overestimated. Here is how it works.

Between setting the meeting and having the actual conversation, relax. Focus on self-care. Stretch your body, take a bath, go for a run. Whatever is decompressing for you, do that.

The conversation itself always starts with love. Tell them you love them. Then, state why you asked for the conversation. Through this, and everything, let compassion and care guide you. Stay calm, stay peaceful. Share the facts of what you see. Then, share an observation. Always, *always* watch your tone so that the things you're saying are factual and nonjudgmental.

After that, sit and listen. You have no obligation to believe their response, but you do have an obligation to treat them with dignity and respect by listening. Remember, their behavior is due to a brain disorder — not lack of moral fiber.

The idea here is that if your emotions and judgment enter the conversation, all the person will hear is your emotions and judgment. That could easily become their excuse to ignore the content. If you get yourself in an emotionally quiet space and a physically quiet environment and then just share the facts, they can hear the facts. They're not clouded by what your emotions are saying under the surface, and they can just listen to your words.

Then, you give them a kiss and go on your way. If necessary, you complete the last step: add a boundary.

QUESTIONS TO PONDER:

1. What are you noticing that concerns you in your loved one's behavior?
2. Stop for a moment to document the facts.
3. As soon as you see a pattern, take what you see to your BALM coach or someone you know understands this work you are doing, and script a conversation.

Part II:
PRACTICAL STRATEGIES

5

Contribute to Recovery
Not the Brain Disorder

WHY THE FAMILY UNIT?

The research (Brown, Lewis, and Liotta, 2000) supports the family's crucial role in recovery. When the family learns new ways to relate, the loved one has a better chance of getting into and staying in recovery. Once treatment occurs, mutual peer support and the family play the pivotal role in a loved one's ability to maintain long-term recovery. According to Dr. John Kelly of Harvard, in an interview with Bill White:

"Acute stabilization of people with addiction is important and can be lifesaving, but this is the easy part. The real challenge is how to prevent relapse and enhance the chances of remission and stable long-term recovery. From my clinical observations and clinical research experience, I can see this happens through "extra-treatment" factors, such as through social networks of recovery

support and family, although short-term treatment can play a critical role in making and strengthening those linkages. So... this is the really interesting and intriguing part of recovery to me; what happens in the days, weeks, months, years, and decades following formal treatment intervention."

The family can be the encouraging or discouraging factor. They can learn new ways of being and speaking and acting that will encourage the loved one, making it easier for the loved one to get and stay well. Or they can put up roadblocks and make that person miserable.

We know that stress is associated with relapse. Our approach involves having the family both work on their own life and help their loved one get well. If you're working on your life, you're reducing your own stress. So, you'll have less stress to sluff off on someone else. Your plate is clean. Your side of the street is clean. So, when you're present with another person, you can be there in a way that's helpful — not harmful.

What does it mean to contribute to a loved one's use disorder or their recovery? Families do love their using loved ones, but often that love is translated through criticism, bitterness, anger and accusation, taking everything personally, blaming, enabling, and staying in denial and pretending nothing's wrong. These things all contribute to the person's SUD. Even if the constant stream of advice and other forms of concern are done in the spirit of love, it's not the kind of love that helps.

Traditional approaches to family recovery in the context of a loved one also getting into recovery say that often, the family will experience a period (sometimes extended) of emotional, if not physical, separation. Researchers and authors Stephanie Brown and Virginia Lewis state in *The Alcoholic Family in Recovery* that it is important that recovering couples understand the "hidden truth" that "the couple 'breaks up' and stays 'separated' — emotionally — for a long time into recovery ... It is this separation and the shift from a focus on the couple and family system to their own individual development that gives the couple a healthy foundation on which to build a new, stronger couple bond. But," they continue, "this takes a long time; so long that some don't make it to the other side".

The BALM posits — and we see the evidence anecdotally as we are growing — that when the family focuses on our two-pronged approach of getting your life back while helping your loved one get theirs back, families can considerably shorten the length of this emotional separation (which can also happen in families where the loved one is a teen or adult child). When the family is using BALM as their primary recovery program or as an adjunct to their Twelve-Step, therapeutic, coaching, or other recovery program, they grow stronger both as a unit and in their individual recovery.

The key is the inner transformation that encourages and allows for an aware, non-enabling, loving relationship with the loved one and the other family members — rather than just a focus on self — before, during, and after a loved one's ongoing recovery process.

BEFORE A LOVED ONE'S RECOVERY

To contribute to recovery is to be peaceful yourself so that you can see the facts on the ground. Once you see the facts, be mindful enough not to take them personally and not to judge the person about them. How do you get to that point?

Families are always contributing: whether you know it or not, you are either contributing to your loved one's SUD or you're contributing to their recovery. They'll always want something from you, even if it's only a response. They will need something. There will be things in their life that will require you to choose to either react or respond. So you'll always be contributing to something.

If you give them money, that money could end up in their veins. If you bail them out of jail without any negotiation of terms (or, as we call it, "leverage") to encourage them to change, you are releasing them to use again. If you ignore them instead of listening, you're making things worse.

Find out what their needs are. Find out what it means to contribute to recovery and move in that direction. If you don't know what those needs are (it can be hard to tell sometimes), remember: we *all* need love and connection. So, if you are pushing them away and belittling or demeaning them because of their use disorder or other behaviors, you're not contributing to their recovery process. You're contributing to the problem.

ONCE THE LOVED ONE IS IN RECOVERY

Once the loved one is in recovery, the same holds true. Honest, aware communication works through BALM conversations the loved one and family member often provide each other. These conversations are shared based on objective observation and only when a concerning pattern is observed. The new relationship is one of acceptance and love, appreciation of difference, and a sense of gratitude for having come through a horrific storm together, with everyone accounted for on the other side.

Perfect? Of course not, but you will be growing together while working through problems individually as well as jointly.

TOUGH LOVE VERSUS BOUNDARIES

Of course, we've all heard about tough love. Cut someone off, isolate them to try to get them on track. The heart behind this is in the right place, but it isn't effective for either party. Isolating doesn't help. There's a distinct difference between "tough love" and "healthy boundaries." Healthy boundaries are essential. The difference, however, is that isolating someone in the name of "tough love" to get them to change is a control tactic; it's about them, it's not about you. Healthy boundaries, on the other hand, are for your own health and benefit — not necessarily for theirs. The actions might even be the same, but it's the motivation that matters.

And if your loved one is a minor? Give them healthy limits along with boundaries. But not shaming, isolating, punishing, or tough love. There is a better way. The BALM, with its emphasis on staying aware of the underlying connection we have with our struggling loved ones, leads the way toward loving relationships in families.

A man came to speak to our group, and he told us about a relapse he'd had. It was a five-year-long relapse, and by the end of it, no one in his family was talking to him, just his best friend. Eventually, his best friend said to him, "I love you very much, but I can't have you in my life at this point, because it's really harming me to watch you kill yourself and be unable to convince you to get help." The speaker said that was the behavior that led to his recovery.

Sometimes, after multiple relapses, families decide they are done being part of a use disorder they cannot influence. Again, the *how* in this decision is as important as the *what*. If it is done with love, a door is left open for the loved one to walk through when they're ready to get help.

One of our BALM moms continually allowed her daughter to come to dinner parties and other events and was very loving throughout the using days. At a certain point, several years into her daughter's use, her daughter's active SUD had resulted in her living on the street. It was painful for this mom, a strong BALMer, to watch her daughter deteriorate — so painful that it eventually created physical stress and distress to the point of illness.

Mom, who had always been very close to her daughter, had a loving BALM conversation with her, explaining that as difficult as it would be to not see her, it was becoming unhealthy for her (the mom) to see her daughter in such bad shape. She said she would always be there to help her daughter find help, but until then, it would be best if they didn't see each other.

This was a painful and challenging decision for the mom, but also very freeing. She had put her daughter through more than ten treatment programs, and her resources were depleted. As a result of her decision, she found herself able to focus on each day without her daughter's challenges interrupting her peace, and she began to feel physically better.

One day, within weeks, her daughter showed up at her door, ready to go to treatment. Mom and her coach got to work and found the young woman a long-term treatment center, and things moved forward quickly from there.

Two years later (at time of this book's publication), the daughter is still living a clean and sober life.

These are just two examples of setting a boundary with love; in each case, the relational connection was preserved because the motivation for pulling away was love. The message the friend and the mother sent was love and self-care. That's not tough love. Tough love is, "We're pulling away from you because your behavior is unacceptable and unless you change it, we're not going to talk to you anymore." There's a subtle difference, and they're certainly not the same. Tough love is about trying to dictate and control behavior deemed bad or shameful. Unconditional BALM love is about family members protecting their own physical and mental well-being while respecting the dignity of all the human beings involved.

When we think about contributing to recovery, the first thing we must do is get our own lives back. Put the oxygen mask on your own face before you try to help someone else. In other words, we must take care of ourselves so much that we are able to relate to the person in a healthier way. That's part of maintaining an inner calm, so that the upset of involvement with this person isn't dictating our lives. For many of us, when we're involved with somebody who is acting out, every moment of our life is, *Should I stay? Should I go? Will they live? Will they die? How do I save them? How do I do this? How do I do that?*

It's panic. Step back from that — on the inside.

The same action can be healthy in one instance and unhealthy in another. For example, take the act of having a conversation.

You could be having a conversation with your loved one about their behavior, and if you're really caught up in the result you want for them, forcing your will on them, making ultimatums, being very aggressive and trying to control them, it's unhealthy.

If you're having that same conversation with them from a calm place, however, describing the facts of what you see, telling them how much you love them, encouraging them to find their path, and if necessary, setting a boundary, that's technically the same action-having a conversation — but from a healthy, loving approach instead.

Boundaries are limits that we set around ourselves for our own health and peace of mind. So, if I'm setting a boundary, that results from deciding what I choose to have in my life and what I don't choose to have in my life; what I choose to be part of and what I choose not to be part of.

For instance, let's say your daughter is selling marijuana in your home, and you don't want to have an illegal substance being sold there (assuming you live in a state where it's illegal or she is a minor). You don't want it in your home or in your life. You are allowed to set a boundary: that if she wants to live with you, she cannot sell marijuana. If she chooses to do it, she'll have to find another place to live. If she lies about it, you will figure it out. When you do, she'll have to find another place to live.

Now, that's a boundary about you — it's not about her. That's a healthy boundary. You're choosing to not be involved in illegal activity, just like you can choose to not have a smoker live with you and smoke in your house because you don't want to breathe that air. (Of course, you can choose to not have marijuana smoking in your home for your own personal quality of life reasons as well, even if it is legal in your state!) It's your boundary. It's not about them, it's about you.

If you're not letting an adult loved one smoke in the house because it's killing *them*, that's an unhealthy boundary — you're doing it to control them. They have the right to choose to smoke if they want to; it's just that simple. If you're doing it because you don't want the secondhand smoke, that's about you, because you have rights, too.

The reason it's so hard to set healthy boundaries, however, is that people will push back. They will often respond as though you're doing something awful, as though it *is* about them (even though you've been clear it isn't), as though you're being too rigid. They will call you names, they will yell, they will manipulate, they will do anything to protect their behavior and their "right" to do whatever they want — even if it infringes on you.

THE PEACE WITHIN

The inevitable pushback from your loved one is why we have a very strict principle about boundary setting: *don't set a boundary unless you're determined to stick to it* (BALM Principle 7). The reason for that is simple: when you set your boundary, no matter how lovingly you do so, no matter how clear it is, the loved one will most likely push back. If you give in, they will see you as someone who can be easily manipulated, and they will further disrespect your boundaries.

So that area of peace within? Boy, that's seems extraordinarily important in this area, doesn't it? Because while that other person is raging at you, your inner peace is all you have. You must be the eye of the storm. Our whole program is about building a level of serenity, sanity, and peace that is imperturbable. That is the key: *being the peace you wish to see in the world* (Step One of seven). When you are the peace, you're able to see the world more objectively (Step Two), and because of the peace, as you see the world more objectively and get upset by your own situation or yourself (Step Three), you work through it, and that deepens your peace even further. All three steps build off each other, but peace is what leads to transformation.

So, the inner transformation is the primary thing. The problem is that total, inner transformation takes a lifetime or more to achieve. You can't necessarily wait to be perfectly peaceful before you start implementing BALM. You can make a huge shift in yourself by choosing a daily peaceful practice and pursuing it, but the BALM's two-pronged approach is simultaneous: get your life back and help your loved one get theirs back, because sometimes you don't have the years it would take to become peaceful first. It's about working on your inner peace as you learn how to shift the way you relate to your struggling relative.

For support in this transformative process, don't be afraid to rely on others. You're not an island in this; there's support all around you. There are professionals who can work with your loved one. There are BALM coaches for you both. There's the BALM Comprehensive Program where you can inundate yourself with information, transformation, and support. There are Twelve-Step programs. There's SMART Recovery and Women for Sobriety. There's a lot out there for a person to learn and practice. Getting support that will greatly enhance your recovery is Principle 8 of the BALM, and in that lesson, we list many places to go for support.

The key is to figure out your needs so you can get some sanity in your life. Get those needs fulfilled. While you're doing that, learn about use disorders, how they operate, and how to contribute to recovery. It's a learning process of going within to get calm while also learning new ways to communicate, finding new ways to be helpful, and using everything at your disposal for yourself and for your loved one.

LEARNING ABOUT SUD

It's important to educate yourself about your loved one's use disorder so you can distinguish what's a part of them and what's a part of their disorder. What you'll need to do in terms of getting help from the outside will depend on a lot of factors, but it all starts with having the clarity and the peace of mind to objectively observe what's going on. This means dealing with the emotional struggles of "Oh, my God! Something's not right here" and getting the education to figure out what exactly that is — and how to cope with it.

To experience a holistic recovery process, be sure to find a program that includes information, transformation, and support. The Daily BALM, for instance, has over 400 recordings of experts talking about use disorders and recovery, along with guidance on how to use a variety of helpful behaviors and tools. We have recordings covering how loved ones can get better, how families can get better, how to cope, how to work with a treatment center, how to find the right helper, and how to get calm yourself — everything. There's a whole gamut of issues when it comes to being in a relationship with someone with these problems, and our goal is to cover them all, including how to contribute to recovery, partner with a treatment center, and advocate for your loved one's recovery. Listening to family members and loved ones who've been there, who are willing to discuss what it took and what they've learned in both individual and family interviews — this is the kind of information that can help. We show people that they're not alone, that they're not the only ones, and that there *is* a way out of this *as a family.*

TRANSFORMATION AND SUPPORT

Of course, the recovery process requires more than just information. That's just the beginning. Information alone is useful, but the transformation part is where you develop a practice of peace. That's where you learn how to objectively observe and work through your emotions. On that basis, you learn the ways to transform your communication. That's the practical application.

Learning how to contribute to the recovery rather than the brain disorder takes a commitment. If your kid had cancer, you wouldn't say, "Oh, I've got choir practice on Wednesday nights. Sorry, can't help you!" You'd do whatever it took to save his life. This is where you invest in support. That investment could mean going to Al-Anon five days a week, and there's nothing wrong with that. But be aware: if you are looking for education and support on how to help your loved one *in addition* to helping yourself, you may need more than what they offer. Yes, you're going to have a lot of serenity and a lot of peace by turning your back on this loved one and saying, "It's not my problem," but we use a different approach. We say, "It *is* your problem." And if it's your problem, let's get to work.

That's what we're here for.

SUPPORT FOR TEENS

I want to take a minute here to connect with teenagers whose parents have a SUD. When it comes to BALM and to boundaries, teenagers have a problem — because of the natural imbalance of authority between you and your parents. If your parent has a SUD, you're not left with much negotiating power. Setting your boundaries can be far more difficult. If you're a teen reading this book about your parent, we invite you to BALM free of charge. You will learn to be the calm in your home, inside and out. Please join us. There is support out there for you. To sign up for the BALM, call (888) 998-BALM, and let us know your situation.

It is not okay if your parents are emotionally or physically abusive. Talk to a guidance counselor, a coach, a teacher, or a therapist. There are adults in your life who care about you and want to help; don't hesitate to connect with them.

If you are in danger of a crisis occurring in your home, be prepared. Find the nonemergency number for fire and police in your town. Call 911 if you or your family members are in danger.

LEVERAGE

We have already discussed the basics of boundary setting. Boundaries are all about what is best for you, the family member. Now let's talk about leverage. Leverage is a form of negotiation we teach our families. It is a give-and-take: you want something, I want something. If your loved one has professional help or is in treatment, you can coordinate leverage with the treatment center. If not, work with your and your loved one's BALM coaches to develop your plan.

Leverage empowers you with the opportunity to encourage recovery behaviors in exchange for things your loved one wants, so it can be a real win-win situation. First, write down anything and everything you give to your loved one or that they rely on you for. Your list can include things like a car, car insurance, a phone, payment for their phone, a roof over their head, seeing the children, the marriage — all depending on who you are and what your relationship is to them. Think of everything you are involved with that is important to them; that's your leverage.

If your loved one says they want to come home from treatment, your leverage could be, "Complete your treatment time successfully, and we'll talk about it then." Using leverage can help you help them decide to do what's best for their recovery.

Here is the caveat: twenty-eight days of treatment is a random construct originally put into place without adequate research. It became the norm since that was what insurance companies would pay for. Many people need sixty to ninety days of actual treatment, followed by six months to a year of recovery residence, therapy, coaching, and ongoing help.

Also, beware of entitlement. You do not owe an adult child a car, a phone, or a roof over their head. You can leverage the things they want against whatever will contribute to their recovery, such as longer treatment time, more months living in a sober environment, getting a job, going to meetings, or working with a recovery life coach.

Here is a chart to help you make your leveraging lists.

DISCOVER YOUR LEVERAGE — AND USE IT!

For this exercise, we define leverage as anything you currently provide or could provide for your loved one that they want to continue to get. To use it most effectively, family members should use it sparingly in partnership with a loved one's professionals as a tool to advocate recovery for the loved one.

In the chart on the next page, use the left side to list everything you provide for your loved one and everything they want you to provide for them or want to get for themselves that are currently out of their hands.

LEVERAGE CHART	
Requests from the Recovering Person	**Requests from the Professionals and Family**
I want to come home after treatment	We want you to go straight from treatment to recovery residence for at least six months before discussing next steps.

With your BALM coach, your loved one's BALM coach, the treatment team, and any other professionals helping your family, create a list of the things you all believe will be best for your loved one's recovery going forward. Also, as much as possible, work with the professionals to determine what agreement terms will be most helpful for that recovery. It is best to go into the final meeting with an idea of what will appear in the columns and with an openness to what your loved one may add.

Most likely, you have started this list on your own, then added input from your professional team and finally, you attend a meeting with your loved one and, if possible, your coach and their coach or other professionals. Together, you discuss what you want and what they want, with each person listing ideas for each column.

Then, negotiate what you want of your loved one for them to get what they want. The delicate balance of respect and fierce advocacy for recovery is one best managed in a BALM frame of mind with professionals present.

To be clear, you don't want to use leverage in a threatening way; it's not something to hold over their head. It is to be used sparingly and strategically, with the help of professionals. Your BALM coach is an expert at working with your loved one's treatment professional. Use your team!

LIMITS

Limits are different from leverage. For example, if your teen is completely out of control, you as a parent have the responsibility to set limits, but that doesn't mean your teen will respond positively. Sometimes you need to bring outsiders in to help you. How your loved one responds to your limits can help you understand how bad the situation is: if they're either unwilling or unable to comply, you'll get a sense of what's going on and what you're dealing with.

Remember that when a person is struggling with a use disorder, their brain is hijacked. Their brain is telling them that they must have this thing, this substance, this behavior — or they will die. Of course, it's really the opposite. They need to stop taking or doing it or they may die, but that's not where their head is.

WHAT ARE YOU CONTRIBUTING TO?

As I've mentioned, if you're not contributing to recovery, you're contributing to the disorder. But sometimes it can be difficult to make that distinction. If your loved one is arrested and you feel that you have to get them out because jails aren't safe, which choice is contributing to recovery? Often, it's impossible to tell without outside help. Of course, to just get them out of jail and back on the streets is enabling, and you are contributing to their disorder.

If possible, get a lawyer and tie any legal action you take to their getting help. This is not the time to advocate for what your loved one wants; this is a very important time to advocate for their recovery. Take advantage of their incarceration to get them the help they need to get well. Yes, they may be an adult, but they are impaired, and you as their caring and loving family member have a choice to contribute to their recovery or to contribute to their disorder by not getting involved. You must advocate for them to get an assessment along with the best level of treatment for their needs. Your job is to contribute to your loved one's recovery by supporting a process that will lead to their getting the help they need.

Once you find out that your child, your spouse, or another loved one has a problem, start gathering your team. It's essential to have a team of players working with you on this process.

Sometimes that team can be made of volunteers, sometimes it's made of professionals, and sometimes it's a combination. For instance, if your child gets into trouble, find out which local lawyers can help specifically with SUD. You're not looking for people just to get them out. You're looking for people who know the judges, who know the treatment centers, who will help you figure out next best steps to help your loved one — just like you'd have a team of doctors and nurses if your child had an immune disorder.

There's a broad range of types of help. There are intensive outpatient programs. There are inpatient programs. There are detoxes. The type of help needed depends on what the drug is and the extent of your loved one's usage. Interventionists (see glossary) can help you get your loved one into treatment. For example, your BALM coach can help you figure out what type of help you need as well as coach you to better communicate with each other and your loved one. They can also help you build the team of professionals so you can better motivate your loved one choose and sustain recovery.

A FAMILY IN RECOVERY

If you want to contribute to recovery, you must be in recovery yourself. From a BALM perspective, family recovery starts with understanding substance use disorder, understanding other use disorders, understanding behavioral challenges and understanding how all those come about. It's not as much about labels as it is about understanding the human condition. It's important to work with people who can help you figure out what's going on with your kid or your loved one. Meanwhile, it's your job to use your BALM tools so you can be calm enough to deal with the situation rationally.

Trust me, dealing with this calmly or rationally is not a natural response. We all have issues in how we respond. Some people are natural enablers. This is true for many parents. Often, one parent is an enabler and one parent is overly rigid. So, one parent's reaction to fear will be, "No! No matter what it is, no," while the other will say, "Oh, come on. Let him do it. It's not that bad."

Getting on the same page with your spouse or ex is a process you can work through with your coach. If family members like parents are opposed to each other, both sides may be having a fear reaction, which triggers a fight-or-flight instinct. The parent who is overly rigid is fighting, and the parent who is enabling is fleeing — and neither is really facing up to what's going on. In fact, they're contributing to the use disorder by creating a toxic, push-and-pull family environment.

HOW TO CONTRIBUTE TO RECOVERY

Once you become fully aware and consciously stop contributing to your loved one's use disorder, the more important task is to then consciously contribute to recovery. The first step, especially as parents, is to make an effort to be in their life. Don't push yourself on them, but remain present. You are an important figure in your child's life with an important role to play. Parents, family members, close loved ones — you always have a role. Remember, you are connected to your loved one on a level deeper than their use disorder (the 5th **BALM** C). Don't be fooled into thinking they don't need you just because they start turning to someone else. Their friends might not have the emotional stability, inner wisdom, or strength to help them the same way a family member could, especially a parent (Neufield and Mate 2005).

So, rebuild your relationship with them.

In the early days of the BALM, I had a mom come to me whose daughter was in jail. "Listen," she said, "I haven't had a kind word with my daughter for eight years. She started using when she was eleven, and I've been screaming at her for eight years. She's now nineteen. She's in jail, and I want to visit her. I haven't visited her thus far because I can't think of anything to say. Can you help me?"

I coached her in class on how she might relate to her daughter differently. I invited her to think of every good memory she could think of with her daughter.

"But they're so old," she said, referring to her good memories of her now adult child.

"I don't care. Let's put them out there."

So she wrote down the memory of her daughter's beautiful smile. She wrote down the way her daughter giggled when she was little, how they used to play Play-Doh together for hours. She wrote beautiful, joyful memories. We built a list of memories that she had shut out for so many years. By the end of this conversation, she was laughing, smiling, and sharing great memories about somebody she hadn't made a good memory with for eight years.

"This is so wonderful," she finally said, "but what do I do with it?"

"When you visit you daughter," I replied, "every time you look at her, see that little girl. Look in her eyes and see that little girl. This person she's been for years, who you've been alienated from — allow that to dissipate and just see that little girl you love. Just share memories with her and tell her how much you love her. Be in the moment, let her talk to you about her life, and don't have any judgment about it. Allow her to tell you what's happening while you just listen and empathize. Don't bring up, 'Well, if you hadn't done this . . .'; leave all that outside the prison door. Just be there with your daughter and enjoy her in the moment."

So she went to the prison, and they had a wonderful time together. They didn't have long because of visitation rules, but all they did the whole session was laugh and giggle and cry and hug. That was the beginning of a new relationship with her daughter.

We all want to make sure we fix it for our loved one, but whether we fix it or not, they're still precious human beings to love and to cherish. So, love and cherish your loved one exactly as he or she is right now, in this moment. Treasure them in the present — and see what happens.

QUESTIONS TO PONDER:

1. Are you contributing to your loved one's disorder or their recovery?
2. Do you have a recovery team in place?
3. If so, who is on it?
4. Who do you want to add?
5. If not, what will it take to put a recovery team in place?

6

Create Your Attitudinal Shift

As you've read by now, our whole program is about empowering families to contribute to the recovery, not to the use disorder. For this to happen, there has to be an attitudinal shift, which is the focus of the first four Principles of BALM:

1. The family has a crucial role to play in a loved one's recovery.
2. Change happens in stages.
3. It is important to let go without giving up or giving in.
4. You can be your loved one's best chance at recovery.

When studied and understood, these concepts create an inner change in the family member that allows a new way of seeing their loved one, their loved one's malady, and the challenge facing their family.

PRINCIPLE ONE
THE FAMILY HAS A ROLE TO PLAY

The attitudinal shift in BALM allows the family to take responsibility for their role. If you don't see your role, then why do anything else? If you don't have a role in this, why work on your attitude at all? Realize that you have a role to play. Part of that role is helping your loved one, and part of that role is taking care of you.

Once the family understands that they have a role, and that they are always contributing to things getting either better or worse, it helps them begin to understand the nature of how change happens when a loved one is trying to change a deeply ingrained habit.

PRINCIPLE TWO
CHANGE HAPPENS IN STAGES

Educating yourself about SUD and other use disorders is very important, and part of that education is understanding how change happens. We use Prochaska and DiClemente's model of the Stages of Change. We teach this to our families so that they can understand their loved one's process, as well as their own.

Here is an article I wrote about the Stages of Change model to help you understand it.

AN INTRODUCTION TO THE SIX STAGES OF CHANGE MODEL

Ever try to break a habit? Not easy, is it?

Perhaps you have counted on the twenty-one-day idea to get you through — namely, that if you practice a new behavior for twenty-one days, you will have momentum that will allow you to more easily move forward to breaking the habit for good. I like that idea and have used it to get me over the hump of difficult changes I am seeking.

But there is more to the picture. The twenty-one days start once you have taken action on the change you wish to make, and those twenty-one days typically last up to six months. But what about the days leading up to the very first day you stop an old habit or start a new one?

According to researcher James Prochaska, PhD, those pre-days are just as important, if not more so, as the first twenty-one of the action steps. Prochaska's research on how people change habitual behaviors has resulted in the Stages of Change model, which is taught in universities and to patients in substance abuse treatment centers and health centers all over the world.

If you want to change a behavior in your life — and according to Prochaska, each of us is in the process of changing three to four things at any given time — you need to become familiar with this model and its stages. How you go through those stages could determine the difference between your success and failure this time around. Most changes take three to four spins through the stages to take hold, Prochaska says.

But by becoming familiar with the stages, a self-changer can improve their ability to handle each stage more effectively and perhaps reduce the number of retreads they will need in order to succeed.

Prochaska outlines the change process in his book *Changing for Good: A Revolutionary Six-Stage Program for Overcoming Bad Habits and Moving Your Life Positively Forward* (Prochaska, Norcross, and DiClemente 2006) and his most recent book, *Changing to Thrive: Using the Stages of Change to Overcome the Top Threats to Your Health and Happiness* (Prochaska and Prochaska 2016). In case these books aren't on your reading list, here are the stages in a nutshell:

Stage One: *Precontemplation* — Prochaska also calls this stage "resistance to change." At this stage, you may not even be thinking about whether you have a problem. You are just living your life, full throttle, enjoying (or not) and doing what you do. The people around you are most likely aware that something is amiss through little hints, like the smoky room due to your chain-smoking, the empty fridge due to your binges, or the diminishing liquor in the cabinet when there hasn't been a party in months. Or maybe you had an injury a year ago and are still ordering (and somehow getting) your prescriptions filled, though most people with that exact injury stopped the pills months before. At any rate, you do *not* see a problem or you are demoralized from having tried to *change* and failed. In Patti Denning's book *Over the Influence: The Harm Reduction Guide for Managing Drugs and Alcohol*, she and her coauthors call this the "Who, me?" stage.

Stage Two: *Contemplation* — At this stage, which Prochaska nicknames "change on the horizon", you have begun to *sometimes* think you *may* have a problem. You are looking at your life, sometimes with the help of others who support your wellness or simply cannot stand watching you kill yourself any longer. And when you look, you think it might be time to think about doing something. At this point, you don't know what it is you want to do exactly. Nor do you have a plan or a change date. You are doing just what the name of the stage says: contemplating. You are still going back and forth between whether or not you have a problem and whether or not you should do anything about it if you do.

This stage is very important as it allows the changer to go over all the pros and cons in their mind. Without help, this stage can go on for a very long time. With help from a recovery life coach, therapist, or supportive friend or family member, the time can be lessened. Prochaska has written his latest book *Changing to Thrive* for people to be able to help themselves through stages of change exercises to quicken the process, and also to offer advice and exercises for those close to the changer. Contemplation comes to its conclusion when a decision has been made to change. Denning calls this stage the "Yes, but" stage.

Stage 3: *Preparation* — Prochaska calls the preparation stage the "getting ready" stage and says that most people in this stage plan to make their change within the month. They have set the date and are involved in activities to help them get ready for the big day.

This stage is important because without the proper planning, the big day may last only that long. The changer at this point may be thinking about what they will do instead of their habit, how they will avoid triggers, how they will begin, and how they will keep going. Whether the changer is a parent who wants to stop yelling at their struggling child, an individual with SUD who wants to get clean, one who wants to keep using drugs but stop sharing needles, or someone who wants to start flossing every night, without adequate preparation, the change they are planning probably will not last.

There may be a support group to join or a Recovery Life Coach or Therapist to hire. There may be new activities and friends to find. There may be clean needles or floss to purchase. Thinking about and taking small steps for these are just the tip of the iceberg of what a changer may need to put into place to make their new habit work. Thus, adequate preparation can have a huge impact on the success of their foray into the next step. Denning calls this stage the "Uh-oh" stage because plans are becoming real and concrete, and the difficulties lying ahead begin to become clearer.

Stage 4: *Action* — Until recently, most people just thought of action as the change. "Why don't you just change?" "Just do it!" Even now, many people unfamiliar with the Stages of Change model don't realize all that must go into preparing for the actual action to take root and become the person's new reality. Prochaska calls the action stage "time to move" — and indeed it is!

At this stage, it is time to put all the preparation into action. There may be some mourning as old friends must be let go of for a time and new types of activities and supports put into place. Depending on the nature of the change, help may be necessary to make this change last.

This stage typically lasts six months as one adjusts to a new way of life. It's amazing how much has to happen before the action takes place, but now the time has come, and if all the thinking and preparing has been done in advance, the action step has a much greater chance of succeeding.

Of course, there is still much to do. Here is where the rubber meets the road: taking it all and putting it into practice, one day at a time. It is a time of great excitement and tremendous adjustments — exhilarating and excruciating at the same time. Denning calls this the "Do It" stage.

Stage 5: *Maintenance* — Now that the action is becoming habitual, the challenge is to keep on keeping on. Prochaska calls this stage "staying there" and for good reason. Ever go on a diet and after a while say to yourself, "I have been so good. I deserve that ice cream!"?

For some people, a diet is all they need, and they can go back to everyday eating. But for those who have worked through Stages of Change to get to this point, or those who did so without much intention, going back now can spell disaster!

This stage, post-action, is the one that will make all the difference. At this point, the changer may have to put new supports in place and get therapy to work on the deeper wounds that need to be healed so they won't be eaten over or smoked over or whatever the changer's drug of choice is. Old friends may have been left behind in the action stage, so in the maintenance stage, it is crucial to form a new community to avoid the loneliness that could lead the changer back to the old, destructive crowd.

At this stage, you are no longer holding off the old habits. Rather, you are building a new life to support a whole new way of living that will keep you alive and healthy and hopefully much happier in the long run than you have been in the past.

To make this stage — which can stretch from two to ten years — stick, you may have to go through some mud. There may be feelings of wishing you could return to the "good old days," some feelings of "I could handle just one" that you ignore and find replacements for. Understanding that just one may take you back to square one is not enough. Putting new supports in place to insure your way of life is a requirement. You may feel like it's just not worth it at times, but unless going back to the truly bad old days is an option for you, you will do what it takes to secure your hard-won victories.

Denning calls this stage "The grind," and it's a well-earned title. There are legions of stories about people who quit drinking, drugging, or smoking and held these habits at bay for a very long time, only to have a life challenge throw them back over the edge. Though there is no absolute insurance against life's traumas and their impact, there is nothing like building a new life with powerful scaffolding to stave off the effects of life's inevitable stresses.

Recycling — When the changer gives up on "The grind," she goes through what Prochaska calls recycling, or "learning from relapse." This event is when a changer, even after great progress, goes back to the behavior they changed earlier. They start drinking or eating or gambling again and their life begins to deteriorate, sometimes slowly, sometimes rather quickly. Relapse may come on the heels of a family tragedy or be due to letting go of the supports that have kept the maintenance going. Or it may be the result of not having been ready to make the change in the first place.

Whatever caused it, when recycling comes, it puts the changer back to the beginning, but not quite. The work and learning she went through is still in her somewhere. Most recyclers don't give up and are willing to start again.

So, this is truly a learning stage. Denning calls this stage "Back to the drawing board," and Prochaska says that his research shows that recycling often leads back to contemplation, preparation, and action again and that most changers need to go through the cycle three to four times before being able to get to the final iteration. If self-change does not work after several tries, it may be time to get help or to try a different path than the one you have tried before, again.

Stage 6: *Termination* — Termination occurs when the changer is finished cycling through the Stages of Change on a specific change. The point is, the struggle is over; the person no longer has the problem in their life. It is resolved. Some say this never truly occurs. Others believe it is possible for areas like smoking and sedentary behavior. Prochaska calls this stage "Exiting the Stages of Change" and Denning calls it the "I'm over it" stage.

Although it can take a while to get there, it is the aspiration of many to do so, and more research and writing points in the direction of it being possible for many habits, but perhaps not for all.

These stages, taught in treatment centers, are useful for the struggling individual to know about and for the family as well. Anything that leads to empathy for oneself and others can be useful as one works through life's challenges.

BOOKS TO CONSIDER:

Prochaska, James, and Janice Prochaska. 2016. *Changing to Thrive: Using the Stages of Change to Overcome the Top Threats to Your Health and Happiness.* Center City, MN: Hazelden.

Prochaska, James, John C. Norcross, and Carlo C. DiClemente. 1994. *Changing for Good: A Revolutionary Six-Stage Program for Overcoming Bad Habits and Moving Your Life Positively Forward.* New York: Harper.

Denning, Patt, Jeannie Little, and Adina Glickman. 2004. *Over the Influence: The Harm Reduction Guide for Managing Drugs and Alcohol.* New York: The Guilford Press.

THE FAMILY'S PATH THROUGH THE STAGES OF CHANGE

In considering the stages, I put together a chart (pp. 96–102) that delineates how family members go through their own Stages of Change in relation to a loved one with SUD. As you can see, the stages are listed in the first column, column two lists characteristics of the stage, column three lists things the family members at that stage may say about their loved one, and column four is about the family member's statements in relationship to self and family in each stage.

Understanding the Stages of Change can complement the work you do in the areas of motivational conversations, asking powerful questions, stopping judging them, and simply inviting them to a deeper look and understanding. This is taught extensively in the BALM, and all our coaches stand ready to help you walk through this process.

You'll also be aware enough to prepare to play a *long game.* Your loved one won't heal instantly, and neither will you. This understanding will help you be patient with your loved one and yourself.

UNDERSTANDING LONG-TERM TRAJECTORY

The Family Member's Stage of Change	What it may look like	Statements in relation to the loved one	Statements in relation to self/family
	Complete denial of a problem.	There's nothing wrong with him.	It's not my problem. I don't see anything wrong with me.
	Drinking and drugging along with the loved one.	He'll grow out of it.	I can talk however I want to talk.
	Defensiveness.	She just needs to get her act together.	Why do I need help?
	Anxiety.	That kid is a bad seed.	Why should I make changes in my behavior?
	Anger.	You wouldn't do this if you loved me.	If you had this going on, you would be crazy too.
	Yelling, screaming, begging.	I hate him.	I am perfectly entitled to behave like this.
Precontemplation	Blaming, bargaining.	He is ruining my life.	
Denial	No understanding or identifying with the disease concept.	He could stop if he wanted to. What's the big deal?	Of course I will help him — he is my child.
Demoralization	Doesn't see a personal need for recovery.	I will do whatever I can so she doesn't experience the consequences of her behavior.	Enabling? How ridiculous.

	UNDERTANDING LONG-TERM TRAJECTORY		
The Family Member's Stage of Change	What it may look like	Statements in relation to the loved one	Statements in relation to self/family
Contemplation/ Ambivalence	Beginning to see that their loved one may have a problem that is more than willful. Beginning to consider that their loved one's behavior could have an impact but not much "will" to shift into a more helpful direction. Stuck. Still thinks enabling is their only choice but seeing it may be hurting.	Maybe he does need help. Maybe it is not his fault, but it is his responsibility to fix it. Maybe the treatment center is right. Maybe the judge is right. Maybe the counselor has a good point. Maybe boundaries would help him.	Maybe I could stop enabling. Maybe it's time to get some help for myself. Maybe if I face this I can be of more help. Maybe if I stop enabling he will have to face his situation. Maybe support would work for me. Maybe my enabling could kill him.

UNDERSTANDING LONG-TERM TRAJECTORY

The Family Member's Stage of Change	What it may look like	Statements in relation to the loved one:	Statements in relation to self/family
	Knows it is time to get help for a loved one and self. Fear of failure. Hires an interventionist. Sets a date within the next four weeks or so. Sets a date for own help: getting a coach, going to meetings, etc.	I've got to find someone to help me help my son. My daughter needs help, not enabling. Could you please help me figure out which treatment center is best? How can I get him to stay in recovery residence after treatment? What would you recommend I say in a BALM conversation?	I can see it's time for me to stop enabling. Starting next week, if Sally asks me for money, I will not give it to her. I am going to find some meetings next Friday. I am going to start listening to the Daily BALM in two weeks. I'll do this to help my loved one — and maybe me.
Preparation/ Planning			

UNDERTANDING LONG-TERM TRAJECTORY

The Family Member's Stage of Change	What it may look like	Statements in relation to the loved one	Statements in relation to self/family
Action/Working a Recovery Program	Takes action to get help for loved one. Takes action to get help for self. Begins to live a recovery life. Stops enabling. Works on staying out of denial. Documents, scripts, shares, and sets boundaries as needed. Gets a coach. Has a sponsor.	No, Jim, I won't tell the treatment center you don't like your roommate. I'm learning a lot about how to be loving to you. No, Sally, I will not get you out of jail. No, Sandy, I won't give you money. I'm sorry you feel that way, but I am not changing my mind.	I heard the most interesting thing on the Daily BALM last week. You should hear lesson seven on boundary setting. My Al-Anon meeting was so great last week. I am realizing how important it is to take care of myself, and I've committed to it!

UNDERSTANDING LONG-TERM TRAJECTORY

The Family Member's Stage of Change	What it may look like	Statements in relation to the loved one	Statements in relation to self/family
Maintenance/ Sticking with It	Has been in action for at least six months to a year. Has formed a recovery community around herself. Has committed to living life in recovery. Is working the Twelve Steps and/or 7 Steps to BALM. Now has friends in family recovery. Working with coach on own issues. Documents, scripts, shares, and sets boundaries as needed.	Could we find a time to talk? Treating loved one with love and respect, whether using or sober. May have broken off ties if the behavior is too difficult to be a part of. Is enjoying a recovery lifestyle with other family members and friends. Has a way of life that is fun and relaxed, even if things aren't better with the loved one.	Is enjoying a recovery lifestyle with other family members and friends. Has a way of life that is fun and relaxed, even if things aren't better with the loved one. Attends classes/ meetings/support groups regularly.

UNDERTANDING LONG-TERM TRAJECTORY

The Family Member's Stage of Change	What it may look like	Statements in relation to the loved one	Statements in relation to self/family
	Has regular slips that turn into a relapse of enabling, in-denial behavior. Believes the lies. Makes excuses. Is angry. May get caught up in another addiction and not be present to what is happening in the family.		
Recycling/Relapse	Screaming, yelling, begging. Crying, coercing, negotiating. Disappointed. Embarrassed. Guilty.	What's wrong with you? You're worthless. You're just like your father. I can't believe this.	I don't go to meetings anymore. They don't help I don't need help. It's not my problem. I'm miserable. If you had my life, you would be too.

UNDERTANDING LONG-TERM TRAJECTORY

The Family Member's Stage of Change	What it may look like	Statements in relation to the loved one	Statements in relation to self/family
		I hear you.	He is doing it his way and I understand that.
Termination/ Completion	The old behaviors are gone; now loving and present as a way of life.	I accept you.	
		I love you.	I am working on changing myself and loving others.
		I may not agree with you, but I know you are on your own journey.	

PRINCIPLE THREE
IT IS IMPORTANT TO LET GO WITHOUT GIVING UP OR GIVING IN

With the realization of the step-by-step nature of change, the family is then ready to face the third part of the attitudinal shift: knowing what it means to *let go* without giving up or giving in. What we mean by that is to let go of your obsession with having the result you want. The fact is, if you love an individual with use disorder, they could die. We all die, but an individual with use disorder has a distinct chance of an early death. The problem with trying to control whether they live or die is not only that you can't do it, but also that it could destroy your life and your relationship with your loved one if you try. Ultimately, the tight grasp of a family unwilling to let go enough to learn a more effective way to help could ultimately rob their loved one of a better chance of staying alive.

This is where the importance of mindfulness really comes in, because in order to let go of the fear, the 24/7 grip, we have to let go of the obsessive thinking about what *could* happen. First, to let go of results, you must let go of obsessive thinking. Then, remember that as long as there's life, there's hope.

So, what does it mean to not give up and not give in? Don't give up on them, but don't give up on yourself, either, under the delusion that you can control their fate. If you throw away your self-care for seven years while trying to help your loved one get better, how will that affect *you*? If and when they *do* get better, they're going to wake up after seven years and see a dishrag. And you're probably going to be pissed as hell for all that you've been through. But there is a better way!

Work on yourself and continue to live *your* life fully! BALM will help you become a better person in many ways:

more loving, more understanding, more patient. You're going to learn how to have conversations that can break through their denial. You're going to connect with resources that can potentially help them. You're not going to give up on them; you're going to learn how to tell them the facts in a way they hopefully can hear. You're going to learn how to be there for them powerfully. You're going to learn how to not give in to the manipulations of their use disorder speaking through them, because the disordered part of your loved one wants to kill them, and you don't!

PRINCIPLE FOUR:
YOU CAN BE THEIR BEST CHANCE AT RECOVERY

The fourth piece of the attitudinal shift is Principle 4: you can be your loved one's best chance at recovery. The way you become their best chance at recovery is to get calm, stay out of denial, become aware of what's really happening, stop enabling, and start helping.

When you help yourself, you're helping your loved one. When you are a role model of recovery in the home, it does have an impact. You become an illustration, an illumination, a beacon. In a situation like this, everything can feel so dark in the household. When you become a role model of recovery, you're a lighthouse who can help your loved one potentially shift.

So how do you bring about that shift in yourself and stay there? It's all about practice.

GET CALM

Developing an inner practice is something that each person does for themselves. In BALM, we teach several strategies, among them the use of the breath and Focus on the Task at Hand.

It's all about developing the ability to be present and aware without becoming overwhelmed, even in very trying circumstances.

What gets you to your calm center? For some people, it's deep prayer. For some, it's meditation. For some, it's contemplation. For some, it's listening to or playing inspirational music.

You'll pick up some calming techniques through this book and more through enrolling in the BALM.

What you choose as your daily practice is less important than simply choosing and using one.

Find some tactic, some practice, to make sure you're engaging in the shift to help you stay calm and quiet on the inside, no matter how chaotic it gets around you.

ESCAPING DENIAL

We have a BALM saying that "denial is the glue of the addictive system." Your loved one has to stay in denial in order to keep using, because if they wake up and realize, "Oh, my God! I'm doing something here that's killing me, and I'd better get some help," then they won't be able to keep using. They won't be able to live with themselves. So, they lie to themselves, and their "inner user" helps them do so.

Then they talk to you. Now, if you have a BALM conversation with them where you're telling them the facts of what you've seen them do, their using-self whispers contradictions. "That's not true," it says, "don't let them get away with that."

So they, in turn, say to you, "That's not true, Mom. Are you crazy? I would never do that. I can't believe you're accusing me of this. That's so not true."

We teach families to believe their own eyes and their own ears rather than their loved one's lies. That is the key to becoming your loved one's best chance: don't let them manipulate you. What often happens to families is they fold. If they didn't see it with their own eyes, and even occasionally if they do, they just allow things to continue. Sometimes they know their loved one is full of it, they're conscious of it, but they just don't want to be bothered. They're exhausted, after all.

So we have a different approach. We remember: the individual with use disorder lies to himself, and he lies to the people around him. The people around him have to either believe him or pretend to believe him in order for him to continue to believe that he doesn't have a problem. If the people around him tell him what they see, then he has to do everything he can to get them to change their mind — or at least stop bugging him.

This is where the peace part comes in again for the family member. If you are at peace inside, if you've taken the steps to foster an environment of peace within yourself, you're a rock. You can't be perturbed by this gaslighting behavior.

Observe the world. Observe yourself. You've got to be wise to your own ways, and you've got to be wise to their ways and the ways of the world. You have to put your perspective above theirs. You have to be very savvy about what the facts are and then remain calm enough that you can clearly tell your loved one those facts. That's where a scripted, prepared, BALM conversation comes in handy. What you say can go under the radar of their denial, from your heart to theirs.

THE IMPORTANCE OF THE BALM CONVERSATION

Coaches can be incredibly helpful in this process. After all, support is key to your own BALM recovery (Principle 8). But it's your own process of mindfulness that will carry the day, that will allow you to do this over time. Remember: this is a long game. Research shows that many people take five years of using before they even recognize that they have a problem — and then about eight more years for the first 60 percent or so to attain long-term recovery (Kelly 2015). This isn't going to happen overnight, but your mindfulness and self-care can carry you through.

Our experience shows that one way to improve those statistics is to train family members on how to help their loved one see the facts and move from stage to stage. That's what we do, and it doesn't happen magically.

The support system here is vital, too, because those outside your family might not be learning the BALM method. They might be pressuring you to take the tough love path. We see many wives come to the BALM because it's a safe place, somewhere they're not being pressured to leave their husbands. Everyone else in their life is saying, "What are you sticking around with this guy for? What's wrong with you?"

These women are trying not to judge their loved one for having this "drug problem," but their friends or community might be judging them for choosing an approach that includes love and connection. There is, unfortunately, a great stigma against individuals with use disorders. A person is not their disorder, and so loving someone who is struggling can require support.

ENABLING VS. HELPING

Once you've moved out of denial and into awareness, it is time to move from enabling to helping. In the past, enabling has been defined as anything you do for your loved one that they can do for themselves. However, we define enabling differently. We define it as *anything you do for your loved one that helps them get and use their substance.* Enabling is something that makes it easier for them to use, or to drink, or gamble. If you pay their rent, then they have money for drugs, and you have enabled their use.

But if you have a loved one who has always had attention deficit challenges and now they're in recovery and trying to get a job, helping them write their resume is not enabling. It is helping. If a person is moving toward recovery and comes across things that are difficult for them — not because of their use but because of their current limitations — work with them! That's helping a person move forward in their life. That's giving them a leg up — but they still have to do the climbing.

Distinguish between behaviors that make it easier for them to get their drug or substance and behaviors that help them move in a positive direction in their life. BALM invites families to move beyond the feeling of being loving to actively being loving in the most positive, life supporting way possible. The BALM method encourages families to adopt an attitude and approach that allows them to support their loved one to move in the direction of recovery through loving interaction and relationship.

One of our families had a daughter who had attention issues, and she couldn't figure out her budget. She kept making mistakes with money. The family's friends were saying, "She has to figure this out for herself. She's twenty years old. You shouldn't be doing this with her."

When the mother came on a coaching call with me and tried to explain, I asked her, "Think of yourself at twenty. How were you at budgeting? What did you know about money?"

"Not much," she admitted.

"Did your parents help you at all?"

"Yeah, they helped me figure it out."

A person with a use disorder may have some developmental gaps because some of them have spent years not learning how to do the things that other people figured out or learned in school. So, they may need that leg up — but that's not enabling. That's helping.

FILLING IN THE GAPS

Use disorder hijacks an individual's brain. Once they're sober, filling that void with a new, healthy meaning is a crucial piece of recovery. They have to reinvent themselves again and again in recovery, because just letting go of drugs isn't enough. What do they want to contribute? How do they want to live?

In the beginning, it's learning the life skills, learning how to live without the substance. Later, it's integrating back into society. Then, there's living a regular life without substances. But after that? It's about getting one's needs met and finding meaning and purpose beyond it all.

Here is a chart I created to help people find meaning so they don't feel a need to move backward to a life of drugs or co-addiction which previously gave them meaning.

WHAT ARE MY NEEDS? ARE THEY BEING MET?

One way of looking at addiction is as a process of getting our needs met in unhealthy ways. Recovery can thus be seen as a process of facing the feelings hiding those needs, discovering the needs themselves, and finding healthy ways to get our needs met.

As we become aware of our feelings, rather than running to cover them up with unhealthy behaviors or substances, we grow into our own power and our own authentic personhood. The chart shown on the next two pages can be a tool to discover what our needs are, find healthy ways to fulfill them, and keep of track of how we feel when we are faithful to getting our needs met in healthy ways as well as how we feel when we don't.

	Spirituality	Connection/ Community	Creativity	Intellectual Growth
Things that help me meet this need				
Things I did today to meet those needs				
Things I did today instead of meeting those needs				
How I felt (or didn't feel) when I found myself out of sync with my own needs				

	Movement	Intimacy	Physical Nourishment	Purposeful Activityy
Things that help me meet this need				
Things I did today to meet those needs				
Things I did today instead of meeting those needs				
How I felt (or didn't feel) when I found myself out of sync with my own needs				

The first steps back toward relapse can be found in ignoring our feelings and the needs they are masking. The first steps toward a long and healthy recovery can be found in uncovering our needs and discovering healthy ways to get them met.

Feel free to change the categories of needs as well as the activities listed. Make this list your own and see if charting your needs and feelings helps you grow in recovery. Let me know how it goes! I'd love to hear from you!

Thank you to Alida Schuyler, often referred to as the "Mother of Recovery Life Coaching," for the ideas that led to this chart. Alida developed the lesson, and I put them into this chart and taught the lesson.

It's very important that the family members understand how the quest for meaning and meeting needs is playing out in their own lives. If you've spent ten years doing nothing but keeping your daughter alive, once she's in recovery, what will *your* life be like?

Finding meaning and purpose in your life not only makes you a healthy model of recovery, but it also provides a beautiful sense of optimism and hope. Believe it or not, this process is something you can begin now, whether or not your loved one has achieved their own recovery yet.

For another way to look at Principle 4 and the journey to being your loved one's best chance, go to page 326 for a link to a free download of *The Ferris Wheel* by Lisa Costa, one of our first BALM coaches.

QUESTIONS TO PONDER:

1. What allows you to be calm in turbulent circumstances?
2. What are your needs?
3. How to you get your needs met?

7

Practical Strategies

THE 7 STEPS TO BALM — THE TRANSFORMATION PROCESS

When you take the time to transform yourself, the potential to transform your entire family and your struggling loved one is staggering. The first part of your shift, creating change, comes from the information learned in the **BALM** 12 Principles and the second part occurs through doing the 7 Steps to **BALM**.

We have a two-pronged approach. You're going to get your life back — that's first. Second, you're going to learn how to help your loved one get theirs back. The guarantee with our approach is that you *will* get your life back — but there's no guarantee that your loved one is going to do the same. We see successes in our **BALM** families all the time, but we can never guarantee them. You can, however, be your loved one's absolute best chance, and the 7 Steps to **BALM** is the road map to doing so. In this chapter, we will look at the first four steps, which include steps one, two and three which are all about self-transformation, and step four which will help you begin the process of transforming your communication with your struggling loved one.

FIRST STEP
BE THE PEACE YOU WISH TO SEE IN THE WORLD

This, the foundation of the entire program, has already been covered in earlier chapters. For an interesting way to learn to be the peace, see BALM coach Michael DeForbes's articles on *Self-Inquiry and the 7 Steps to BALM* and *Pointing to the Peace That Is Always There: The Promise of Step One* in Appendix II on page 281.

SECOND STEP
OBJECTIVELY OBSERVE WHAT YOUR LOVED ONE DOES AND SAYS

This means observing just the facts you see and hear as unemotionally as possible. Of course, this takes effort; it's easy to have negative feelings toward someone who is doing negative things. But as we practice this, we're learning how to see the world through the eyes of peace. Just look for the facts in each situation. Observe what your loved one is actually doing and saying because it's in the facts that we'll find solutions.

The facts will reveal what the problem is. Our opinions and our emotions tell us how we feel about it, which is irrelevant to helping our loved one. It is not irrelevant to us, obviously, but it is regarding our loved one. Observe the world around you objectively.

Certain charts we use can be particularly helpful with this. In addition to the Clear/Unclear chart shared on pages 41–42, we use a chart called My Business, My Loved One's Business, God's/The Universe's Business.

MY BUSINESS, MY LOVED ONE'S BUSINESS, GOD'S/THE UNIVERSE'S BUSINESS

Sometimes our own behaviors or circumstances or those of other people make no sense to us, and we simply want to change them. At those times, it is good to assess whether we have the right or the power to force change in the situation. This chart can help. We recommend going through it with your BALM Family Recovery Life Coach or other caring recovery professional.

At the top, summarize the problem in a sentence or two. For instance, *My son will not stop using.* Then, list who is responsible for what in that situation.

First, what is *your* business in this situation? Your business is to share the facts with him about what you see. Your business is to protect yourself and the rest of the family. Your business is to be loving. Your business is to stop enabling him. If your using loved one is living with you, it's also your business to protect your property and family from illegal behavior.

Next, what's *his* business? His business is to figure out what he wants to do with his life. His business is to figure out how to stop using, or how to support himself if he's going to continue. None of that is your business. (And yet, using the BALM, you can learn communication tools to invite him into recovery without alienating him.)

Finally, God's business. Whether or not your son is able to choose recovery and follow through is between him and his God. You can do the things the BALM teaches that will make it easier for him to stop and harder for him to keep using, but ultimately, his choices are between him and his God.

The challenging situation I am facing is: *ex. My Loved One will not stop using*		
My Business	**My Loved One's Business**	**God's/The Universe's Business**
ex. Share facts about what I see	*ex. Figure out how to stop using*	*ex. Whether he chooses to recover*

THIRD STEP
BECOME AWARE OF YOUR INNER EMOTIONAL LANDSCAPE WITHOUT JUDGMENT

When you know somebody who has a problem and you're objectively observing the facts of their behavior, that doesn't mean you're not going to have feelings.

You may feel, "My God, I can't stand this. I can't take it." Your heart may palpitate. You may start sweating; your breath might become shallow. Whatever it is for you, understand that you're going to have feelings. So become aware of your inner emotional landscape, and don't judge yourself for it. If you can do that, if you're willing to look at your emotions objectively, that gives you a little distance. As you work more deeply on this step, you will learn ways to heal your feelings as well.

FOURTH STEP
DOCUMENT WHAT YOU SEE AND HEAR

This means *just the facts*. Document what your loved one says and does. This can be extremely difficult emotionally, which is why step one is so important. These steps build on each other. Steps one, two, and three are the inner transformation tools. We say "the inner transformation" because we believe inner transformation is necessary to achieve the true transformation of our communication and relationships with others.

Without step one, you can't do any of this long-term.

If you can't get calm, you can't see things objectively. If you can't see things objectively, you can't observe your emotions without judgment. If you can't get calm, see things objectively, and observe your emotions without judgment, it will be very hard to document the facts without opinion and judgment slipping in.

When my clients document the facts, I recommend they keep a little notebook in their purse or pocket, or use their phone if they're more comfortable with that. Keep track of everything your loved one does and says that seems a little off or that bothers you. Then look for patterns.

Here's an example: One day you see your husband do something just a little bit off — nothing huge, just something strange. Maybe he's short with you when he normally wouldn't be. Maybe he's sleeping a lot. Whatever it is, it feels off. Write it down; if you don't write it down, you'll forget it. A few days later, you might see something else — write that down, too. The third time you see something, write it down, sit down with him, and have a conversation.

By the time you get there, you have a pattern to reference. One of our clients did this and realized her husband had relapsed into porn. She was able to have a conversation with him and point to a very specific, documented pattern. Yes, your loved one still might deny it, but it's hard to argue with dated notes, especially observations by more than one person. Document what you observe, and watch your own ability to stay out of denial grow!

MORE PRACTICAL STRATEGIES TO ENCOURAGE THE SHIFT

When something happens, most people react instinctively. We teach families how to *respond* instead. That requires sitting, considering, breathing, and intentionally deciding what you're going to do or say.

Clear/Unclear (p. 42) is particularly useful in this arena, because instead of reacting, you're thinking things through. What are the *facts*? What do you know for sure, and what is frustrating you that you don't know yet?

Setting boundaries that work for you is another way to get calm. Planning the boundaries, respecting other people's boundaries, figuring out where you end and the other person begins — boundary setting is essential to your health and recovery. It's also a skill many people have trouble with. In fact, the key to being a good boundary setter that many folks miss is to not set a boundary until you are determined to stick to it— and our whole program is designed to strengthen your ability to do so calmly and powerfully.

Learning what it means to be loving often starts with understanding and implementing structure in your own life. Having a clear structure helps eliminate stress and keeps you focused. When your loved one has use disorder and you're not living a structured life, you may feel completely out of control. Solid structure, then, is crucial to coping with your loved one's problem.

Of course, you don't want to be so busy to the point that you can't think, but you do want to be able to have other activities outside of your loved one, and structure can help you do so.

MANAGING FLOODING

Flooding is a natural response to stress. In *Conflict Unraveled: Solving Problems at Work and in Families,* author Andra Medea explains flooding and provides tips for dealing with it. She defines flooding as that adrenaline rush that accompanies stress, that triggers an upset response and sends your blood to your feet. Your heart is pounding. You can't think, you can't speak, you can't tell a story from beginning to end, you can't sequence anything.

A simple way to detect whether you're flooding is to try to assess whether you're thinking logically. You might not be able to; flooding throws logic out the door. You might be fighting, you might be yelling, you might be shutting down, but in any case, you're being led by emotional responses with no ability to access logical ones. If you are too upset to assess if you are flooding, you probably are!

Flooding is also very contagious; people who are struggling with a loved one's use flood a lot, and then the family members around them will flood even more. It's contagious. Even I have to catch myself when my clients start to flood; when they turn to attack mode (which is common when people are flooding), it can get me escalated quickly if I don't consciously turn it off. Here is what I do to de-escalate. See if it works for you:

When you start to flood, there are a few things you can do to stop it. If you're sitting at a heavy desk or table, you can put your fingers on the top and your thumbs under and pull up. Of course, you can't do anything with the desk, but it gets your large muscle flexing and your blood flowing again. Or try making large circular motions with your arms and moving your legs. The large muscle movements will get your blood flowing. Count backward from one hundred, say the ABCs backward, breathe deep breaths — do anything to focus your mind on something else. With those techniques, you'll notice the flooding start to fall away.

But what about the person you're with? If someone is flooding badly and you're with them, just walk out. Walk out gently and lovingly, but walk out. "I'm sorry. I'm starting to flood here," is a perfectly valid explanation, one that our families use a lot with each other. That's taking responsibility for your own stress reaction to the situation, as opposed to saying, "You make me sick and you're driving me crazy!" If you're making blaming statements, you're probably still flooding.

MEDEA'S QUICK GUIDE TO CONTROL FLOODING

WHAT TO REMEMBER

Flooding happens to everyone. It happens in different ways, with different styles, but no one is immune to it. We're wired for this. When it hits — when, not if — you have got to be prepared to bring yourself out. Only then do you have any chance of getting back to problem-solving and a sane, functioning life.

TO CONTROL FLOODING IN YOURSELF

› **Watch for physical symptoms first:** Pounding head, racing heart, short breath, sweaty palms, dry mouth. Make a list of your personal signs. Check the list when you're under stress. Checking the list is more important than yelling at someone.

› **Watch for mental symptoms:** Jumbled thoughts; rotary thinking; or an inability to see options, to sequence, or handle math. Also watch for sudden inarticulation, disjointed speech, or suggestibility.

› **Use large muscles:** Go for a walk. Close the door and do jumping-jacks or swing your arms in windmills. Use isometrics if you're stuck in a meeting.

› **Reverse symptoms:** If your breathing goes short, breathe deep and slow. If your fists are clenched, open your hands and stretch your fingers.

› **Focus on specifics:** List facts and read them back to keep your mind focused. Slow the pace.

› **If you can't break free of flooding at the time:** Recognize that you can't think and stop arguing. State clearly that you'd like to talk later, then leave and re-group. Try again after you have repeated the earlier steps.

› **Prepare in advance:** If a tough situation is approaching, practice taking yourself out of flooding. Your mind learned flooding; it can unlearn it. You can develop a resistance to flooding or train yourself to snap out of it.

TO HANDLE FLOODING IN OTHERS

› **Watch for symptoms,** such as flushed face, pulsing veins, or disjointed sentences.

› **Don't talk at them since they can't hear you.** Instead, let them talk; give them time to vent. Ask sequence questions: What happened first? What happened next? Use a low, calm tone of voice.

› **Don't crowd them,** don't touch them, and don't make fast movements. If they want to leave, let them.

› **Be prepared for thinking problems.** Don't demand math from someone who is flooding, and don't give complicated directions. Keep it simple, or wait until they calm down.

› **Avoid jargon.** Use short, clear sentences.

› **With chronic cases, talk pain control, not anger control.** High levels of adrenaline are toxic; this isn't a comfortable feeling. But the process will take time. They didn't learn flooding in a day, and they won't unlearn in a day.

› **Work on yourself first.** Flooding is contagious, but so is calm. You can't hope to stop someone else's flooding unless you can stop your own.

From Medea, Andra. 2004. *Conflict Unraveled: Fixing Problems at Work and in Families.* Chicago: Pivot Point Press. Reprinted with permission. With special thanks to Dr. John Gottman of the Gottman Institute for his work on flooding.

PRACTICALLY PROMOTING PEACE

MOTIVATIONAL INTERVIEWING

Motivational Interviewing (MI) is a way of interacting with our loved ones that helps them explore their own motivations so they can determine their own best path. Holding these motivational conversations can be extremely powerful, especially when paired with a BALM conversation. MI was developed to help counselors address their clients' ambivalence toward change. In the beginning, MI emphasized technique. But today, the emphasis is more on the value of a compassionate relationship that can evoke a loved one's *best* inner knowing (Miller and Rollnick 2012).

We introduce MI to parents and family members as an adjunct to a BALM conversation because both methods recognize the quality of relationship as essential to encouraging a person to move from ambivalence to willingness to change. The BALM conversations share the facts of what you hear your loved one saying and see your loved one doing, and a motivational conversation provides guidance on how to ask questions that give a loved one the ability to go deep within, beyond the lies and self-deception, to what they really want, what may be keeping them back, and what they feel will help them get there.

Motivational interviewing and the Stages of Change model covered in Principle 2 do complement each other, though they are two distinct methods.

The key to both MI and BALM is not in asking the "right" questions or sharing the facts perfectly. Understanding the steps of a process is helpful, but more important than what you say is your motivation, your loving approach, your tone, the way in which you approach your relationship with the person who is suffering.

In BALM, we talk about be the peace you wish to see in the world and seeing your loved one through the eyes of love rather than judgment or resentment in order to be their best chance at recovery. We emphasize a loving respect combined with an understanding of what is best practice to help a loved one move toward recovery. We use the brief intervention known as the BALM conversation to provide objective facts in a loving tone.

Motivational interviewing emphasizes compassion, collaboration, acceptance, and evocation as its underlying spirit. Neither program is about manipulating an individual to do things your way. Both start with an understanding that under all the apparent dysfunction, the loved one has an inner knowing and an inner peace, an inner guide of their own.

A compassionate counselor or loving family member who is willing to educate themselves and address the person in a respectful tone, with words and intent that respect the person's right to make their own decision, can be there for the struggling individual most powerfully. Does this guarantee a specific result? No. It does not.

But as we say in BALM, educating yourself and experiencing the attitudinal shift will empower you to be their best chance at recovery. Remember, it is all about contributing to recovery, not causing it. That is beyond the ability of any human other than the struggling person himself or herself.

Self-awareness is essential, and to that end we also include an ongoing journaling workshop in our offerings. Some families attend regularly, some just listen to the recordings at their leisure, and many get a lot of benefit from it. It's called *Journal Your Way to BALM Recovery*, and it uses journaling to keep you applying all you've learned toward your daily life. The focus of the BALM Journal is to provide another way to help BALMers Be A Loving Mirror. Only in this case, they are learning to Be A Loving Mirror to themselves.

Self-awareness can also come through mindfulness. Once you start to develop a quieting practice in your life, you will become an observer of yourself and others. One exercise you can do today to grow your self-awareness is to simply watch yourself as you move through your day. Then, document what you have said and thought and done — just the facts!

As you do so, don't allow judgment. Don't say, "Oh, I'm terrible. I'm awful." Instead, simply say, "Oh, look at that. Look what I'm doing now. So that's what it's like to behave this way. Isn't that interesting?" (Patent 2007).

Become an observer in your own life. See what happens, and see how nonjudgmental awareness can lead to mindfulness.

Developing a daily practice is very important: a practice of mindfulness, a practice of *something* that gets you to calm yourself and grow your awareness each moment. If you don't like the idea of meditating, it could be something simple, like cleaning. It could be painting the house or taking a walk. As long as what you're doing calms your mind as well as your body, you're on the right track.

All of these practical tactics are really about going back to that basic foundation: there *must* be peace within. That is the grounding for everything.

Be intentional and promote a sense of peace and stability inside yourself.

QUESTIONS TO PONDER:

1. What happens to you when you start flooding?
2. What can you do to disengage from losing your mental balance during stressful times?

8

It Takes What It Takes

One of the most important lessons you will need to take away as you pursue recovery is this: *it takes what it takes.* Know yourself. What is it going to take for you to have the attitudinal shift that's going to make all the difference in your family's life? How willing are you to do what it takes?

Each person's version of "it takes what it takes" will be different. Everyone will be different in this. Some of you out there might just need to read this book, and that'll be it. That's all it will take for you. Others may need to take a class or get a coach. Someone else may need to be in therapy twice a week. Another may need to go inpatient. Yes, there are inpatient programs for families, too! This malady takes its toll on everyone in its path and taking personal responsibility to find the solution that best fits us is what our journey requires!

Whatever that is: It takes what it takes.

We see a lot of families enrolling in the BALM's comprehensive online family recovery program. Some do that and have a life coach, and others have a therapist as well. That's what it takes for them. I've had a few families who, over the years, needed more; I've worked with them to get them to an inpatient family recovery treatment center for a week or two, or even longer. It takes what it takes. What are you willing to do to walk the Loving Path and make a difference in your and your family's lives?

It takes what it takes is about knowing there's a range of needs, and it's essential to honestly assess yours. We all want it to be easy, but it's not. What will it take for you?

VARIOUS STRATEGIES

Some people listen to our BALM recordings of a program called the Daily BALM. Others listen live. We have over 250 digital recordings of family members, recovering persons, and recovery professionals telling their stories and sharing their expertise. These can be hugely helpful, and some of our families wake up in the morning to them, listen to them as a backdrop all day, or listen to them all night. Some people take our program as they would a college course. Some people take the 7 Steps to BALM over and over and over again, come to every coaching group and journaling workshop, and have a private coach. There's no judgment. It takes what it takes. We all need to be aware of our own needs so we can consciously decide the breadth of strategies we want to implement to get into recovery.

The thing is, recovery is a lifelong journey. A lot of people don't want to hear that; they want an easy solution. For some people, it might just be learning a few new skills. For others, maybe those who have generations of use disorder and dysfunction in their families or those who are traumatized by what's happened to them, every moment is a struggle. They need additional support.

Some people need therapeutic intervention. Others need a Family Recovery Life Coach to help them move forward. It takes what it takes. We respect whatever it takes. We encourage people to decide how important recovery is and then figure out what it's going to take for them to be there most powerfully for themselves and their loved ones on this journey.

Unfortunately, family members tend to underestimate this part. Often, say when their loved one goes into treatment, they think, "Oh, good! That's done. They're in treatment. Everything is fine now," and the family stops BALMing. They don't do anything more. They don't think they have a problem. Then, should a relapse come, they're not prepared. It will probably take more than you think at first, and that's okay — because it just takes what it takes to reach recovery.

As my sponsor, Dawn, once told me, "The good news is we have our whole lives to do this work. The bad news? It will probably take that long."

The reason we offer the BALM Comprehensive for a full year is that when a loved one leaves treatment, the family is on a honeymoon. They leave the BALM program, and everything seems wonderful. But when the loved one has a slip, it's terrifying, and they come back. We teach family members how to cope with these slips so they don't turn into relapses. You can contribute to recovery when a loved one has a slip rather than inadvertently making things worse.

Recovery is a lifelong journey, and we make it one of love and inner discovery.

QUESTIONS TO PONDER

1. What will it take for you to consistently Be A Loving Mirror to yourself, your loved ones and others?
2. What are you willing to do to make that happen?

Part III:

REAL FAMILIES RECOVERING

9

The History of BALM®

MY STORY

My family has given me the opportunity to learn how to love, regardless of differences. What a precious lesson I've learned: to know that I don't have to be the same as them, that they don't have to be the same as me, but we can both be loving. And that's really the BALM methodology: we're called to be loving, to actually be the love and peace we wish others would be for and to us.

When I was very young, I experienced a severe emotional trauma that led me to cope by eating, and I developed a food use disorder. Often, people with use disorder are trauma survivors. From a very young age, I used food to numb myself. When I was nineteen, my mother took me to my first Overeaters

Anonymous meeting. For me, that started a lifelong love of the Twelve Steps.

I cherish the Twelve Steps. The distillation of worldly wisdom, they encapsulate the three most important relationships, as shown in this summation of the steps: Trust God, Clean House, Help Others. I was always a seeker, to be honest. I sought wisdom and truth from many different religions and spiritual traditions, and the Twelve Steps became the bridge between them all. It taught me the importance of having a spiritual relationship, along with a healthy relationship with self and others.

And when I looked at all the different spiritual paths I had studied, they were all saying those same three things: have a relationship with God, have a relationship with yourself, and have a relationship with other people. For me, the Twelve Steps distilled all of that so I could better piece together the understandings I had been raised with and had studied.

When I was twenty-six, my sister told me about her substance use disorder. My sister has thirty-four years in recovery now, and she has been one of my greatest teachers. We fought like cats and dogs from the time we were very little, and we've both had our own issues and challenges over the years — but she unconditionally loves me, and I her. It sometimes looks tense when we get into arguments, and we can't spend a lot of time together in person due to geography, but we talk on the phone almost every day. She's a treasure to me. She's a very spiritual person, and we've walked the spiritual path together.

When she told me about her use disorder, I started going to Al-Anon. By then, I had been around other people who used, often my dates and boyfriends. I'm not saying I looked for people who used, but as I've said before, they seemed drawn to me. Maybe they weren't all specifically individuals with use disorders, but I had a habit of dating guys with issues. They all seemed to face different challenges. But so did I and so did my family, so it didn't seem like too big a deal for me at the time. I remember being in Al-Anon, listening and saying to myself, "Oh, so that's how you handle it. Okay, I could marry an alcoholic. I'm in Al-Anon."

Which meant, when I met my husband, I wasn't afraid. Of course, people told me I was insane. But I felt that with what I had learned, I had all the tools. Obviously, I was wrong on that point. I had to find more tools. But my advantage was this: I knew where to look for them.

MEETING MY HUSBAND

When I met my husband, he was active in his substance use disorder. There was lying and deception and all that goes with the life of an individual with use disorder. My family liked him (everyone likes him), but they were scared for me. No one wants their daughter dating an individual with active use disorder. Stigma, of course, is one reason; fear of the mayhem of active use is another.

We met on New Year's Day in 1985, and we started dating immediately. We basically moved in with each other after three dates, which I had never done before. Alan and I just clicked; we were good friends from minute one, you know what I mean? I wish you could meet him. When we went on our first date, I started laughing at dinner — and I didn't stop laughing for months. He's hilarious. This became the tragic comedy of our early married life: that this vibrant, smart, wonderful, funny man also had a disease that was killing him. It made him a liar, a con artist who didn't have energy left for a relationship because everything was going into maintaining his SUD. And yet, he was very loving, as he is to this day in his recovery.

All of this seems like a lot of contradictory information. But that's part of loving someone who's struggling with a disease such as this: it feels like a contradiction. Alan is someone who came into my life to bring me great joy — as well as great sorrow.

We started dating in January and got engaged in June. My mother had the wedding planned in about two days because, funnily enough, I had been recently engaged to another man and had broken it off only a few weeks before I'd met Alan. At first I told Alan, "You know, I'm not gonna get involved with you for a long time because I don't want you to feel like a rebound."

His response? "That's all right. I don't mind being a rebound." It made me laugh, I'll tell you that much. So, when we got engaged, all my mother had to do was call the vendors and say, "Same thing, different date, different guy."

After we got married, we moved to DC, where his job was based. I mentioned we'd been living together before, but because we were commuting across cities, we didn't get the full effect. Once we were married and I was living with him full-time, I saw it. I finally saw how truly impaired Alan was.

He was in bad shape. He was a salesman, which meant he wasn't subject to typical work hours. He could work hard for a day or two, make a lot of money, and then just lie in bed, wasted... and that's exactly what he did. He tried to hide everything from me, but I knew something was wrong. From the minute I got to Washington, I was going to Al-Anon meetings almost every day just for sanity. Everything was off, and I knew it — I just didn't know what to do about it.

About three months after we got married was when I changed my own perspective and unknowingly started practicing what I later called BALM. By May 1, nine months after our wedding, he was sober. It was an incredible relief. Of course, he would then go around telling people I was the reason he got sober, which made me terribly uncomfortable. In Al-Anon, you never take credit for that sort of thing — because you don't cause it, you can't control it, and *you can't cure it.*

But what I discovered over years of research is that my love, my strategies, and the tools I learned through studying what other spouses had done were what had helped me help him. So, no, I did not cause him to get clean and sober. But I certainly contributed to his ability to get clean and sober.

I stopped contributing to his SUD, and I started contributing to recovery.

THE RELAPSE

At that point, however, I wasn't practicing a formal method — the word "BALM" hadn't even occurred to me. I hadn't gotten into coaching by any means; I remained in a completely different career for the next couple of decades.

For the next twelve years, both of us were doing really well. We reached extremely high points in our careers, but that ironically led to some deterioration. Because we were so overwhelmed and busy, we stopped going to our support group meetings. We weren't taking care of ourselves, and so we didn't have the quality of inner life and coupledom that we'd enjoyed before.

Slowly but surely, things fell apart. By the time we'd been married eighteen years, Alan was beginning a full multiyear relapse. During that time, our daughter was growing up, with all the experimentation and challenge *that* entails, so we were focused on her. I didn't even notice his relapse, to tell you the truth — or I didn't want to. I'd also been in a food relapse toward the beginning of all this. I gained an inordinate amount of weight and was simply eating my way through life. I became completely miserable; I was deeply unhappy in my career. The stress level at my job was high, and I wasn't using adequate tools to cope. It was the infamous golden handcuffs: I was making a tremendous amount of money and didn't see a way out. I used food to cope, which went on for several years. As I came out of my active use, Alan was just going into his.

And that's when I started to notice how sick he was. It was around the time I got an even more stressful job that required a move out of town. Part of the year, he joined me — sort of — and part of the year I commuted. His decline became more apparent from a distance. Yet, still, I was unsure about what was really going on.

When I left town, he was supposed to move with me, which he didn't do. Instead, he just packed a few things and visited for a few months. That should have been my first clue. But denial can be so thick, like a dark storm cloud over your head. It's the glue of the using system. If the family stays in denial, nothing changes. It is the hallmark of substance use disorder and other addictions; denial is what keeps everything in place.

They say that the family relapses first. Well, in addition to everything else, I had not been attending meetings. I believe that if I had continued to Be A Loving Mirror, he may have had a chance of not having that relapse. And I don't take responsibility for his relapse, but I do take responsibility for having stopped working my program which led to my contributing to his relapse.

At first, I thought all the signs were about my marriage — I thought our relationship was dying. A spiritual director guided me through what I later realized was a sort of Clear/Unclear process, although it wasn't labeled as such at the time.

"Ask God about the truth of it," she said, "and just write it out." So, I started writing. As I did so, more than fifty different facts came flooding out of me — that deep denial had been holding them all inside like a giant, crumbling dam. They were all things I'd never confronted him about because I was too terrified of his reaction. But I knew I had to do something.

So I did what I had done originally to help him get clean so many years before. At one point, about five in the morning,

I called him from the apartment I was living in. He wasn't picking up at home. So, I called his cell. When he answered, I could hear the cars of a highway in the background.

"Where are you?" I asked.

"I'm in my bedroom," he replied — a flat-out lie.

"No, I know you're not," I said calmly. "And here's what else I know." Then, I just started reading the list of everything that he'd done over the past five years, but dispassionately. Without judgment, without emotion — just sharing what I'd observed. He had to hear it. Of course, he started yelling so much I had to hold the phone away from my ear.

"You're screaming at me," I said. "I'm going to hang up now, and I love you." I hung up. And I repeated that process daily over three or four months. Finally, I left my job to go home and help him. I knew he might die if I didn't.

I knew this because my daughter graduated from college up north and went home first. Soon after, she called and told me how badly he was doing and to please come home. They had been very close throughout her years growing up. Alan had been her trusted advisor and guide, someone she could count on for wise counsel. And thank God, that role has been restored today. But at that moment in time, he was unable to finish a sentence, let alone stick to any plans they made. So, I left my out-of-town job, and soon we were all home together. When I arrived, my daughter and I exchanged a nervous glance. Things were bad.

After a few days of observing the scene, I sat down with Alan. "I love you very much, and here's the story," I said. "You're in really bad shape. I don't know exactly what it is. I don't know if it's drugs. I don't know if it's other women. I don't know if it's gambling. I don't know what you're up to, but I know it's bad, and I am really concerned. Long-term, it's not something I choose to live with. So I'm giving you three months to go to treatment and restart your recovery. After that, I'll stay by you for the first year in recovery. But I have no idea if this marriage can last."

He said the same thing about our marriage right back at me. At that point, you could say, we had very little hope for our union.

But very slowly, our marriage started to come back. That summer, I wrote him a letter. I described the amazing man who had been my best friend all those years. And then I listed all the ways that I knew something was very wrong. In black and white, he saw those fifty things.

"I know this isn't really you," I wrote, "and I want my husband back." I remember giving him that letter, and then he put it on a shelf. Then he started sweeping the carpet. All over the house, he swept, and I watched him clean the house from top to bottom.

Meanwhile, I was determined that I was going to do everything I could to help my husband save his life and to save our marriage. In the end, if none of it worked, I would be okay. But I would work like hell for things to get better, and I used the experts to help me.

For the next three days, I met with all my coaches and advisors, including my infidelity coach, my personal coach, my peer coach, my sponsor, my therapist, and my spiritual director. And I utilized them. When I say "it takes what it takes," I mean it.

I didn't always like the advice I got or the package it was wrapped in, but I did my best to do what they said, and in time, it did make things better.

At one point, my sponsor told me that if I didn't get strong enough to speak directly with my husband, she would drop me. Later in the process, she told me how important it would be for him to go to treatment and then stay out of the home for many months in a sober environment before returning. She expressed how important it would be for me to continue working on myself at that time, because if I didn't, I would hurt — not help — myself, my husband, and our family.

I didn't like the message, but I took it. I wanted what she had in her life: many years of family recovery that included a husband in recovery. Their example of a life lived in recovery was the model I held through all of those dark, frightening days.

I knew then and I know now that there are no guarantees a loved one will get and stay in recovery, no matter what the family says or does. But I was also realizing once again the truths I had learned so long ago: I was my husband's best chance at recovery and could also be his worst nightmare. I was no longer willing to be his worst nightmare. The cost was too high.

Eventually, my husband agreed to go into detox, thinking he would stay a few days and come home. The professionals and I had a different plan, though. I worked closely with the detox to get him into a treatment center that would work best for him. Fortunately, over his eleven-day stay, his detox counselor acquired a clearer picture of the type of treatment that would be best for him. Again, I listened, putting my own tendency to control on the back burner. I advocated for his recovery, partnering with the professionals on my husband's behalf.

Some people might say that's the sort of thing a loved one has to figure out on their own; that by coordinating I was enabling him, helping him too much, making it too easy for him. You know what I say to that?

Bullshit.

When somebody is that sick, they need their loved one to advocate for them, just like if he'd had a heart attack or diabetes. Would I desert somebody who had a heart attack? Would I desert somebody, God forbid, who had leukemia? Hell, no. I'd be here with him all the way. I believe that our job is to be there with our loved ones, powerfully, as much as they need it, in a way that contributes to their recovery, not their use disorder. I don't know about your loved one in the throes of their addiction, but for mine, the actions I took were both helpful and appreciated, in the long run, if not completely in the moment.

After detox, Alan went to a treatment center, and having been a treatment professional himself, he had a special connection to the staff there. But, God, was he sick and so was I. In there I joined him in all family therapy and even signed up for my own.

Every Wednesday night from 6:30 PM to 11:30 PM, the center had a family night. I would come in every week with my list of all the things that drove me crazy about him, all the facts of what his SUD had wrought in our lives. The joke among the staff was, "Oh, man, what's she gonna bring *this* week?" I would essentially take him apart every week and tell him all this — and then they would put him back together. Their only rule for us was "no parking lot therapy," and we followed it to a T, discussing our disagreements in couple's therapy and groups only.

For the first month, he made it known daily that he would come home after thirty days, and I let him know he would have to go to a recovery residence (known at the time as a halfway house) for at least six months first.

One night, a therapist asked Alan, "What will happen if you choose not to go back to recovery?"

"I'll love my family."

"And where will you be sitting?"

"I'll be sitting on a park bench by myself."

"Is that what you want?" he asked.

"No."

And that is when he stopped advocating to come home and began getting to work.

We went to weekly therapy together while he was in treatment and of course, each on our own. At least once, the therapist sent me home for being so venomous at the start of our couples' session that he felt it would be harmful to my husband and unhelpful to our process.

"Go home and do your work," he advised. That was an eye-opener for me.

I remember the room, the feeling of abject rage, how they brought my husband in, his shock at the level of my anger, and then how they took him out. The moment was etched in my memory. I was reaching a bottom with my rage about what had happened. It was time to start doing the inner work to heal it and stop taking it out on Alan.

So I did.

A BALM® CONVERSATION

My husband went to inpatient treatment for a total of three months and to the halfway house afterward. The plan had been a six-month stay at the halfway house, but the entire halfway house relapsed during a weekend when Alan was at home with us. On his way back to the halfway house on Monday morning, I got a call from the treatment center telling me about the relapse, and that they thought he was ready to come home. They asked if it would be okay with me. I could see the difference in Alan by then, and since the treatment center could too, it felt safe for us to have him home. Once I agreed, they called Alan in his car and told him to turn around and go back home, that the halfway house had become drug and sex infested over the weekend, and he was to not go there.

When he came home, he was doing okay for a while. He was going to his meetings every day and I was going to mine. Then, a couple months later, he was suddenly sleeping all day long. It was startling. I tried not to freak out; rather, I just observed it and jotted down my observations every day. A few days in, I initiated the conversation.

"Honey, there's something I need to share with you in a loving way," I said.

"Okay."

"You know I love you."

"Yes," he said, waiting.

"Last week," I said, trying to be as unbiased as possible, "you were going to meetings every day. You were so energetic. And this week, you have barely gotten out of bed every day. I just noticed it."

We didn't talk about it any more than that. The following week his energy began to return, but still, we didn't talk about it. I just figured he started going to more meetings because of what I had told him and so he felt better. Not until years later did I discover the truth. When we were doing a talk for families in Ohio, he shared that when he heard my observations, he actually took them to his doctor. He shared in his talk that, based on my conversation with him, his doctor examined his medication and adjusted his antidepressant, and that fixed the issue. He didn't tell me this at the time; he just dealt with it.

This is why it's so essential that, in a BALM conversation, we don't give our advice and opinions. We can't risk that, because those opinions may be wrong. Everybody has a blind side. We just share the facts. Alan didn't see what was happening to him, but he did see the facts when they were delivered in an unemotional, loving way. And he made a decision to go to the doctor and find out what those facts meant. That was ultimately the solution he needed.

I contributed to his recovery, but not in the way I thought.

BECOMING LOVING

Around this time, I began to truly understand that the best chance for him was for me to be loving — partly because of Dawn, my Al-Anon sponsor. I met Dawn early in my marriage, and she had a husband who was sober. She has been on the Twelve-Step speaking circuit. She's spoken in Al-Anon and OA all over the country and the continent, and she has an excellent Al-Anon program. She is the person who taught me the importance of being loving.

Whenever things went crazy, when my husband seemed to go nuts, she would just say, "Are you being loving?" Or (as you now know) she might say, "Your only obligation to another adult human being is to be a loving person. That's it." Another one of her favorites was: "Are you staying in present time?"

As I mentioned earlier, most of the time I just wanted to kick her through the phone. I did share my anger and she encouraged me to share it with her, not with my husband. Yet her persistence eventually helped me understand the role of being loving in supporting a loved one's recovery. I found a way to live happily, regardless of my husband's choices. Once I was able to do that, I started to live with greater purpose and intention in my marriage and in my life.

That teaching, "Your only obligation to another adult human being is to be a loving person," became a mantra of mine that paved the way to my next career twenty-one years later when I started training to be a life coach.

Early in my coaching career, I took a wonderful coaching course on finding purpose, and through that I found my deepest purpose: to help families of individuals with use disorders find their way, and to help people on the recovery path find their purpose. Those have been the two areas I have focused on in my coaching career.

For the families, I developed the BALM program, and today we are developing a BALM program for individuals with use disorders as well.

STARTING BALM®: ALAN'S STORY AND MINE

As you might imagine, Alan considers himself the star of the BALM because of our history, and without him, the BALM may have never happened. When Alan comes and speaks in our groups or classes, he jokes, "I'm very happy to be here as the inspiration for the BALM program," and everyone will cheer. He's teasing, but it's true. People adore him, because if it weren't for Alan, there wouldn't be BALM. Alan taught me what it takes to help a person who's suffering with this disease and asked me to choose to help families. Throughout the years, he's been very supportive of my recovery and of the BALM program.

I have always considered him a big soul with a crucial role in a mission of mercy for people affected by use disorder and their families. For nine years in his first go at recovery, he worked his way up the ranks of treatment center leadership and was a pioneer in the in-patient treatment of adolescents. Since renewing his recovery a decade ago, he once again worked his way up the ranks of treatment administration. A humble and giving person, he has never had entitlement issues.

Two years after coming out of treatment, he decided it was time to get back to his purpose of helping suffering users get well. He was immediately offered a job in administration and instead chose to, once again, work his way through the ranks.

"I'm newly sober," I remember him saying. "I will work as a tech and see how I can serve there."

Within a couple of years, he was the Tech Training Coordinator, writing policies and procedures and getting systems in place throughout the center.

He has earned a reputation as someone to call to help a treatment center improve its systems, personnel policies, and practices for the good of the clients, and today, he continues to do that work in a new town, helping the local population of individuals with substance use disorder as CEO of a local treatment center.

My journey too, has evolved. When I first started my coaching career, I discovered that many of my clients didn't want to go to Al-Anon. I wanted to encourage them to recover with or without the Twelve Steps, so I started blogging. I prayed for inspiration to write blogs that would help people who wouldn't go to Al-Anon, and it all started pouring out of me. Eventually I produced a set of blogs that were all about our four BALM foundations: self-care, being loving, setting boundaries, and getting support. I started writing and talking about that, but my clients were still resistant.

That's when I first coined the phrase "Be A Loving Mirror." Every time I wrote that term, I got a lot of responses; I knew I was onto something that could help people because they seemed intrigued. It had struck a chord somehow. "Mirroring" is a coaching term, which means to reflect back what someone says. They might say, "I'm in so much pain." You can respond, "I can see that you're in pain. I hear that you're in pain." It's being a mirror to them. They say it, you say it back. The idea of adding love and reflection to the facts of a loved one's behaviors became the core of Be A Loving Mirror and became what I wrote about, and what I taught people. I discovered that if you can teach people to be loving and to be a mirror, they will recover — and their loved one will have the best chance of recovery.

I was a trained life coach, but to deepen my understanding, I went to five different schools to try to figure out how to specifically help families facing SUD. None of the schools were specifically for families, but they were still helpful. One of the most impactful was a school that focused on Recovery Life Coaching. I learned a lot there and I became a teacher for them.

I wasn't Al-Anon. I wasn't a Twelve-Step program. I was just a coach who developed a method based on what I had learned, researched, and experienced. Because I had been an educator in my previous career, the coach training schools I went through wanted me to either mentor or teach their coaches. So, I was working for two different schools, and some of the clients I had who were life coaches wanted to work in recovery and asked me to coach them on that, so I did. Before I knew it, the coaches who wanted to work with families affected by a loved one's use disorder were coming to me, asking me to open a school for people who want to coach families.

The first time I taught BALM, I just taught the BALM 12 Principles. I tried to put everything into an hour and a half every week: coaching, group coaching, Q&A, and partner time — all in an hour and a half! I was trying to cram too much in. That soon evolved into two weekly classes, one focused on teaching and interviewing people on the BALM 12 Principles, and the other focusing on the 7 Steps to BALM: the practical step-by-step guide of how to Be A Loving Mirror. Supportive coaching groups were added, where members could just come and share a problem they might be facing and even have a coach walk them through how to handle it differently. And, finally, we added the Journal Your Way to BALM Recovery course, designed to help people go within to process their recovery through writing. The entire group of offerings eventually grew into the BALM Comprehensive Family Recovery Education Program.

As you've read, our approach is two-pronged: help yourself, help your loved one. The mission of our company is to help all families blaze the trail to recovery in their homes. That mission holds within it the potential to eliminate relapse, which is at the core of our vision. Families are big contributors to making things worse; for instance, when their loved one behaves "badly," the family is so traumatized that they freak out in ways that discourage peace or calm. There is no judgment meant in sharing this observation — just an opportunity to choose what to contribute to: the disorder or the recovery. Based on the understanding that stress is a big factor in relapse, families can choose to shift from increasing the stress level in their house to increasing the level of peace.

So, do families cause their loved one to use? Hell, no. Do they contribute? Absolutely.

FINDING LIFE PURPOSE IN RECOVERY

What I learned and am committed to passing on is that if I live from a calm vantage point, where I can be objective in my observations of my loved one, I can be their best chance. I can deal with and work through my own emotions without blaming my struggling loved one for my inability to cope. The fact of the matter is, when our loved one's behavior bothers us, it often acts as a trigger for our own past hurtful experiences or memories.

That isn't to minimize the impact of a loved one's behavior. It's just to say that we often carry emotional burdens that are much older than any relationship we're in. So when I'm willing to work through my own stuff on all those levels — getting calm, being an objective observer, becoming aware of my inner emotional landscape — when I'm willing to do that, I can see much more clearly.

When Alan got sober this last time, back in 2008, I remember saying to him, "Listen. Here's what I realized. For five years you were deteriorating, and I never said a word because I was afraid of how you would react. But I will never be afraid of you again. I will tell you what I see. I will lovingly give you the facts that I see." That's how we relate to each other now: we lovingly tell each other the facts we see. Does that mean we never fight, we never yell? Of course we do. But when it comes to the important stuff, we do our best to be there for each other in an honest way, and to be there for ourselves.

When Alan first got out of treatment, I was in coaching school. There was no BALM; I was just practicing good recovery with my husband. Within a year, I had found my calling as a True Purpose® coach through my mentor Tim Kelley, the founder and developer of the True Purpose® method. I'm one of fourty-four Certified True Purpose® Coaches in the world. Going through this process led me to find that I have two life missions: the first is to help all families blaze the trail to recovery in their homes, and the second is to make Life Purpose a given on the recovery path.

The BALM programs have come about because of that first mission. Life Purpose in Recovery™ is what I call the True Purpose® work I do with families and individuals affected by use disorders (which I will be addressing in an upcoming book by that name).

Guided by my connection to Source (one of my names for the God of my understanding), I developed a program designed to end relapse by helping all families blaze the trail to recovery in their homes. And now that that is established, we are preparing to offer Life Purpose in Recovery™ to groups in addition to individuals as we always have.

By 2010, BALM was what we were all about.

WHAT IS BALM®?

When you are BALMing, you are nonjudgmental, and this is reflected in the tone, cadence, and pitch of your voice. You are not making any threats, verbally or nonverbally.

You're simply observing what you're seeing and reporting on it. You're just noticing the facts, what's happening, without adding your opinions. You're aware of what's going on around you. You breathe through any flooding you're experiencing.

You report back in a calm, objective, dispassionate way. You're not emotional in your presentation. You may have emotions to work through; this you do with your BALM Family Recovery Life Coach, with a therapist, in your journal, with a loving sponsor, or with your friends in recovery. You do not take your emotional reactions out on your loved one.

As you now know, that will not be productive. You exude the unshakable power of calm presence based on your daily practice of increasing the peace in your inner life. You deliver your message without expectation. You simply share a different perspective on what's happening. And in some cases, if they've blacked out, you are letting them know that something is going on at all—what we call helping them see through their blind side. In the beginning, this is how I taught it to people.

Still, I knew something was missing. Then I heard about someone who had a group every day online for individuals with use disorders, and I thought to myself, "Imagine if families had something every single day! What a difference that would make!" So, in 2013, I developed the first daily BALM course. Monday, there was a lesson. Tuesday, there was a discussion about that lesson. Wednesday, there was a demonstration of how to Be A Loving Mirror. Thursday, there was a family member or individual with use disorder speaking. On Friday, I conducted an interview with an expert.

When the coaches I was training pointed out that there wasn't anything to teach families how to Be A Loving Mirror in a step-by-step fashion, I developed the 7 Steps to BALM. Eventually, it became a course that every BALM family goes through: first the BALM 12 Principles, then the 7 Steps to BALM.

Now, there are six to eight BALM classes and coaching groups offered a week, with plans afoot to provide streaming BALM recordings to make our huge archive even more accessible to families.

But why do we even need BALM? Al-Anon has been providing support for years to families. Isn't that enough?

BALM® IS MORE THAN SUPPORT

Support is crucial when it comes to getting your life and act together, but at the end of the day, we need more than that. A simple support group isn't enough. We family members need actual skills and tools to communicate and be helpful to our loved ones in a constructive way — we want to contribute in a healthy way to their recovery. I created BALM because I needed to figure out a way to get those skills to my clients.

I knew it was possible, that the "tough love" route didn't represent the way in which I had been taught Al-Anon from my sponsor, nor did it represent my understanding of the importance of love and connection. I wanted people to learn what Dawn had taught me. With her guidance and my own research, I had helped my husband lovingly. Why shouldn't other people be able to help their loved ones, too? I just didn't buy this idea of drop him, leave him, get out of there, don't waste your life. That's not the path I chose, and more and more, I was meeting others who didn't want that path, either.

Plus, there was already a place for people who *wanted* to leave. There were plenty of support groups for those family members who chose tough love. But there were no places, no tools, no resources for people who wanted to stay and help their loved one and family get their collective life back.

When I was first in Al-Anon, and my husband and I were in early recovery together, I was speaking at a meeting and someone said, "What's wrong with you? We *have* to stay together. Why would you stay voluntarily?" I looked up and noticed that the speaker was part of a couple. Turns out they were the parents of a struggling loved one.

"Because I love my husband," I said simply. "Why wouldn't I stay? I can't even imagine my life without him, so why would I be looking for a way out?"

"Well, it's gonna be a very hard path. Why would you want that?"

"I don't know," I said honestly. "It's just my path."

Of course, it would have been nice to find and marry somebody who really had their act together and have a wonderful life where everything's perfect. But that wasn't my path. My path was to meet someone who had a lot of challenges — and, by the way, I also had a lot of challenges. Some of those challenges we sorted out together, and some we had to sort out separately. We both had our ups and our downs. There's a lot of stigma out there, but just because the stigma says that an individual with use disorder isn't worth waiting for or sticking with doesn't mean it's true.

I set time limits on myself, as I already mentioned. It's very painful to watch someone kill themselves. It's painful to be involved with someone who is engaged in self-harming behavior. You feel like you're giving more than you are getting. The person isn't there for you. They aren't able to be. They're very ill.

What's more, you want to have a life. If things get too rough-and-tumble, it's easy to become hopeless, miserable, and unhappy. That's why it was very important for me to figure out, first of all: How long was I going to give this? And second, what would it mean to give it my all? What would it mean to be there in a meaningful way so I had the best chance of helping him? That's where all the research came in, the experimentation, the action. Once I did it and saw that, in this case, it helped him — after something like that, how could I not want to share this with other families?

What I ultimately found was that choosing to stay is hard. How do you stay without enabling? How does one be helpful and loving, and successfully work with a struggling loved one to build a life together? That's a challenge, yes.

But I believe it's a challenge worth embracing.

QUESTIONS TO PONDER:

1. What in this story speaks to you? Journal about it and see where it takes you.

———

Here's an article printed in a national web-based recovery magazine that shared one reporter's findings about our program.

A Healing B.A.L.M. for Families Dealing with Addiction
By Michelle Horton

After dealing with my husband's addiction for ten years, I was tired and hopeless. When I found a new recovery community that promised to help me salvage our relationship, I had to give it a try.

Walk into any Al-Anon room and ask, "What do you, as family members of an addict or alcoholic, ultimately want in your life?" and you'll hear, across the board: peace.

Oh sure, we might use other words — words like "stability" or "contentment" or "living with someone who doesn't steal my money" — but it all points to one basic need: peace.

Living with or simply loving someone struggling through an active addiction is like living in hell, and we assume peace will come in time, right? It will come after our child admits she has a problem or our husband goes to rehab or our mother sticks to a Twelve-Step program. When they change, then our lives can go back to normal.

Or maybe we know, through our own recoveries and programs, that "happiness is a choice." That we didn't cause the addiction, we can't control the addiction, and we can't cure the addiction — all the "C's" of Al-Anon. Maybe we've discovered that the hell continues, even after recoveries begin. Loving someone who is struggling with inner demons, and realizing, through loving that person, that we ourselves have inner monsters to wrangle, is tough work.

I've read all the literature and recognized my codependent tendencies, and yet all the intellectualizing in the world won't stop the anger from rising in my throat whenever my recovering husband nods off on the couch. When I'm lying awake at 3 a.m. listening to his wheezing asthma, I'm rarely repeating mantras and working on my breath work. No, my mind is replaying that time EMT workers were in my bedroom, sirens blaring, with my 4-year-old son sleeping in the next room. Then I remember the medical bills. (*Deep breaths, Michelle.*)

Despite standing by my husband for over a decade of addict behavior, I'd asked for a separation three times within the first year of his tumultuous recovery. I came to the conclusion that in order to love my husband the way he deserved — to truly accept him as he is, whether he uses or not — I needed some safe space. His actions and behaviors were still affecting me, and I wanted off the rollercoaster of recovery. I wanted to love him, and I wanted to love *me*, and I thought the best way to do that was in separate houses.

But then I spoke with Beverly Buncher, the founder and head coach for *Family Recovery Resources,* based in Coconut Creek, Fla. She developed a program called the BALM, which stands for Be A Loving Mirror. The course is designed to help family members of addicts and alcoholics get their lives back. It also promises to teach skills and tools to effectively help loved ones get and stay sober, not through controlling or nagging or wanting it *really really* badly, but through "being a loving mirror."

I was skeptical, as one is when she's at the end of her rope, dangling toward the perceived freedom of separation, but I took a call with Buncher anyway. Within the first 20 minutes of our conversation, she completely changed the trajectory of my thoughts and intentions. Not only did I realize how few recovery tools I had for myself, but she convinced me that her approach — the entire philosophy of the BALM — was sensible and life changing.

"It's possible to lead a sane and happy life while living with a lunatic," Buncher promised, with compassion and kindness toward said lunatic. With the right tools, the right perspective, and the right support, it's possible to live alongside a struggling, sometimes crazy person and not morph into an even crazier person in the process.

In our first conversation together, Buncher gave me something I'd been missing for a long time: hope.

We are their best chance at recovery, when we focus on our *own* recovery.

"You have a crucial role to play in their recovery."

That's the message Buncher gives in her introduction to the BALM, a general overview on her 5-year-old program. It's a monumental thing for a family member to hear. You see, we're often told that we can't play a role. It's out of our control. It's up to *them* to get help, and the best we can do is accept and let go.

Through the BALM program, acceptance and letting go are still crucial, but Buncher argues that when family members get their own lives back — when we find true, radiant, infectious recovery for ourselves — then that's our loved one's best chance at wanting and finding recovery, too.

Not only that, but when we learn the most effective tools and strategies for dealing with our loved one's behavior — when we can trust our own eyes and ears, when we have a healthy amount of compassion and understanding, and when we have the personalized support to put our tools, mental scripts, and boundaries into action — it has the potential to change everything.

Buncher knows this to be true professionally, as a recovery and life coach who has helped families transform not only *their* lives but their loved one's as well. But she also knows this personally, as a 29-year recovery veteran, Al-Anon devotee, and wife of a recovered addict. She and her husband have been through hell and back, and she credits the BALM method for saving their marriage not once, but twice.

The BALM isn't a replacement for Al-Anon or another program; it's a supplementation. It's another tool (or rather, it's more like a pre-packed set of tools). In fact, Buncher's program addresses the one thing I couldn't find in my local meetings:

Al-Anon PLUS.

"It's refreshing to hear that a recovering marriage is possible, because it seems like everyone in my Al-Anon meetings are divorced or separated," I said to Buncher over the phone. "It's discouraging."

Buncher laughed. While she very much understood what I meant ("I couldn't find anyone under the age of 50 who was still married to the alcoholic, either"), she does credit Al-Anon for saving her life, and virtually all of the experts and speakers in the BALM program are part of Al-Anon, too.

"I consider the BALM to be Al-Anon PLUS," she said. "Do you know about the 4 C's?"

Hmmm, I knew about the *three* (you didn't *cause* it, can't *control* it, and can't *cure* it), but there's a fourth?

"The fourth one used to be much more prominent in the original Al-Anon literature, but it's quietly faded over the last couple of decades," she continued. Here it is: you can *contribute* to your loved one's recovery, and you *don't* have to *contribute* to their addiction.

So the BALM is basically all of the wisdom and support of Al-Anon and similar compassion and common-sense-based programs, but it emphasizes the long-lost 4th "C": you can *contribute* to your loved one's recovery in a practical and meaningful way.

Be A Loving Mirror

The way we do that is through reflecting — mirroring — what we see. Not what we feel or think or fear, but what we're truthfully seeing, from a place of love and peace. Because the BALM is designed to help family members achieve peace (which is all recovery really is; our inner radiant peace), we can reflect that peace onto our loved ones, like a mirror. That's what relationships are, after all: mirrors. For better or worse.

Other books, therapists, and programs advocate the same thing, but the BALM is strategically designed to facilitate this through three main components: information, transformation, and support, all of which is focused on not only the family member, but the family member's relationship, too. Al-Anon tells us to keep the focus on ourselves, not our loved one, but the BALM says that it's *also* about our loved one. The program recognizes our inherent interconnectedness.

The program starts with the Daily BALM, which is the "information" component of the program. Each week, participants receive one of the BALM 12 Principles in an email, including an hour-long lesson with Buncher, as well as all sorts of reference materials — corresponding PowerPoints, interviews with experts, past support call recordings around that topic, and stories from people who have walked the walk and made it through. Participants also receive journaling prompts, printable handouts that correspond to each lesson, and note-taking templates.

Every Wednesday there is a "support call," where Buncher further explains the principle, interviews an expert or inspiring recovered person, and gives participants a chance to ask specific questions or share our struggles. Not only do we hear valuable advice from smart, inspiring people, but we then get to talk to them directly. Additionally, participants get two coaching calls each week, where we chat with a BALM coach more in-depth about current issues, or any questions they might have about the weekly lesson.

Then comes the "transformation" aspect of the program: The 7 Steps to BALM, an 8-week course that promises to teach family members how to "get calm from the inside out." We're also paired with a weekly partner to practice, and there's more discussion and support available throughout.

"It's not about the strategy, it's about the recovery."

I'm only four weeks into the BALM program, but it's blowing my socks off. The support and personalized attention is incomparable, and the lessons are really, truly helpful. I was hesitant when I heard the price ($1800 for the full year; $999 when they run their occasional specials), but when I broke it down on a monthly payment plan (which they offer) and considered that it includes up to four family members, it was almost cheaper than therapy.

The most valuable part, for me, is having access to a wide variety of people who made it through to the other side. Access to the radiant peacefulness of recovery, acting like an outstretched hand, saying it's possible, it's available, *just jump*. It's also inspired me to keep going to my meetings and to deeply commit to my recovery, knowing I have a weekly schedule to keep me on track.

And so then maybe I, too, can embody that kind of peace I'm seeing in the BALM community.

Maybe I, too, can have my hand outstretched to my husband, saying *look what recovery looks like; it's safe to jump, my love.*

But even if he doesn't take my hand, if he doesn't choose to join me, at least I'll still be here, dancing in my own blissful peace, radiating in recovery.

————

This article appeared in *Renew* magazine in September 2015 and has been reprinted with permission of the magazine's publisher. The article can be found online at http://www.reneweveryday. com/a-healing-balm-for-families-dealing-with-addiction.

10

The Early Recoverers

In the very beginning stages of BALM, I had clients who I taught this method to, but I really didn't know how to transfer it. I didn't know how to give them the transformation. All I really knew how to do was to script a conversation.

For example, if one of my clients had to talk to their loved one, or to the juvenile home or treatment center, I scripted it. They practiced it with me, then they went and had the conversation with my script. They'd come back, we'd script the next conversation, and on it would go. And it worked. People *were* helping their loved ones. The problem was, that system is not sustainable — for them or for me. I can't script every conversation for every person who comes to BALM.

In the early days, it would take me two or three years to help a family in the way we are able to help them now in a much shorter period of time. Today, our BALM coaches participate in the BALM as part of their training, practicing what they learn so they can benefit from BALMing and effectively share it with the families they serve. Many of them are now also BALM teachers online and in person to ensure that we move toward our collective company mission of helping all families blaze the trail to recovery in their homes.

Getting back to the beginning, in the earliest years of the company, one of our BALMers had a daughter who had been struggling with substances for many years. I kept telling the mom what to do, scripting conversations, and showing her how to do it. She kept going against the professional advice and not following through, again and again and again — over the course of her daughter being in three or four treatment centers. (Her favorite line was, "But she's an adult; she gets to choose" — and the result was relapse after relapse.)

Every time I worked with her, I'd ask, "Okay, remember what happened last time when the treatment center told you your daughter needed to spend more time in treatment or attend aftercare and you followed your daughter's wishes instead? Now, what are you going to do this time?"

It took about four experiences of working through these relapses together over a three-year period, and a month in an in-patient family treatment facility, for her to finally cry uncle and do what I had been coaching her to do all along.

I often think of what I could have done for her if I had then what the BALM offers now. Her daughter did get sober, but throughout the whole process, she didn't know how to do any of it herself. I did it all for her — I held her hand through everything, which some people naturally resist. In the long run, she did learn how to 'sit down, shut up, and smile' as we say, contributing less and less to making things worse, just by not saying whatever came into her head. Being able to control one's words can help a great deal.

Today, though, our members learn how to create and have conversations through the 7 Steps to BALM course. They then use their coaches to help them refine their scripts and review their communication skills as they transform from the inside out. In the early days, my families didn't transform. I transformed their conversations, and that's why it took so long to effect change — and the change often didn't last without sustained help for the family along the way.

Years later, during her daughter's relapse, the mom's growth is evident however and there is less resistance to her (the mom's) part in moving things toward recovery. Plus, her attitude is one of love and understanding.

The missing piece for the early BALMers was often that BALM transformation that our newest members demonstrate much more quickly and powerfully, and that the pioneers did not have the opportunity to experience as quickly or deeply during their family's most difficult times. The program just wasn't there yet. Without the Information (**BALM** 12 Principles) and Transformation (7 Steps to **BALM**) classes and concepts added to the coaching, the road to family recovery can take so much longer.

Nevertheless, these amazing early BALMers are the people who inspired — as much as my own family — the development of the **BALM**.

THE STORY OF MICHELLE

Michelle came to us sober. She'd been an individual with use disorder for years, but she'd been sober for more than two by the time she came to us. Now, her daughter's SUD was heroin.

She came to BALM asking for help. But when I told her what it cost, she backed out immediately. She didn't want to pay, which is understandable. That always breaks my heart as I know the life-and-death nature of this illness. At the same time, we have to respect people's choices. Of course, when there is need, we do our best to accommodate.

Well, much to my relief, she came back six months later. By that time, her daughter was close to death, and she knew if she didn't do something fast, the worst could happen. I worked with her for a year, and at the same time, she went into the BALM Comprehensive, which by then was a year old. Over the years that followed, her daughter went through three more treatment centers.

But Michelle? All this time, that mother grabbed onto BALM like *she* was the one dying. She worked diligently, and it transformed her. We weren't the only ones to notice, either. After her daughter got sober, she looked at her and said, "Mom, there's something different about you. Something good different."

Michelle was practicing BALM. In fact, she became a BALM coach and is studying to teach the BALM 12 Principles in her town.

And now, several years later, her daughter has three years clean and sober, and is working in the treatment field. Will wonders never cease!

THE STORY OF MALIK

Malik's wife was using heroin when he came to BALM. He took my weekly class, "The 12 Keys to Family Recovery," and eventually started coaching with me. Malik was incredibly frustrated. He was a professional man with a big job, but his wife was using heroin. What's more, his in-laws kept giving his wife money and supplying her habit! At one point, when his wife was arrested, it was her parents who bailed her out. They just kept giving her money; they showed love by giving her whatever she wanted. He did not want them to keep enabling her, but they were forceful. They insisted. They also had a nasty habit of blaming Malik and putting him down, all the while making things worse.

One day, he came into my class and was really angry at his in-laws. He was furious at them and at his wife for her choices. He was frothing. It was my job to ask the simple, but difficult, question:

"How is your anger helping you help your wife stay sober?"

And he just sat there. "Well, I guess it really isn't," he finally admitted.

"So what might work better?"

We went through a coaching process that day that allowed him to move from total anger to acceptance and love, and he became a BALMer, even before BALM was fully formed. He was working with me in BALM's infancy. While his wife was in treatment, he committed to setting boundaries in a powerful way. I taught him how to have loving conversations, how to reflect back.

When his wife got sober, he was always there to support her. When she had surgery for an unrelated illness, he took time off work to stay with her, to make sure she wouldn't go back on drugs. He did everything he could, all while practicing BALM. He practiced engaged detachment, which is really what BALM is about. People say, "Detach with love," but we say, "Engage and detach." You detach from the anger. You detach from the obsessive thinking. You detach from the nonproductive way of being. You detach from enabling. But you don't detach from your loved one.

His wife has been sober now for five years.

THE STORY OF HALLIE

When Hallie came into the BALM, she was referred to me by one of my coaches. After I got on the phone with her, she said hello and immediately started crying. She sat on that phone and cried with me for half an hour.

I waited. I just listened to her cry, until she was ready to tell me her story. This is what she told me:

At that point, her sister was sober. But the treatment center her sister was in had convinced the family to detach from her physically — to not have anything to do with her. Apparently, she wasn't doing things the way the center wanted her to. They wanted the family to teach her a lesson, saying the family should take care of themselves and separate from such bad behavior.

Hallie was torn. She felt like boundaries were important, but there was something not sitting well for her about this plan. Over the course of our work together and her own immersion in the Be A Loving Mirror program, she discovered that she could have boundaries that did not involve physical detachment or anger.

Everyone in her family was detaching from the sister out of fury. They were so angry at her, and it's understandable why. She had brought a lot of grief and sadness to an otherwise happy family life. But through the BALM, Hallie learned how to see her sister differently. Instead of seeing her as an individual with use disorder who had destroyed the family, she saw her as her wonderful sister who was very ill. Instead of seeing her as someone she had to avoid, she saw her as someone she could slowly move back toward in a healing and healthy way.

She always told me that the real turnaround for her was learning the fifth C: you are *connected* to your loved one on a level deeper than their use disorder. At that point, she started to look at her sister through the eyes of love. Her sister was acting terribly, yelling at her, using her, or trying to get her to do things she knew weren't healthy. Instead of looking at her as a pain in the butt who was really hurting the family, and destroying her life, Hallie saw her as her wonderful sister to whom she was connected, who was going through a very difficult time.

Hallie communicated with her sister differently. She stopped doing things for her sister that her sister could do for herself, but she didn't disappear from her life. She was still engaged and involved, went to counseling sessions with her when needed, and advocated for her.

That sister has been sober now for quite a while. It doesn't mean there haven't been slips, but a slip doesn't have to become a relapse. When a family member is able to be there with the person, to listen to what's going on with them and not judge them, oftentimes the slip will melt away. We've seen that again and again with families. But a slip often becomes endlessly chaotic in a relapse where the family cannot be kind or loving. BALM is a different way of relating.

SUD is a very stigmatized disorder, so unfortunately, family members are often judgmental. Everyone's judgmental about this sort of thing. You judge an individual with use disorder; they judge themselves. But when the family stops judging them, they can be themselves. They can develop, and they can think clearly. Being accepted and loved by somebody is like having a home base. That's what our families give their loved ones. That's what families are for. But in non-BALM families where there's an active use disorder, things are often so twisted that home base isn't there anymore.

That doesn't mean this loving approach guarantees recovery; nothing can guarantee recovery. But it can make the time you have right now meaningful. We've had families who have been told for years to stay away from their use disordered loved ones, to cut them off — and they've listened. But when they practice BALMing, they find ways to connect with healthy boundaries. Some of those loved ones still don't make it. This is a terrible disease. But the beautiful truth is, those families were able to create some precious memories in those last few years, all because they reached out.

THE STORY OF SASHA

Sasha had a husband who couldn't get sober. She came into the BALM, and we coached her twice a week. She worked the program like crazy and was incredibly loving to her husband. However, despite her work, he kept slipping for a solid year. The whole time she was in the BALM, he would slip.

Instead of handling it badly, freaking out or stressing out, she handled it as a BALMer. She was loving, she was matter-of-fact, and she consistently told him what did and didn't work for her. There was a point at which she even said, "This slipping has happened several times, and I don't think this is healthy for our son. You may have to spend some time away." She was serious about her boundaries! It took an entire year of her consistently doing all that, but you know what? He got sober, and it stuck.

We see so many different patterns. We see people who find recovery immediately, and we see people like Sasha. But it's the family member's consistency in BALMing that makes a huge difference. If three or four family members get involved, it's really something. There just isn't anywhere for your loved one to hide.

At the same time, we believe very strongly in the power of one. Even if just one family member changes, the whole dynamic changes. Many folks come to us thinking this program won't work if they're the only one doing it. On the contrary; if you practice it diligently, everything will shift. Just as important, you'll get your own life back.

QUESTIONS TO PONDER:

1. Which story in this chapter do you relate to?
2. What are you willing to do to experience and sustain an inner transformation?

Part IV:
PULL IT ALL TOGETHER

11

From Family to Loved One: How Shift Creates Change

Transformation is the key to all we do at BALM.

As you go through this process of transformation, one way to truly mark and measure your progress is your conversational tone. Tone is critical in a BALM conversation; there is no room for sarcasm or accusation.

WATCHING YOUR TONE

Some people who have been traumatized are sarcastic. Some are timid. Some are angry. An effective BALM conversation requires a tone of loving calm throughout. And when you script your BALM conversation, none of the emotional baggage can show up. You must completely let go of any sarcasm, blame, accusation, anger, or malice — or don't have the conversation at all.

Recently, I interviewed a woman on the Daily BALM program who is a master at boundary setting. She's one of our old BALMers; her son has been sober five years. She shared with us how when she first came in, she was very sarcastic and very angry, but she got rid of it.

When I asked her how she did so, she said it was through the honest coaching conversations we had.

Her observations in our initial coaching sessions six years ago were often spot-on, but the caustic delivery made me shiver to my bones. I asked her permission to point out the tone I was hearing, and she was willing to learn not only new words and phrases but also a new delivery tone for her communication.

We don't realize that our own sarcasm, anger, meanness, yelling, or whatever it is can be harmful to the people we love. BALM coaches get permission from their clients to give feedback on tone, sarcasm, and more, and when clients are willing, the transformation is often noticed appreciatively by their loved ones. In one case, a client reported that the change in her tone was so profound that her children were willing to be in her life again after many years of distance.

SUPPORT DURING TRANSFORMATION

The three parts of BALM, as you know by now, are information, transformation, and support. Earlier in this book we dealt with information. At this point, we are well into discussing transformation. But the third component of BALM is critical as well, since transformation is difficult to attain or sustain without support.

How are you getting the support you need? If your BALM coach gave you this book, you already know that a BALM coach can be an amazing source of support during this time — for instance, when you're scripting your conversations. At the beginning of the coaching relationship, we script with our clients, modeling tools and tricks for them as they learn how to do it themselves. Eventually, in the 7 Steps to BALM, they learn to master these skills — but they often benefit from a coach's support during that transition.

It is important in a BALM conversation to come from love. If you connect with that, if you connect with yourself, your inner spirit and your Higher Power, and you develop the observation and emotional awareness tools, your BALM conversations will often become mini interventions.

If you don't have your own coach yet and are enrolled in the BALM, you can attend the coaching groups available in the BALM Comprehensive program. If you need more support, of course, you will want to hire your own coach. Give us a call and we will pair you with one of our many certified BALM coaches, all of whom can help you grow in your ability to apply what you are learning in class.

After a while, you might even learn how to have spontaneous BALM conversations. For instance, your husband looks up at you in the morning and his eyes are bloodshot, and you tell him so. That's it.

Not, "What the hell did you do last night?"

Just, "*Honey, your eyes are bloodshot*", stated calmly in an even, conventional tone. You are simply reporting a fact, not making an accusation.

Of course, if your loved one is drunk, you really don't want to have a BALM conversation at that time. You jot down the facts, but you don't want to speak about matters of consequence to a person who is inebriated. The right time and place for a BALM conversation is when a person is lucid. And as you grow and transform, you will get better at spotting times when those spontaneous conversations will work.

Imagine how much more effective that growth will be and how much more easily you will be able to see those opportunities if you have support throughout the process!

Remember that denial is the glue of the addictive system. It holds it all together. Your using loved one needs to believe their lies, so they tell themselves a lie that allows them to keep using. They also need *you* to believe their lies so they can keep believing their own lies. So they tell you the same lie they are telling themselves. When they tell you the lie, if you say, "Well, that's not true," then it becomes your loved one's job, as a person struggling to hold onto their use disorder, to defend the lie and tell you that *you* are the crazy one. This is when you may hear responses like:

"What? How could you say that about me?"

"I would never do anything like that."

"You must be crazy! Are you seeing things?"

But if you can say something to your loved one in a way that does not promote their denial, that does not get their defenses up, then they might be able to hear you. These conversations can have a quick, shocking, life-changing impact — or they can be like an IV drip, where it takes a long time for anything to change from one tiny drip. But the more drips there are, the faster change can occur. Likewise, the more correctly implemented BALM conversations (well planned and well executed) you have with your loved one, the greater the impact your conversations can have.

That said, there are times for quicker action. Leverage must be applied, motivational questions must be asked, or an actual interventionist must be brought in sooner rather than later.

Your BALM coach will work with you to figure out when your BALM conversation is a pure sharing of facts or when it may be best to incorporate these other powerful tools and/or when to add more people to your family's recovery team.

And there are times when you may incorporate different tools but your loved one will not budge. If the situation is dangerous for you or your loved one, all bets are off with the slow and steady approach. Get help immediately. Call 911 and move the situation forward.

TRANSFORMATIONAL BOUNDARIES

There are times when your loved one's behavior, though not an immediate emergency, may irritate you and make it extremely difficult to go on as things are, yet they seem unable or unwilling to change. In those cases, your BALM conversation may need the addition of a boundary. Boundaries are part of the "get your life back" aspect of the BALM method. There is an actual script for it taught in the 7 Steps to BALM course.

Again, boundaries are about you, the person who is setting them. Helping your struggling loved one is a potential side benefit of setting a boundary, not the main reason for implementing it.

That is an important distinction, because often, when people think of setting boundaries for a person who is struggling, they think of fencing them in. But that intention — of controlling the uncontrollable (remember the second C, you can't control their SUD) — just increases their defensiveness. Your boundary is a fence around *you*, not anyone else.

A boundary is something you can set to allow yourself space in your life. Boundaries describe what you choose to live with and what you choose to not allow in your life. As stated, they can help you get your life back in the middle of the hell of a loved one's struggles.

Many people think that setting a boundary is only saying, "Get out! Leave my house!" But there is a wide range of possibility in boundary setting that also includes things like what you will and won't pay for, what times people call you, what time your door gets double-locked at night, and who may and may not visit your home.

The key to BALM boundary setting is the same as in a BALM conversation: *tone*. Tone is the difference between mean and kind, arrogant and humble, angry and calm.

As long as the boundary works for the person setting it and is stated in a kind and loving way, it works.

Will there be pushback? Most definitely. To deal with however your loved ones and other family members respond to your new words and behaviors and to have the greatest impact on yourself and your family, we BALMers recommend that you make *your* transformation a priority.

WHY YOUR TRANSFORMATION MATTERS

The 7 Steps to BALM are all about changing yourself, changing how you are oriented toward the world and your loved one. It's about transforming yourself and then transforming your relationships with other people in the world. You could use steps four through seven on your boss, on your coworkers, on your best friend, on your sister, on your wife, on your husband, on anyone.

Be the peace. Have a daily practice so that you can cope with what's going on in any stressful situation, whether that's your home life, your work life, or just watching the news. Observe the facts. Become aware of your angers and judgments, and take off your buttons so they can't be pushed. Jot down what's happening, but only the facts. Set a boundary if you need to. Take specific action if you need to. But to be effective, do so from a quiet place.

The attitudinal shift that's required is the shift from contributing to your loved one's use disorder toward contributing to their recovery. Where once you may have thought, "This is not my problem and he's an asshole," now you realize, "He's impaired, and I have a role in making things better, too."

That attitudinal shift is where you realize you *can* handle this. It's just one foot in front of the other to go from chaos to sanity. From turmoil to peace. The attitudinal shift of your thoughts and feelings is what will change the talk, the tone, and the behavior. First you change your attitude, then you take action. You might make a new commitment to your self-care, or to being loving, or to setting boundaries, or even to getting support. Those are all actions.

You can see why a yearlong course can be helpful and sometimes necessary. This type of transformation takes time and work. But the truth is there's no magic number when it comes to the time required. Some people will read this book and that will be all they'll need; some will need constant coaching, courses, and intensives. You can't know who you are until you try; it just takes what it takes. The transformation is about you.

FROM FAMILY TO LOVED ONE: HOW SHIFT CREATES CHANGE

Again, the BALM program contains three parts. The first step, information, is made up of the BALM 12 Principles and all the interviews with our experts. The second part, transformation, is the seven-step process to create your own inner shift, a shift that can ultimately lead your loved one to transform. The third part, support, includes individual coaching and group coaching available to families so they don't have to walk it alone.

When a family transforms through this shift, the whole dynamic of the family changes. Often, the loved one is surprised at first, maybe even bothered by it because they can't push buttons the way they used to. But in the long run, most are deeply grateful.

We've seen BALM restore marriages, save children, and unite families — we see it again and again and again. Of course, as said before, there are no guarantees that a loved one will find recovery. Even then, there can be healed relationships and peace. One mom said that even after the loss of her son, she saw the program as a healing BALM for her with its focus on peace, unconditional love, and nonjudgment. She also said she considered the time she and her son spent together, before his death, to be a time restored to them due to her participation in the BALM. (See Maryann Williams's article "Peace in the Midst of Grieving" in Chapter 11.)

Many programs provide the information aspect. A woman spoke at our class a couple of years ago explaining how when she first came to BALM, nothing we did seemed unique. Her husband had been in four treatment programs, and a lot of what we taught was available in those programs. The difference was and is the transformation piece and the ongoing application of all you have learned. If you do one workshop, or even a weeklong class, once it's over — it's gone. There's no follow-up, no transformation, no support.

In the BALM, she pointed out, she worked on it all for a full year, transformed as she faced each challenge along the way, and had a whole team to support her through the process. Her willingness to do deep work even inspired a structural guide that our coaches use to take family members through the 7-Step process.

As Maharishi Mahesh Yogi used to say, "Knowledge that's in the book stays in the book."

It is information combined with experience that creates transformation. The 7 Steps to BALM are all actions: a step is something *you* take. We call the 7 Steps to BALM the pearl of our program, because it's hidden. It's something that you have to unwrap, that you have to choose to be a part of, and the radiance it creates is beyond belief.

I've worked with families who were on the most destructive path you can imagine; communication was reduced to screaming, all the time, in every direction. I've seen those families transform through the 7 Steps to BALM so that the way they communicate completely shifts. The transformation is so evident, even when the individual with use disorder doesn't recover. As a result of working the 7 Steps to **BALM**, the family members find out how to actively love each other again in a way that is enjoyable. They want to be together and be around each other; they delight in each other.

THE TOOLS FOR TRANSFORMATION

Although I've touched on some exercises already, in the context of this essential transformation I think it's worth reiterating some of the tools that can make the biggest impact on your journey.

One of the first, most powerful, and simplest exercises we teach our families is the Four-Four-Eight. You breathe in for a count of four. You hold in that breath for a count of four. And you let it out to the count of eight. It's really just breathing. Depending on how upset you are, you might need to do it once, twice, three or four times, or for five minutes. For some people, that's their meditation practice. They wake up in the morning, they open their eyes, breathe into the count of four, hold it to the count of four, breathe out to the count of eight — for five solid minutes. We invite people to do it for five minutes in the morning, five minutes at lunch, and five minutes when they go to bed. If I can't sleep at night, I do Four-Four-Eight, and it puts me right to sleep.

One time, a client called me extremely upset. Her ex-husband had just told her she wasn't welcome at their daughter's wedding. His family was paying for it, and even though *he* was the individual with use disorder, she was not welcome. She was sobbing so frantically over the phone, and I felt myself flooding. I had been working with her for a good long while; everyone cared about her, and I had an extreme emotional reaction to her distress. As I felt myself flooding, I jumped into the Four-Four-Eight. I did it four times before I could even answer her.

Then, I was able to listen without yelling, screaming, crying, or blaming. I was able to be there for her.

These kinds of things happen all the time. In families where there is an individual with a use disorder, there is unpredictable behavior. Breath can make a surprisingly huge difference.

Another tool we teach is breathing through transitions. If you're upset when the phone rings — because, for a family member of an individual with use disorder, you don't know what's going to be on the other end of that phone — breathe through that transition of going to pick up the phone.

We practice breathing through transitions to be prepared for those events. For instance, as you're about to walk from the living room to the dining room, breathe. Breathe in as you're approaching the archway to go to the next room. Hold it as you're walking through, breathe out as you go to the other side.

If you're opening the fridge, breathe in as you open it. Hold it as you take out a food item, breathe out as you close it. Or maybe you breathe in as you're walking into your bedroom, and you breathe out once you get in there. Then, after all this practice, you will know how to breathe when the phone rings. Breathe in when the phone rings, pick it up, breathe out. And say hello.

The idea is to prepare for the times you're afraid of by practicing Four-Four-Eight daily, when things are calm. You will become conscious and mindful about breath, and you will have that resource and strength available to you if and when something happens.

HOW TOOLS CAN SHIFT YOUR BODY AND MIND

The remarkable thing about these tools and exercises is what an immediate, visceral difference they can make in your emotional state. Take the watching your hands trick, for instance, which we call *Focus on the Task at Hand*. If something upsets you, look at your hands. Watch what your hands are doing and describe it to yourself — so that it becomes what you are thinking about. "I am now peeling the carrot. My right hand is pulling the peeler down the side of the carrot," and so on.

You can also practice being in the moment to calm yourself down. For instance, you can focus on the world with an innocent awareness, just looking at a picture for instance, as if you've never seen it before. Michael Brown discusses present moment awareness in his book *The Presence Process*, as do many others, and we practice being in the present moment as part of our practice of Step 2. Allow your eyes to soften; just stay with it for two to three minutes. See the texture, see the color, practice observing objectively. Not only does this immediately lower your blood pressure, it teaches you long-term skills. You learn to differentiate between what you know for sure and what you don't know, which leads to another remarkable tool: the Clear/Unclear (p. 42) chart.

Clear/Unclear, as mentioned, is one of the most important ways to observe what's going on around you objectively. Normally, when we observe, we instinctively bring in knowledge of the past around that person. For example, you see a loved one who smokes coming and say to yourself, "*She's going to smoke a cigarette and drive me crazy!*"

If I'm doing that, I am not seeing you. I'm seeing my bias about you.

Instead, practice Clear/Unclear. She walked across the room. As she approached I could smell the smoke on her clothes. She reached over to give me a hug and exhaled her stale cigarette breath. As I breathed in, I felt it up my nose and down my throat. She lit a cigarette in the living room and started coughing as soon as she inhaled it.

It's just the facts, which is infinitely helpful in observing your own inner emotional landscape without judgment. You observe your feelings of anger, judgment, and resentment. You observe your need to control a situation and fix it. You breathe through the intensity of it. You learn to become patient in a truly powerful way.

BODY WISDOM

Lion Goodman, developer of the Clear Your Beliefs® program, is a teacher of mine, and I've seen miracles with his Body Wisdom technique, which we use in the BALM as a Step 3 exercise. We ask our clients: What are you feeling right now? *I'm feeling angry.* Can you find that anger in your body? *Yes, I can.* What color is it? They spend time describing it, and soon the emotion leaves — as a result of dealing directly with the physical sensation. You go deeper and deeper, and eventually even the physical sensation leaves. Sometimes it takes more than once. Sometimes you do it again and again and again for every feeling, and it's powerful.

I had a client who had a terrible feeling of anxiety in the pit of her stomach for twenty-five years; she couldn't get rid of it. We did forty-five minutes of Body Wisdom, and that feeling went away and never came back.

The idea behind Body Wisdom is that feelings come and go, like thoughts. And, like thoughts, we can manage them. Feelings and thoughts create problems only when we glom on to them or push them down, where they get lodged deep within you.

We teach people to think of thoughts or feelings as clouds going by. This is a mindfulness practice. When a feeling comes, allow it to be there, whatever it is. Just observe it until it goes away; be light with your feelings. In other words, don't fight them. They will eventually pass. But if you are fighting your feelings or pushing them down, they will lodge in your body somewhere and create physical illness and/or anxiety.

MAKE IT DIFFICULT TO KEEP USING

In the BALM, we teach you how to make it difficult for your loved one to keep using and easy for them to stop using. Often, families are doing just the opposite.

For instance, if the person doesn't have a job and you give them rent money, food money, and a car and pay for their phone, they don't have to worry about survival. Any money they do have can buy their drug or process of choice, and they can sell what you give them to do so.

Once you start to pull away the supports they're using, they have to fend for themselves, and often that makes it tougher for them to get the money to use.

Meanwhile, you're showing them a lot of love. If you pull away all the supports but are not showing love, they'll feel like you're abandoning them, judging them, or trying to hurt them. Instead, you show lots of love but pull away the things that are enabling their use. You lovingly start to allow them to take responsibility for their life.

Learning this balance, of course, is difficult. What is enabling? What is helping?

When my husband had anger issues, he would yell a lot, and I was stressed out. I would go to therapy for short periods of time to work through it, but the therapists were always trying to get me to leave him — even though I had decided I wasn't leaving. Was that wise or not? I don't know. It's just what I wanted. It's what I chose. And yet every therapist made a concerted effort to get me to leave my husband.

I told them we both had problems. I said I was going to work on mine in therapy; he was going to do what he chose to do. But I didn't hire them to get me to leave my husband! I hired them to help me cope with my life on life's terms. If they didn't want to do that, I went to somebody else. I made a choice about how I wanted to be supported.

IT WILL TAKE TIME

Realize this transformative process will take time. A transformation from inner chaos to inner peace cannot happen overnight. Each baby step you take will grow your reserve of inner calm. The practice of being present to each moment, and many others included in the BALM, will help you grow. But if deep transformation from constant inner turmoil to abiding inner peace is your goal, a commitment to dedicating daily time to practice and study may be required.

It takes what it takes.

QUESTIONS TO PONDER:

1. Where are you in your journey?

12

Be Your Loved One's BEST Chance at Recovery

Love is the answer. We believe from the bottom of our hearts that love is the key. It's a *state* of being who you are, and it's a *way* of being in the world. It's the thoughts you think, the words you speak, and the actions you create — all are part of this loving person that you are. We believe that bringing the love out of yourself from the deepest part of you and being that love will change everything.

Love is the single best way to apply the lessons in this book to create a truly meaningful life. I created the BALM to help families of loved ones the way I had been helped. The people who first used it started reporting that they were using it at work, using it in school, using it with non-using relatives. It was transforming every part of their life! As you can see from the family and coach stories in the book, the experiences of our BALMers show that the BALM 12 Principles and the 7 Steps to

BALM have the potential to affect all of your life, even beyond your relationship with your loved one.

We say to families, "We will teach you how to get your life back and how to help your loved one get theirs back. At the very least, you'll get yours back if you do this — and hopefully you'll help them get theirs back, too." Meanwhile, if you continue to apply these principles and steps in your life, you will be at peace. Yes, it's that transformative. You *do* have a very important role to play, and this is the work of the Loving Path. The work of the Loving Path is to find out what it means to be your loved one's best chance at recovery and to practice it each and every day of your life.

LOVE IS A VERB

Love is a verb. All these things you do to Be A Loving Mirror? They are love in action. Lovingly setting a boundary? That's love in action. Love for yourself? Scripting a conversation? Treating your loved one with dignity and respect? All these things are love in action.

Let me be clear: just because I'm teaching this does not mean I've mastered it. I'm by no means perfect at it. I have to say that I've been doing this for a lot of years now, and I've had some difficult years. I've had some years where I've been better, or worse, at it than others; that's just the human journey. What's been really wonderful about it, though, is this: when I falter, the people around me lovingly tell me so. And what a relief that is! What a relief to be accepted and loved; not judged, but still *seen*. That's the biggest gift we can give each other.

I'm a person in recovery. That's a daily gift. I'm spiritually fit enough to live a happy and sane life for today. Will I own that same sanity and serenity tomorrow? If I continue to do the work I'm choosing to do today, probably. That goes back to love: when I love myself from within, the work I do impacts my own life quality and is able to radiate to my loved one and to the world.

There is a lightness of being when you're at peace like that. It's not just light as in wattage, but it's also light as in *nothing's weighing you down*. You let it go, you're acting from love — and that takes a burden off the person in recovery, too. Our self-care gives our loved one the freedom to take care of themselves. When we have our claws in them, they're completely sapped of any energy to assess their situation and move their life forward because we're working so hard to keep their focus on us (even though we rarely see it that way). We need a lot of energy to be that obsessed, and they have to put all their energy into getting us off their back. By taking care of ourselves, we actually free up the other to take care of themselves. That's power. That's connection.

You are connected to your loved one on a level deeper than their use disorder (BALM's fifth C). If your child or loved one is acting out, remember that. When you realize that, you can just look at them in peace. You know they love you. You know you love them. You're connected. You're not adversaries.

If the energy that's flowing both ways in this connection is anger, then the true connection isn't felt as love. It's like an electrocution instead of an electrical loving connection. Restore the loving connection on your end, and allow it to replace the electrocution and its negative connection. That's what creates the opportunity for the person who's struggling to actually recover. Instead of battling you *and* their disease, they're just battling the disease. How do you bring this about? The BALM 12 Principles and 7 Steps to BALM.

THE POWER OF ONE

Sometimes the loving conversations need to happen with other people, not just the one struggling: a husband, a brother, an aunt, an uncle. This work goes beyond just your relationship with your loved one. If the people around you are fighting you, are still enabling, are making it difficult for your loved one, that makes your peace even more difficult to attain. It makes it harder for everyone. But the power of one means you can make a difference; you can have BALM conversations with every member of the family.

That's another reason people often hire a coach. I had a client whose wife was a real enabler, and all the children followed suit, too. I worked with him to be able to have conversations, to help her stop enabling, and to get the kids to stop enabling. To get them all on the same page, we had meetings together. I met with the brother, the sister, the mother, and the father to help them cope with what was happening.

It takes a massive amount of bravery to have some of these conversations with your family; that's why your own peace is the first and primary step. In the beginning, a good coach can help you develop your peace and develop your conversations. Over time, you'll be doing it yourself, but your coach can get you started. It does require bravery, but when you know it's your next best step, it's the only thing.

DOES TRAUMA CHANGE YOU?

Of course trauma changes people. Once trauma strikes, it can change one's whole path both inwardly and out in the world.

As family members of people with a life-threatening malady that tells them they don't have a problem, we can feel sucker punched by several things at once.

> The dangerous things they may be doing to themselves or exposing others to
> The lying that goes hand in hand with the disorder
> The shame resulting from the stigma associated with a disease that is often criminalized rather than treated

› Our own lack of clarity about how best to help, if we should help, if we even can help

Recently, I was interviewing candidates for a job at the BALM Institute. As each one sat down, I asked them what brought them to our company. Almost everyone had some connection to recovery or the desire for it.

One person in particular will stay with me for a long time. A lovely woman in her fifties, she sat across from me and started crying as soon as I asked the question. She couldn't stop crying. As she began to calm herself, she explained that for the past few days, in preparation for the interview, she had been reading our blogs online and it hit her that her past had completely traumatized her in ways she rarely faced or allowed herself to consider.

Throughout all the years of her childhood, she had endured an alcoholic parent who had brought instability into the family, making it difficult for her to focus on her schoolwork or share her world with others. Her sober parent made it clear that she was not to *ever* say *anything* to *anyone* about what was going on in their house. And to make things even worse, she went to Alateen (the Twelve-Step program for teens affected by a loved one's drinking) but was threatened that she had better not share what was going on at home even there!

There really was no escape for her, no safe place to share and heal. And so, forty years later, she walked into a job interview, a highly professional woman with an impressive resume, and cried, and cried, and cried.

Yes, of course, the trauma of being raised in a home where there has been verbal or physical or sexual abuse, or where there has been constant drinking and yelling and confusion, and the often uncertain financial conditions that can go with the disorder can have long-standing effects.

And on the other hand, hearing about another family's trauma is always sad and difficult.

But when you're on the inside experiencing it, developing a new mindset can affect the degree of trauma's impact on you. As Scott Kiloby of the Kiloby Center says, "I cannot begin to express how important it is for families to be educated and to experience their own transformation."

It is so important to have tools and a structure within to understand and cope with what is happening to you. Then, you're living life, and as you're learning a new way to handle your life, you're handling it. It's not *oh so sad, oh so horrible, oh so difficult* — it's just life. One foot in front of the other. Do the right thing, right now, for the right reasons. It does take courage. And it also takes skills and an understanding of the resources available to you as you move forward facing the family disorder.

The bravery it takes to have a BALM conversation is only one aspect of the bravery it takes to walk the path of a BALMer.

Family members often have decisions to make in life-or-death situations.

The opioid epidemic has turned the slow to fast speed of SUD development into supersonic speed.

Getting trained to administer Naloxone to reverse the effects of an overdose is only one action families of opioid users may decide to take. And people like Ginny Atwood Lovitt, Executive Director and Co-Founder of the Chris Atwood Foundation in Virginia, and Justin Phillips, Executive Director and Founder of Overdose Lifeline in Indiana, have had to use all the bravery at their disposal after losing loved ones to opioid addiction so they can advocate for opioid reversal availability in their states.

These two individuals expend tremendous energy and time fighting stigma and shame at every step to bring families the Naloxone reversal training they need and to advocate for eliminating the stigma of a medically recognized brain disorder, whose sufferers are still treated as subhuman in many areas of society. They, and others I know, including Barbara Theodosiou and her team at The Addict's Mom and Joanne Peterson of Learn to Cope, care deeply about eliminating stigma and making it easier, not harder, for our loved ones to recover and to be family members who are supported and educated fully to face the challenges of SUD.

This book is here to say that love is the answer to the hatred and misunderstanding facing our loved ones and us. Love calls us to be brave in our conversations and in our actions.

Advocates see the value of families getting educated about the disorder and how to contribute to a loved one's recovery. Some are even insisting that the families they work with learn to Be A Loving Mirror so the families can help those struggling with opioid disorder to first survive overdose and then move beyond overdose to long-lasting recovery.

If you think about it, all of us humans go through things that other people can't even imagine going through. SUD is just *our* path. There is a gift even in great sorrow. *Be A Loving Mirror* is the journey and the destination. This is what it takes. Be the peace you wish to see in the world; be objective in your observations. Be emotionally aware without letting your emotions overtake you. When this is your path, you do what's necessary to be your loved one's best chance, namely: document, script, share, and, if needed, set a boundary. You advocate for their recovery, never letting their recovery fall to the bottom of a professional's to-do list.

Living these steps is critical not just for your loved one but for all areas of your life. Because if you don't live your life at peace, objectively observing the world, you stagnate in the worst way possible.

I know someone who treated his employees very badly. Then he became ill for several years. Everyone thought that would change him, that he would treat his workers with at least a little more kindness. They were sure his heart would shift with such a life-altering disease. He was at death's door for seven years — but it didn't change him. Not one bit.

Most people think that *of course* a trauma to one area of a person's life will change that person. But I've met a lot of people, and the reality is many don't automatically change as a result of hardship. They get right up there to the brink, and something in their heart doesn't shift. It's too calcified. That shift has to be a choice, no matter where you are in life, and it isn't always easy to bring about. But it can be done.

In the same way, the experience of having a relative challenged with use disorder isn't always enough to create a shift. We have the **BALM** 12 Principles and the 7 Steps to **BALM** to create that shift, because sometimes people don't know how to go about this loving approach and need education to achieve it. You can't always shift on your own. Maybe that employer, if he had had something like the BALM, would have been able to change.

Of course, a program experience won't magically change you. You have to change yourself, and it all starts with willingness.

QUESTIONS TO PONDER:

1. How willing are you to make an attitudinal shift?

13

Pull Your Family Through Trauma

THERE IS ALWAYS HOPE

At BALM, we help families blaze the trail to recovery in their homes. When everyone else has told you there is no hope left, we will always say that *as long as there's life, there is hope.* We help families who have reached the stage of hopelessness come back from the brink and become their loved one's best chance.

Most of the families who come to me say they have no hope. Sometimes their loved one has been through treatment three times, sometimes ten times. I spoke to a mother the other day who wasn't sure she could afford the BALM, but she'd spent almost $100,000 on her son's multiple treatments.

"What have you learned about how to help him and be his best chance?" I asked her.

"Well, I've learned to mind my own business and leave him on his path."

"Okay," I replied. "How do you feel about that?"

"I do wish there was something more that I could do. . ."

She wasn't satisfied with just leaving her son to fall. To hit rock bottom. We can't be satisfied with that, not when rock bottom can mean a loss of life.

Yet that mom, and many others, have adopted a limited philosophy that, while noble, is neither true nor compassionate, nor is it practical.

There is something more we can do, and that's what I told her. There is no guarantee you can save your loved one, but you *can* give him his best chance. Families can either be a toxic influence or a loving influence. We all love our children, but there is toxic love that enables them. Then there is BALM love, which is unconditional and wise at the same time...and often, it really does help.

THE POWER OF FAMILY

Your loved one's fate is up to him and his understanding of a Higher Power; you can't control it. But you can be the force for change. As stated, we in the BALM program believe very strongly in what we call the power of one. One person in a family can make the difference in the lives of every person in that family, including your loved one — but not limited to them. By being a loving person, Being A Loving Mirror, being the peace you wish to see in the world, you will be that beacon of light for your entire family, a beacon that can allow them to walk through their trials and, in many cases, bring them back from the brink of destruction.

As shared earlier, research shows that as the loved one gets sober, the family and loved one will inevitably part ways for a while — often for years. But at BALM, we offer a new way to change the inevitable to the unlikely. Ours is a path for people who would like to save their loved one *and* their family; we encourage our families to grow strong together from the very start. Even in early recovery, we see everyone growing closer together.

Sometimes people don't want to save their family, but they would like to help their loved one. Or they feel they can't do either. They may find that if they really are disinterested in keeping their marriage together, keeping their family together, this path might feel odd at times. But it's the path of love. You can define how to live your life, and you can even have an uncoupling that is loving. You can have a goodbye that is loving. The point in it all is love.

We had a family who was really deep in the BALM, and their son was apparently using after living with them for a while. They lovingly wrote him a letter that empowered him on his new path and said, "We love you. We're always here for you," but they didn't allow him to use in their house. As a result, he chose to live elsewhere, but he got better on his own and remained emotionally close to them.

It's not always about everybody staying close physically. There are ways to be close spiritually and emotionally wherever you are.

FREEDOM FROM THE BRINK

When you love someone who is caught up in a SUD cycle, it feels like at any moment the world could fall in. At any moment, they could die. At any moment, they could relapse. At any moment, everything you've spent your whole life building or believing could completely fall apart. It's an unconscious, often pushed-down, abject fear that families affected by SUD carry with them as part of their day-to-day life.

The brink is different for everyone, but the ultimate fear we all have is that we're going to lose them. That hopelessness is the real brink. The BALM is the soothing path that allows families to restore hope in a possible future. They know they cannot ensure that their loved one is going to be okay, yet they decide to walk a path that will empower them to be their loved one's best chance.

This is a very simple idea, and you'll notice we state it again and again: you can be someone's best chance at recovery. Most families with a loved one who's using or new in recovery have no idea what to say to their loved one. They don't know what to do. They may be spouting off all kinds of stuff, but they're aware that they don't really know what to say. They want to say the magic words or do the magic thing that's going to help their loved one, but they have no idea what that is.

There is no magic, but there is a healing BALM.

A BALM that teaches them how to better understand their place in the challenge their family is facing. As a result of better understanding their role, their place in it all, they start to see which thoughts, words, and behaviors could be most helpful and which ones must be left unsaid and undone.

Before BALM, the affected families are living in a war zone. The brink is falling over the edge into hopelessness. But the BALM is something to cling to, to learn, to start to live, even if the loved one hasn't recovered; there's still hope because we're using this method. We are given tools to be able to balance ourselves and be okay regardless.

This program is not, "You're going to be okay no matter what. So just get okay." But neither is it, "Here's how you fix them. Forget about you." It's the ultimate combination of those two philosophies. You will be okay, and that, along with the communication tools you put into practice, will potentially help your loved one be okay. Step by step, moment by moment, the family restores their hope, restores their faith, restores their relationships with each other and with their loved one, and begins a new journey into recovery.

OBSTACLES MOST FAMILIES FACE

With so many families who come to us, we've been able to observe the most common obstacles they face as they begin this journey. The first is always their own inability to say *yes*. There's a lot of resistance to simply getting started, making that leap, especially for families who have been going through this for a while. They've tried other things, people have made promises, they've gotten their hopes up — but nothing has "worked." Their loved one has been in treatment center after treatment center, and as far as they can see, all hope is lost.

But the first obstacle on any path is the obstacle between our ears, right? These families think they've heard it before, because that first piece of the BALM program, information, is something a lot of programs offer. They don't realize that the BALM doesn't stop there. What a difference the transformation and support pieces of the program can make.

The second obstacle is the ingrained habits families have to get past. They're in their own lifestyle, their own rhythm — chaotic though it may be — and new change is difficult. In a sense, joining the BALM or doing the work to Be A Loving Mirror is about breaking a habit. If you're looking at breaking habits, you're looking at a change process.

If you're looking at a change process, the first thing we recommend is you look at where you are in that stage process (Prochaska and Prochaska, 2017). Are you in precontemplation where you don't think you have a problem? Are you thinking maybe you do need help? Are you preparing for that help? Are you in action? Family members soon find this out in the BALM and learn how to move from one stage to the next so they can get into the action of helping themselves and their loved one. (See The Family's Path Through the Stages of Change: Understanding the Long Term Trajectory of Family Recovery chart on pages 95-102 and the Stages of Change Assessment on pages 263-266).

The third obstacle or challenge family members face is how to break those habits that are no longer working. To help you do so, your BALM coach will work with you to set goals and will be your interactive partner to help you reach the goals you set. When you're breaking a habit, you have to decide how far you are willing to go to achieve the desired result. At the beginning, when someone comes to me considering the BALM or coaching, I always ask them to tell me three changes they'd like to see in their life as a result of using this program. They'll tell me their goals and then we coach on those goals.

I hear a lot of common ideas in these sessions; there is nothing new under the sun. But any goal can always give me an idea of where the person is in their process. Some people will have completely internal goals such as, "I want to have peace of mind regardless of what happens with my son." "I want to develop my faith." Some might have external goals like, "I want my daughter to get sober." "I want my health to improve." "I want a new job." "I want to repair my marriage."

Sometimes the goals have to do with something fun. I had one mom with three goals: "I want my son sober, my daughter healthy, and I want to get better at tennis, my husband's passion, so we can share that together." Those were valid goals for her.

There are some people who say, "Wait a minute, you can't have a goal for your son. That's not your goal, to get your son sober." I disagree. That is a completely valid goal. But what's at the *root* of it?

When I meet with people, I always take them through a process of narrowing it down to see what their deepest, core goal is. So, I might ask, if you get your child sober, what will that give you? "Well, then I'll know he's happy." If you know he's happy, what will that give you? "That will give me a rest."

If you have a rest, what will that give you? "Well, that will give me contentment." If you have contentment, what'll that give you? "That'll give me peace of mind." If you have peace of mind, what will that give you? "That's it; that's all I need. Peace of mind."

When you get to that point where the person says, "That's it. We're there," you know that that's really their core goal. So she wants her son to be sober and she wants peace of mind. The son being sober, that could take some time. It isn't completely in her hands. Peace of mind, on the other hand? That's something we can start working on immediately in this moment without relying on her son or anyone else to get there. And by working on her goal of peace of mind, she may gain greater inner clarity with which to learn how to help her son directly.

QUESTIONS TO PONDER:

Look at your own goals now. Take three goals. Examine them, and discover what the root goal of each one is. For each, ask yourself:

1. What do you really want out of this program?
2. What do you want out of reading this book?
3. What do you really want on your journey toward recovery?

14

Recovery from the Trenches
BALM® Coaches Share Their Journeys

BEV'S INTRO

The best present I received on my sixtieth birthday last year came in the form of a Facebook message:

"Today is my son's 5th anniversary of recovery. Couldn't have done it without you, the treatment center, and of course, without my son."

Seeing that note brought back so many memories and tears and so much hope for families everywhere. It reminded me of the importance of sticking with families going through the ups and downs of early recovery (often two years or more).

It reminded me of the importance of reminding families who sometimes feel as if they are being dragged through the mud to:

› Persist with everything they are learning in BALM
› Continue to work with their coach
› Continue to love loved ones going through the ups and downs of the struggle

Then, when a slip hit in year six, mom used everything she had learned to get her son help quickly and not overdramatize the process. That story is not yet complete. Yet, mom's ability to listen, think, get help, and follow directions is serving her well as she walks through it with her son and other family members.

To watch a loved one first fight against recovery and then repeatedly fight to get recovery takes so much out of a family.

Here in the BALM community, we do everything we can to help families learn new skills and tools so they can stay sane through it all and give their loved one the best chance of recovery.

Loved ones and families can do well in recovery and then lose their way.

Family recovery is a practice. We never get perfect at it. But every time we do the work of cultivating our deep inner calm, it grows deeper and calmer.

Every time we help rather than enable, stay out of denial and choose awareness, and treat our loved one with dignity and respect even through their struggles, we are contributing to their potential recovery.

Traveling this path with a community, with a coach, makes it so much easier.

That's why I'm so grateful to have the BALM to offer and why it's so good to have so many families and coaches working to help each other grow in BALM skills.

I am so inspired by the growing number of coaches reaching out to families all over the world, teaching them how to Be A Loving Mirror, and increasing the amount of peace and recovery in families as they do so. As the coaches grow in their personal practice as BALMer's and broaden the scope of their work with families, they are truly partnering with us to achieve the BALM mission of helping all families blaze the trail to recovery in their homes!

In this chapter, we will read the stories of several BALM coaches who have chosen to share their inspirational journeys with you.

A DREAM COME TRUE

Marissa Arber, CBC
Grateful Be A Loving Mirror Mom
Certified BALM Family Recovery Life Coach
Florida

I am the mom of a person recovering from a substance use disorder. For several years, my beautiful, brilliant son was caught up in a world I was unprepared for and horrified by, and I woke up each morning just wanting to know if he was still alive and how I could help him.

By the time I found BALM, he was finishing up a third or fourth treatment experience, this time at a world-renowned center. They insisted that we completely cut him off from all contact with us, though he was sober. Their tough love approach had been successful up to that point but did not sit well with me.

Wanting more than anything for him to stay sober, we did what they said, and I cried pretty much all day every day, waiting for this severe version of boundary setting to end and our family to return to the unified unit it had been so long ago.

This was not the first challenging experience in my life. Years ago, I had lost my mom and brother to cancer and had experienced my own bouts of cancer myself. As a result of years of chemo and many alternative treatments, I slowly returned to myself.

I was and am a strong woman of faith, but the fear of losing my son was sapping my emotional strength immensely. All the manipulation my family members had fallen prey to was depleting me. My son later told me that in those days, he would go to whoever would hear him about how bad I was, and they believed his lies, while I was believing my eyes and ears.

During that last treatment stint, I sat in a family group, and I looked at my son and said aloud, "I have dug six feet of ground and now I am sitting in it, and the last thing that is left is for them to put the dirt over me. I am done." I remember the looks on my family members' faces. I did not realize how bad things were within me until that moment.

The next weekend, they asked us to write down five things we had not completed that we intended to accomplish in the next five years of our lives. Since I had recently talked about being done with my life, at first it took me aback. But then, as I thought about it, I realized that what I had always wanted to do was become a life coach and help others with the wisdom gleaned from the challenges of my life, and so I wrote that down.

A few weeks later, by divine design, when we were about to completely cut our sober son off, I received a text from someone who knew our son well.

She simply wrote, "Here is a number to someone I believe could help you. May I give her your number too? I gave you her number a few years ago but I don't think you called her."

And when I looked at my phone, I did see there was the text from three years before with the same number.

Since things hadn't gotten better for me in those three years, and my son had been sober and lost it twice since then, I decided to make the call. Bev and I talked for at least an hour, the first thirty minutes of which were nothing but her listening to me cry.

I couldn't see spending money on a family program when we had already invested so much of our time and resources on treatment centers, but I knew we needed help, and I intuited that this would be money well spent.

The first thing that happened was she told me to go into a live online BALM 12 Principles class (called the Daily BALM) and listen, to see how it hit me. There was no BALM book to read at that time, so I really knew nothing about the program.

Suddenly I was finding out there was another approach to loving my son besides the tough love approach the treatment center insisted on. I had tried to go to Al-Anon over and over again, but it, too, was too harsh for me. Until finding the BALM, I had found only one person or program willing to listen to my perspective and talk with me, but she was no longer our counselor. Everyone else talked at me, telling me I had to give up my perspective for the one they had.

BALM resonated more with my own affectionate approach and also included leverage and boundaries, and it guided families away from enabling behaviors. Finally, I was home.

I chose to sign up for BALM Family Recovery Education, BALM Family Recovery Life Coaching, and eventually BALM Family Recovery Life Coach Training. Bev said to take as long as I needed to recover before starting the life coach training.

I didn't think I would start for a year, but I felt so much better so soon that I was ready to start preparing for my new career within a few months.

My tears began to lessen as I studied the BALM and worked with my coach. We met twice a week for the first six months and soon moved down to once weekly as I began to find my solace, answers, and strength within myself, the BALM, and the BALM community.

For the first time, I was being heard. People cared about me, my growth, and my feelings, and they understood the compassion I wanted to have for my son. This alone was revolutionary for me. It changed everything for me and my family.

My husband joined me for some of the coaching sessions, and together we shifted our relationship with each other and with our son to one that was good for us and simultaneously good for him. Even my other children had a session or two as we shifted our collective stance from distance and anger to healthy boundaries based on love and respect for ourselves and the man my son was working to become.

Over time, we watched our son grow up. With Bev's help, we built a team that included his own coach and therapist and a local team who helped him through his initial independence and continues to be there for him today. I cannot emphasize enough the importance of having the right people on the team. In our case, the two people who have worked with him have understood and supported him as lovingly as the BALM has supported us.

As Bev always says, recovery has different faces for different individuals and families. My son found his recovery through his work with his team. We found ours through the BALM and our work with our coach and BALM community.

This process of building a loving team to help a family and loved one grow in recovery is one of the most powerful benefits of BALM that I have seen. No one is left out, and so the family stays intact, even through the most difficult days.

Behind the scenes, my coach worked with us to be his best chance at recovery and does to this day.

It hasn't always been a smooth path. Growing up never is. But with the BALM, my coach, and the BALM community, my life has meaning deeper than I could have imagined.

Today I am a certified BALM coach, working with families and helping them the way my coach helped me.

I am so thankful for the BALM and all it has done for us and for the training that is empowering me to be there for families all over the world.

Even though Marissa's husband, Isaac, isn't a BALM coach, he sent us his BALM story, and we wanted to include it with her story.

FROM DESPAIR TO HOPEFULNESS

Isaac Arber
BALM Parent
Florida

According to the way I was raised, being a husband, father, grandfather, and entrepreneur required a person to have leadership skills and the expectancy of respect and obedience.

It came to be that our son, a bright, handsome, well-educated young man who had the world at his fingertips, for no certain nor understandable reason, found himself in the grips of an opioid addiction.

Although my dear wife, Marissa, presented me with clear evidence of this fact, my natural reaction was to go into denial. After all, being our only son (we are also blessed with two daughters), the apple of my eye, the follower of my footsteps, and the one I expected to improve upon that which I have accomplished, it was impossible for this to be true. It didn't make sense and I refused to accept it.

Slowly, I fell into despair. I found myself in a situation where my skills as a leader didn't work, and the expectancy of respect and obedience was nonexistent. His lies, thieving, and manipulation threw our entire family into turmoil, and my being in denial created a huge gash in my relationship with Marissa. Our son's addiction was a Damocles sword that dictated our daily existence.

We went through several cycles of detox and rehabilitation, family meetings, and other support systems. Each treatment center offered their own approach and philosophy, with a pretty much common theme of setting up harsh boundaries that rather than provide for positivity, loving, and caring, proved to create animosity, distrust, aggression, and disengagement.

We were torn by the fact that although our son was progressing in his recovery from this terrible disease, our yearning for a return to our previous family structure of loving and caring was not to be. We found ourselves in total dysfunction. There was no desire for anything entertaining. Our family life with our other children and grandchildren suffered. Even though we knew that his actions were out of control, every minute was consumed by anxiety and fear of the unknown. What we were experiencing was not family life.

One day, Marissa told me of her conversation with Bev regarding a program called the BALM. We decided to give it a try and after our first session, we realized that this approach was what we were yearning for. Healthy boundaries were set, conversations revolved around building of trust and sharing love and respect. The program immediately began to bring Marissa and myself together again. Our other children participated in several sessions in order to learn how to reconnect with their brother in a healthy manner.

The BALM team helped to guide our recovery and arranged for a coordinated effort with our son's therapists and counselors.

Today our son has returned to being a heathy, handsome, bright young man and a responsible member of society.

The BALM, true to its acronym, has coated me in a reassuring, loving, tender environment. The team has taught me how to interact positively and live a healthy life. It has brought about a tremendous change in the manner that we deal with our son's recovery and has enabled my outlook to have changed from despair to hopefulness.

GREAT PAIN LED ME TO HELP OTHERS

Ginny Atwood-Lovitt
BALM Coach Trainee
Virginia

I lost my brother to a heroin overdose in 2013, and in his memory, my family and I started a nonprofit organization called The Chris Atwood Foundation to fight the opioid crisis by training friends and family how to use a medication that can revive someone from an overdose.

We've saved over fifty lives since last year. This work has been very therapeutic for me in my grief, but running the organization on a tight budget, with no staff, and no experience in nonprofit management, has been a crazy, stressful, uphill battle for me.

The BALM coach training forces me to look deeper into my feelings, to take time for myself, and has given me better coping tools to deal with stress. It has grown me as a person as well as a leader. I'm not taking coaching clients yet, but the BALM program is showing me how to provide proper support to families who come to us looking for help.

My family had such a hard time finding adequate education and support when Christopher was alive, and I am very grateful to be able to point other families in the right direction.

COMPASSION AND CONNECTION MADE THE DIFFERENCE

Andrea Arlington, ACC, CBC
Certified BALM Family Recovery Life Coach
California

As the mother of two heroin addicts in recovery, the sister of a young man who died at age seventeen and had been an IV drug user, and having been married three times to men who suffered from substance use disorder and other addictions, I can honestly say that in each case, my relationships with these wonderful human beings would have been positively enriched and benefited by having had the BALM Family Recovery program and a BALM coach.

It is heartbreaking to love someone and not know how to help them. More than the drugs and alcohol, I believe my brother Ben was driven to continue using and ultimately died because of the lack of understanding of our family and the way we approached his — what we perceived as — bad behavior and stupid choices. My parents, out of lack of understanding, used shaming, blaming, guilting, venomous tones of voice, and judgment rather than compassion, a calm presence, and language that families learn to use in the BALM. These tools create connection rather than widening the wall that is created by lack of understanding and unhealthy interaction.

I honestly know that as a mother, I failed to understand what my daughters needed, just as my parents had not understood what my brother Ben had needed. They were in and out of jail and living on the street at times.

When I finally gained the tools and strategies that do work, our family was able to help inspire my second daughter to choose and sustain recovery after five treatment programs. We finally understood that what she needed was connection and compassion, and as soon as we began to approach her using the tools that the BALM teaches, she chose to get off heroin and crystal meth and has now been in recovery for five years.

If I had had these tools when I was in relationship to the men I was married to, I believe there is a chance that they would have chosen recovery because I would have not been the crazy, insane wife and mother as I was trying to navigate and control the insanity that addiction can cause in families without the support of a community like the BALM and the tools that are provided.

Today, I navigate through all of my relationships and decisions in life using the amazing tools that the BALM has taught me, along with having worked for over a year with a BALM certified Family Recovery Life Coach.

My relationships feel connected and rich and rewarding for the first time in my life. It took me fifty years to achieve that, but it would've never happened had I not had this program.

I am so grateful to Beverly Buncher, her amazing program, and this beautiful community of families who are all working toward their recovery and being their loved one's best chance for recovery.

"I DIDN'T KNOW WHAT I DIDN'T KNOW"

Lisa Costa, CBC
Certified **BALM** Coach and Recovering Family Member
Massachusetts

As a mother of two sons suffering from opiate addiction, my life was filled with hopelessness and despair for several years. I was a loving, caring mother who always nurtured, supported, and unconditionally loved her children. They were raised in a "good" home, with devoted extended family and friends. It made no sense to me — I feared I had truly failed as a mother, and I found myself living a life of shame, isolation, hopelessness, and misery.

Many of you who read this will say to yourselves, "That sounds like me." In truth, my life was exactly like anyone else's who has a loved one suffering from addictive behavior.

It was several years before I found the BALM. On my own, I had joined a support group, read books, and attended parent programs of the treatment center that my children attended. I started to understand that to help my sons would take a new form of parenting that would require a serious commitment, which I thought I had but found that it was much harder than I had ever dreamed.

I continued to make some serious mistakes while not realizing that I was still enabling and still in denial. I tried not to listen to the requests of my boys but rather to the professionals. Nothing was changing. Although I didn't understand this at the time, I was suffering from trauma. Anyone who has lived this life is truly a victim of trauma...subjected to abusive behavior, tirades, theft, and constant lies, while holding our breath praying for a change — but devastated with each relapse.

Many of us learn the Al-Anon mantra: I didn't **cause** it, I can't **control** it, and I can't **cure** it. I tried to believe it because it certainly helped me relieve some guilt, but deep down, I still thought somehow it was my fault, that I could control it (after all, I had done pretty well controlling most situations) and certainly could figure out a way to cure it. What I hadn't yet fully understood, that while those three C's were statements of truth, I wasn't completely removed from the outcome. The big truth that I would come to know so well from BALM was that I *could* **contribute** to my loved one's recovery. Or, just as easily, I could unintentionally contribute to his continuing to use. Such a terrifying reality.

Fast forward a couple of years. Through some sort of divine intervention, I was introduced to Bev Buncher, and hence the

BALM. What is this BALM? I asked myself. I thought I knew about family recovery.

What happened next was life-changing. You know that phrase "You don't know what you don't know"? I had only scratched the surface, and scratching the surface will not help save a life. Certainly not my own life.

The BALM is more than comprehensive learning — it's fast-track learning, which is vital when you have a using addict. It is intense support—providing the self-care we all need desperately. Most definitely, the BALM is transformational. I can honestly say that I am transformed as a parent in the way that I interact with my children (not just the two in recovery). My relationships in general are stronger. I always thought of myself as nonjudgmental and empathetic, a problem-solver (except for this nightmare), a shoulder to lean on, and a good communicator. Again, I didn't know what I didn't know.

Through the BALM, not only have I learned so much about addiction and the proper role of a loving mother in this situation, but I have had access to hundreds of interviews with addicts and professionals. Most importantly, I have become able to communicate in a way that I didn't know was possible. I know how to contribute to recovery rather than contributing to the problem.

My two sons now each have five years of recovery, and their lives are transformed through their journeys more than I could have ever imagined. My relationship with them is something I could only dream of. I can honestly say, although I wouldn't wish this nightmare on any parent, their lives are richer, and they are better human beings because of recovery. There truly is hope for all, and I am so proud of them. I am also so proud of my own recovery as a parent.

I have become a BALM Family Recovery Life Coach and Teacher and am able to share this incredible program with other families as well as to guide them not to make the same mistakes I did. I cringe when I think of those mistakes, as they were life-threatening, albeit well-meaning. We absolutely are our loved one's best chance, and it's vital that all parents understand this fully.

Everyone learns recovery in their own time, but we can help them embrace change sooner rather than later. To witness other parents as they learn to practice the BALM is inspiring beyond words. Although there is never a guarantee that your loved one will recover, I have witnessed many situations where the family has been able to see what they once believed would never happen: a loved one in recovery!

The other day, my best friend of thirty-five years said to me, "What I love the most about you is that you continue to become the best version of yourself." I can truly say that the BALM has been my inspiration. Thank you, Bev.

*Go to page 326 to download Lisa's guide to getting off the wheel of denial, titled **The Ferris Wheel.***

HELPING FAMILIES AND LOVED ONES

Mike DeForbes, MFA, LCDP, ACC, CBC
Certified BALM Family Recovery Life Coach
Rhode Island

I have been working in the substance abuse treatment field for over ten years and prior to that was a professor of fine arts at a local community college. About seven years ago, I decided I wanted to add the coach approach to my work. I went to coach training school and soon met Bev, who became my mentor coach. She was, coincidentally, a Recovery Life Coach, which was of great interest to me as someone in recovery and working in the field.

During that time, I was so impressed with the coaching field and the opportunities it presented for entrepreneurship that I began to coach with Bev not only to improve my coaching but also to figure out if there was a way to transition out of the treatment field and into full-time coaching and public speaking.

Bev was a True Purpose® Coach as well as a mentor coach, and when I explained that I was trying to find my calling, she offered to take me through the True Purpose® process. We spent the next six months exploring my destiny. What started as a search for an escape out of the career I was planted in at that time evolved into a deep communicative relationship with a trusted source that I could call on to guide me through the ups and downs of my career and my day-to-day life. I also began to deepen my own spiritual work through classes, prayer, meditation, and self-inquiry that allowed me to experience a deeper appreciation of each moment.

As a result of my purpose work and other inner work, I was able to find out that I was being called to help addicts through my new skills as a coach exactly where I was planted.

The work I have been able to do with my clients has deepened over the years through my inner work, my purpose work, and my work with the BALM, even though the time I have been given to work with individual clients has decreased. This is because of my growing ability to deeply connect with them in each moment of our time together.

In 2013, when the BALM Family Recovery Life Coaching program opened its doors, I was in the first cohort of advanced students. I was able to give vital input to the development of the 7 Steps to BALM because of my own inner work and experience, and I became Bev's assistant teacher in the course and eventually the lead teacher. This program has opened up opportunities for me to help families around the world through my teaching, coaching, and writing in an area dear to me: deepening recovery through inner growth.

As one of the original BALMers, I have a powerful understanding of how this program can help those affected by another's use disorder as well as their own, and I look forward to the addition of the Life Purpose in Recovery for individuals as I am already using the principles and steps with my clients at work and know it will be an important addition to the BALM program.

For the link to download and read the self-inquiry guides that Michael wrote specifically for the BALM program, go to page 326.

A FAMILY MEMBER BY CHOICE EMBRACES BALM®

Jen Fisher, ACC, CBC
Certified BALM Family Recovery Life Coach and Coach Educator
Illinois/Colorado

I came into the BALM community in a different way than many others I have met here. Rather than coming in looking for answers, I was attracted because I learned the BALM method was teaching a few things I already knew to be true. Through our experience with a young man named Dale, I knew that a family significantly contributes to the state of being of someone suffering from substance abuse disorder, and I knew that when it comes to those individuals in our families, the most important job we have is to love them. I came to the BALM so I could learn more, and I wanted to be able to help others learn as well.

On an otherwise "normal day" in 2012, my husband came home from work and told me he'd met a young man on the streets of Chicago who was homeless, alienated from his family, and struggling with substance abuse. My husband wanted to get involved. I was floored. I was standing in my kitchen thinking, "What? What are you talking about?"

We had no experience with addiction and recovery...we had heard stories of other families struggling, but by the grace of God, we had been spared. Although I was afraid and skeptical, I was immediately drawn in by this young man's story and the fact that he was completely alone in the world. As much as I could never imagine the circumstances, what if one of my own three sons were lost and alone somewhere? Wouldn't I want another mother to step up? Do something? My husband and I were now on the same page.

If someone would have told me that night that Dale would become over the next few years like another son to my husband and me and a brother to my boys, I would have told them they were crazy. But for two years, he spent weekends at our house, celebrated holidays with us, and became part of the fabric of our family. We were with him when he served jail time, went through recovery, lived in sober living homes, and struggled with independence.

Knowing nothing about addiction and recovery, my husband and I did the best we could to love and support this young man because at the core, we felt what he needed first and foremost was a loving family, a support system, and a set of strong advocates who would both guide and fight for him. Wasn't that the foundation of how we'd raised our own sons? We decided we would figure out the rest.

And we did. He got a job, worked a Twelve-Step program, and created a social life with other people in recovery who supported his new choices. For years it worked really well...and then we got the call. It was the Sunday before Thanksgiving and he was on his way home from a retreat with his AA brothers. He confessed to them and then to us that he had relapsed. Despite much effort on our part, we were not able to get him into a detox facility that night. We were uneducated, uninformed, and it was 2 AM on a Monday morning.

There were many things that happened during the next two days — cryptic messages, unanswered texts, reports from friends — but the very short, very sad ending to our story came in the form of a call on Thanksgiving morning from his sponsor informing us that this "bonus son" had passed from an overdose. We had loved a boy, and he had loved us deeply. He had made such progress, and now he was simply gone. To say that we were devastated is an understatement.

His passing was a forceful turning point in our lives. I know that while we had been uneducated, our efforts to love this boy and give him a support structure was effective. Without knowing it, we had in many ways contributed to his recovery rather than his addiction, and we had loved him without expecting a certain result. In some ways, we were Loving Mirrors before I knew what that was!

Although I am at peace about his passing, I humanly wish I had known more than about a true BALM way of being. I see now we had much to learn about boundary setting, manipulation, and getting support, and I wonder how that knowledge might have altered his path.

I am forever changed because of Dale and am incredibly passionate about educating families so their learning can come, as much as possible, before heartache. I know most families simply want to help, but they don't know how. The BALM holds keys to helping families get the kind of education that can affect outcomes. Although it's "rearview-mirror" learning and too late for our boy, the BALM helps me work with families and teach them how to be their loved one's best chance. I am committed to passing it on.

BALM COACH TRAINING HELPED ME HEAL WOUNDS I DID NOT KNOW I HAD

Frumma Rosenberg-Gottlieb, BFRLC
BALM Coach
Author of *Awesome Aging; Happier, Healthier, Smarter and Younger than Yesterday*

I have been a middle and high school principal, and am currently a relationship coach, and a spiritual mentor with a good sized following. I had just decided to take a couple of years off to write my book when Beverly contacted me about joining the BALM community. I thought BALM coaching would prove a nice source of supplemental income, and I had some issues in the extended family that made me particularly sensitive to matters of addiction.

But I had no idea what I was getting into! The coach training was on a level that I hadn't experienced in my former coaching classes. The other members of my cohort were profound and thoughtful. The self-examination was intense. I found myself counting down until the next session. It was healing old wounds that I didn't know I had! I was hungry for the unguarded conversations with people who had been through a thing or two! Every encounter was so real in comparison to the surface level conversations with my friend next door.

And I grew as a listener, an empathetic human who wanted to really know the other members of my planet. I grew in my self-acceptance, loving myself in spite of my flaws. I grew as a professional. My coaching skills have been honed and my antenna is up to deepen and further my clients' self-knowledge in a way I hadn't imagined to be possible. I grew as an advocate rather than a judge of the addicts in my world and in the larger world. It has been a worthwhile journey.

To download Frumma's guide to Judaism and the BALM, go to page 326 for the link to the free BALM online appendix.

WHEN WORK AND HOME RELATIONSHIPS COLLIDE

Jim Graham, ACC, CBC
Certified **BALM** Family Recovery Life Coach
Illinois

Today I am in my twenty-second year of sobriety. I am very grateful for the direction that has been given to me, to be a more effective and loving human being.

The BALM has played a major role in the expansion of not only recovery but of my business and personal life as well.

For my family, the cycle in generations of addictive and dry drunk thinking and behaviors has been broken. My wife and my three boys, who are now over twenty years old, have witnessed a father who continually looks to Be A Loving Mirror.

Today critical conversations are thought out and scripted. Facts from all parties are sought out so that fact, not story, is the narrative, where solutions can form. In the past, those same critical confrontations were met with anger, judgment, and mistrust. Today there is no reaction but a process that promotes solution and healing.

Using the **BALM** 12 Principles and the 7 Steps to **BALM** has me finding fact through loving questions, including active listening to truly understand and moving to what is clear and unclear so that facts are addressed, not story. It leaves interpretations out and loving solutions in.

When these critical events come up, all parties feel they have been heard and understood. They see the work behind being understood. They see the fairness in what is clear and what is unclear. They come to know everyone's involvement and where they can improve their part as well as others. Anger and judgment are no longer successful. Loving conversations and solutions have taken their place.

At work, these principles have saved me, my company, my wife, and my brother. Past events once puzzled me and left me with toxic reactions that caused more problems. Now those same events that once puzzled me get turned into loving, long-lasting solutions due to the tools the BALM has given me.

For instance, we had a situation where my wife and brother found themselves in an argument that escalated from anger to rage. Both were yelling and crying, and a total loss of control took over. I was able to act calmly because I knew I had the tools. An event that once controlled me was quickly diffused into a lifetime of lasting solution.

What do I mean by lasting solution? On that day, a very real relationship threatening was happening. My wife could have quit. My wife and brother could have stopped talking with each other. The business and our private lives would have been guided with anger, toxic behaviors, and resentment over an entire lifetime.

Instead, in a matter of four hours of going through one of the many methodical tools we study in BALM, this time like Medea's tips for controlling flooding, we all met with relief and release from the drive of anger and emotion. All parties were able in this relief to see their part. Because they felt heard and acknowledged, they now wanted and were willing to find and work on a solution. Once the angry energy passed, they remembered that they really loved each other, and that was the driver to the solution.

That was three years ago, and a lasting narrative of solution prevails. Our old way would have been, "Have you heard this one?" "Remember that day three years ago when you did this?" and *bam*, just like that you are right back to that same day. But who really wants to live like this for three years? Instead, because of learning to be the peace, we relate to each other on an entirely different level, as peaceful cooperative colleagues and loving relatives.

Because of the BALM, I am a better leader, husband, father, brother, son, and friend and all other roles I play. Every day I use the BALM to be an attractive safe solution compared to the solution of addiction. The BALM helps me to remember what my niece said so well: "There's a better way to do this."

Today I'm grateful to know there is a better way. Today when I have a good day — and there are many, it's because the BALM guided me to loving solutions and behaviors versus angry solutions and behaviors.

BALM®: THE RECOVERY COMMUNITY THAT GOES WHEREVER I GO

Elizabeth Gross, ACC, CBC
Certified BALM Family Recovery Life Coach
and BALM Parent
Illinois/Utah

The BALM is a pillar of my recovery. As I prepare to move across the country, what brings me so much comfort is that my BALM community will come with me! It doesn't matter if I'm traveling or moving or not at home, I can always access the BALM on my phone or my computer.

It was no coincidence that I stumbled upon the BALM when I was looking for a Family Recovery Life Coaching School. I had no idea that I had found the most amazing treasure trove of recovery and personal growth, starting with the BALM Comprehensive. Our nineteen-year-old son was living in a sober living house for recovery from heroin addiction, and my husband and I became immersed in the BALM Comprehensive. I love that it's online because my husband was more willing to listen to the Daily BALM on Wednesday nights in the comfort of our home. I had done Al-Anon and been to the family recovery programs at the various treatment centers my son had been at since age thirteen, but the transformation that I was about to experience would change *everything*!

I love the BALM 12 Principles because of the insights and the language around the journey that we as families face when we have a loved suffering from substance use disorder. The Daily BALM on Monday afternoons and Wednesday nights are staples of my family recovery program. I love hearing the speakers and the comments and conversation afterward. I always walk away with new insights, new recovery buddies, and the reinforcement of the feeling that I am not alone.

I love the 7 Steps to BALM because it's a deep dive into learning the communication skills we need to have to become our loved one's best advocate. It's taught me to honor my voice, to express my observations and truths in a curious, nonjudgmental way. I'm not always good at it, but I'm willing to keep trying to get better at it. I have loved having a buddy to practice with and have developed friendships with my buddies.

The coaching groups are another way that I have created community for myself. Whether I have an issue to bring to the table or am just listening and offering support, those sessions are so powerful and create the sense of community that I need.

My husband, Brian, and I hired Beverly Buncher to be our Family Recovery Life Coach for a year, and wow, transformation seems like an understatement! She helped us see how we could work better together instead of working apart. She asked us powerful questions that created more awareness about our behaviors and attitudes, and what we needed to work on! The coaching combined with the BALM Comprehensive has brought so much healing to our family. I am so very grateful, and our family is forever changed.

Coaching school was an incredible experience of personal growth, learning a new skill set, and realizing my passion for helping other parents. Learning to coach is an intense and joyful and painful and transformational experience! Even though I graduated from the program, my former classmates are still part of my life, and they are my extended family.

I love the BALM, its loving nature, and its vibe of meeting people where they are. The BALM continues to teach me so much about being in relationship with others, with myself, and with my Higher Power. Thank you to the BALM recovery community for being there for me, teaching and guiding me, and loving and accepting me as I am!

THE BALM® HELPED ME MAKE PEACE WITH MY MOM

Liselle Hill, PCC, CBC
Certified BALM Family Recovery Life Coach
California

My mom was truly an amazing person and mother. She was dynamic and interesting. She was outgoing and very involved with us and our lives when we were young.

She was also very social and was really a party girl.

Over time, the alcohol claimed her. It became more and more important to her, and we became less and less a part of her world. By the time I was in high school, I no longer felt I knew her at all. By my college years and my young married years, she was never available to me anymore.

When we tried an intervention, my mother told us that if she had to choose between alcohol and her kids and grandkids, she would choose alcohol.

As a result, I had a lot of anger toward her. I felt she had deserted me.

But then I reached a point where I didn't like the way I was treating her. I didn't like the anger and resentment. I wanted to change, and that is where BALM came in.

The BALM helped me make peace with my mom. It helped me learn how to love her regardless of her addiction. It reminded me of everything wonderful about her and gave me the ability to love her despite the chaos.

The amazing thing it did was to mend our bridges before she passed away. My mom died still using. But I was able to have a loving relationship with her despite the fact that she was still drinking.

Beyond that it helped me develop into the person I wanted to be. It taught me how to act from love and to see my part in the craziness.

I dropped all resentment and have come to understand that my mother is largely responsible for my being the person I am today.

Today I am grateful for the gift she gave me of learning how to love unconditionally. And that gift has positively impacted every relationship I have today.

BEING GIVEN THE BALM® CHANGED MY FAMILY'S LIFE

Stacey Karchner
BALM Family Recovery Life Coach
Pennsylvania

I began attending Al-Anon, October 2012, after the recommendation of my daughter's rehab and the urging of my daughter. My life was unmanageable. I was so reactive. I was addicted to my loved one and so scared. It was helpful to walk into the Al-Anon room and know I was not alone, and I continue to have Al-Anon as one of my wellness tools.

It was 2014 and I had been in Al-Anon for two years. I was practicing tough love and was still crazy! My life was centered on and enmeshed with my children's. My daughter was in early recovery, and my son was continually relapsing and had gotten kicked out of another rehab and had come home. I lived as a prisoner of fear and was gripping tightly, attached to outcomes.

In July of 2015, I put my son on a plane from PA to a treatment center in south FL (I believe his sixth and his last at this point). I flew to visit him in September 2015, and the first day I was there, I got a call a few hours after dropping him off after supper that he had used an abundant amount of an over-the-counter drug and relapsed.

I was able to see him a few days later in the morning before flying home, and I was crying and told him how disappointed I was because I spent the money to visit and hardly saw him. How could he do that? The way I reacted brought shame and guilt to him.

When I got back home, I was a wreck. I had relapsed too! I called his therapist crying. She asked me if I was signed up for the BALM and said it would help me a lot. She signed me up that day. I immediately dove in and began soaking up the BALM, using notebooks and taking notes during all the lessons, recordings, and live calls.

I could not get enough of the recordings, the live calls, the BALM 12 Principles, the 7 Steps to BALM, etc. It was Al-Anon on steroids! The recordings of addicts telling their stories brought me so much hope. I have notebooks full of notes from live calls and recordings.

BALM brought me so much compassion for my children, especially after learning the Stages of Change. BALM has changed my life and relationships. I do wish I could go back to that day in FL for a redo. By the grace of God, my son celebrated two years sober in September and my daughter five years in August. I know now that if I do have to go through them slipping or relapsing in the future, I will *not* handle it as

I did before BALM. I am now a loving responder who gathers facts and has loving conversations. I have learned so many ways to stay calm, and I love the Clear/Unclear chart.

BALM has been such a blessing in my life, so I made the choice to take the courses to be a BALM Family Recovery Life Coach in order to help families be their loved one's best chance at recovery. If I could have had the program and a coach in the beginning of my journey, in the midst of all the crises, it would have saved me lots of wrinkles and aging.

A FATHER'S DAY TRIBUTE

Lynn Mackin, ACC, CBC
Family Member and Certified BALM Family Recovery Life Coach
Minnesota

Dear Father of an Addict,

Today is Father's Day 2017 and I am feeling overwhelmed with many thoughts about being a mom. Perhaps that doesn't make sense, but, to quote my own dad, "Without mothers there would be no fathers." For whatever that's worth.

This day marks the first Father's Day since roughly 2008 that I don't live in fear for the health or life of my (adult) child who has struggled with addiction and co-occurring disorders. Today, by God's grace and her strength and tenacity, she is in early recovery and has nine months of sobriety. She is working a strong recovery program, which she embarked on of her own choosing on September 8, 2016. This road to recovery was, she would say, completely of her own choosing — unlike her three prior treatment attempts.

Today, she has been walking a recovery journey that began with a flight to a detox facility in Tampa, Florida, that she would describe as very good for "easing" her withdrawal from a drug that would have taken two years to get off on her own. She describes the process as "hell"; both the twelve days she was there, as well as the ongoing months following with PAWS (post-acute withdrawal symptoms). Her body has been through hell both by drug abuse and its aftermath, and yet she hasn't turned back. She is an amazing woman. I am grateful and blessed.

She embarked upon this road with the commitment that she would do "whatever it takes this time." She was afraid of dying from addiction. Following detox, she has completed two and a half months of residential treatment, one month of day treatment, and seven months of outpatient treatment while residing in three different sober living environments. (Some were not so great, and yet she remained sober and committed to her program.)

She is taking her treatment team's recommendations and living them out to the best of her ability. She has a sponsor, is working the Twelve Steps of AA/NA, and attends AA/NA meetings. She is of service to others and looks for opportunities to share, as they say in the Twelve-Step programs, her experience, strength, and hope. She was recently asked to be a speaker at meetings at three of her treatment center's locations.

Many days are difficult for her as she navigates life with the body she betrayed with substances and associated behaviors. And yet she hasn't turned back. She is a strong woman. I am hopeful and blessed.

On the family front, I must be completely honest: loving someone in active addiction was pure hell. It was consuming, frightening, and confusing. It was lonely and chaotic. It could bring me to gut-wrenching tears and fears of her death. It divides families, siblings, and former friends. But it never stole my hope. I don't know if that was born out of denial, but I did come to understand that as long as there is life, there is hope.

Through the BALM approach to family recovery, I have learned how to let go — without giving up or giving in (letting go of the outcome.) I have learned how to get out of denial by focusing on "just the facts" without adding an emotional charge or using the past to inform the present. I have learned to let her own her journey while I own mine. I have learned that she is a person, not a problem. I have learned that we are connected to each other on a level far deeper than her addiction, and I believe that fact helped drive her toward recovery.

She wants a relationship with her family more now than she ever has, and she is sorry for the pain her illness brought into our life. Of course, I don't know her thoughts and feelings. I only know what she tells me, or what I witness. What I know is that she wants the opportunity for second chances: the opportunity to share what she has learned, and to show us how she is evolving into a person who could be trusted, truthful, and counted on. All she is asking for is our time and our interest, so she can find her way back. She wants to sit down eye-to-eye and heart-to-heart and know that we are still here after "all of this." Progress, not perfection.

So now, on Father's Day, I live amid answered prayers, and so does my child. She is in recovery. She is committed to her program. I get to have a relationship with someone I never knew as she grows into the woman God will have her become. She is dreaming of a future now and trying to mend fences while dealing with the shame and regret that grew out of her choices. I can't even begin to imagine how hard that is. She is a work in progress and yet, she hasn't turned back. She is a determined woman. I am hopeful and blessed and grateful for her strength.

Thank you, dear husband, for giving her to me. I am eternally grateful for her, for her sister, for you, and for the growth this journey has produced in me.

ADVANCING MY INNER WORK

Lisa McDonald, CBC
Certified **BALM** Family Recovery Life Coach
Pennsylvania

For years, I have been actively involved in my own recovery through a Twelve-Step fellowship. I have grown leaps and bounds in this program by working steps and being of service. It led me back to my First Love, Jesus. It helped me build a foundation of personal responsibility and community. Honestly, it saved my life because first and foremost, it enabled me to stop using, lose the desire to use, and find a new way of life. However, as I ambled through my life, I found that there were a few behavior patterns, defects of character, that I just couldn't seem to get a handle on. That is where the BALM comes in.

As I entered the **BALM** Family Recovery Life Coach Training Program, I thought that I had myself under control, and I was quite sure that everyone in the program was going to benefit from my years of recovery knowledge and experience. I was in complete denial of the amount of work that was left to be done in my own heart.

I was reactive, unpredictable, easily frustrated, and prone to angry outbursts, but I had been this way for so long. I just thought it was the best I could do, and the people in my life were just going to have to accept me this way. The 7 Steps to BALM changed all of this for me.

After the first class, I did the "Inner Work" assignment, and the Buddy Assignment for Step 1, and I was hooked. My attitude changed, and I began to listen intently, not just for the information but for its application in my own life. I was no longer only a coaching student taking a required class. I was an involved participant. I saw in that week my reactivity decrease and my ability to be present in each moment increase. At that point, I realized how much work I had left to do, and I got to it. Using the 7 Steps to BALM in my life has changed the way I interact with the world, for sure!

I have since taken a family member through the class, and I am currently taking the class again with a new buddy. Each time I take the class, I find that my growth deepens and solidifies. The Twelve Steps for me have been the "hook," if you will, that I hang the 7 Steps to BALM on. I have all the wonderful information found in both the BALM 12 Principles and the Twelve Steps of my recovery fellowship to anchor the practical application found in the 7 Steps to BALM.

Today, I can say that I am less reactive, more at peace, and able to handle life's challenges in a way that keeps me connected to my loved ones. My children are BALMed regularly without even knowing it. It is teaching them to be responsible for their emotions and choices, which at four, six, and eight will serve them well all their lives. My eighteen-year-old feels empowered to get out there and live the life that he wants. The BALM has given me the ability to respect the process of all of the lovely, flawed people in my life and love them right where they are!

GIVING FAMILIES A CLEAR PATH TO RECOVERY

Chris Prevas, CBC
Certified BALM Family Recovery Life Coach
and BALM Parent
Pennsylvania/Maryland

My family recovery journey started in December 2008 when we discovered that our daughter (seventeen years old at the time) was caught in the grip of heroin addiction. Although my wife and I suspected that our daughter was dealing with difficult issues, never in my most fevered nightmares did I think that we would ever be face-to-face with opiate addiction in my family. It rocked my world. Fortunately, my wife had enough experience as a high school nurse to know that we were in way over our heads, that we should put our daughter into what would be the first of several in-patient rehabs.

Upon our return home from that first rehab, I was now having to deal with this discovery. My biggest issues were fear, shame, and anger resulting from that toxic combination. I felt isolated and alone without a clue where to turn next. Thankfully, several friends recommended sources of help, mainly Al-Anon, family counselors, and our faith community.

From these kind folks, I learned that I was not alone, that there was help from people who had "been there," and that I could experience inner change to regain both the serenity and the wisdom to move forward. I learned that although I didn't cause my daughter's substance use disorder, couldn't cure it, and couldn't even control it, I came to understand my part in it and how I contributed to her using due to my anger outbursts and controlling ways.

My old ways of coping had become just as compulsive as an addict's compulsive use of drugs. I needed help. As a friend of mine once put it, I had become sick from drug use and I had never even used myself. Thank God for recovery. I still attend Al-Anon on a weekly basis because I need continuous help to keep my head straight.

Long story short, our daughter eventually came to grips with her illness and sought recovery. She is seven years clean and sober as of this writing, and our relationship has gratefully been restored through both her work and my work. I know that this is not everyone's story and that drug addiction is claiming lives every day. It's a heartbreaking reality.

Family recovery is a difficult process because there are painful personal truths to face, a dizzying and confusing array of expensive treatment options, months to years of hard work, and very high stakes: our loved ones' lives are on the line. Our family's recovery story is marked by many "ad hoc" attempts to find help, some of which were effective and others that were not. For our family, we kind of pieced it together by praying hard and making our best guesses.

As the years have gone by, I have met many people who have a story similar to mine. While some people dive into recovery headfirst, many others struggle in silence, secrecy, and shame. It is hard to watch this when I know that there a better way. I'm thankful for the guides I met along the way who pointed out the better way to me. My heart goes out to families who are still stuck in this painful place.

I was first introduced to the BALM in early 2015 when my wife, Jill (see her story on page 238), found the BALM and enrolled in the Family Recovery Life Coaching program.

I got to witness up close the power of the BALM program: both how Jill's approach to her own recovery shifted into high gear and how much enthusiasm she had at finding a more effective way of helping people like us. The teaching I heard was spot-on, the focus on changing the inner landscape was exactly what I had experienced in my own journey, the use of online meetings and recordings provided both convenience and anonymity, and the community of support provided encouragement to the BALMers to continue in the face of adversity. It is a well-designed package.

In early 2016, Jill suggested that I consider becoming a BALM Family Recovery Life Coach. After prayer, research, and conversations with Bev Buncher, I enrolled in the coaching program. So glad I did. I was already involved in both Twelve-Step sponsorship and recovery ministry at our church: the BALM has provided another way to serve and to give back what I was given so freely in my own journey.

I am currently a part-time Family Recovery Life Coach and have several clients that I am serving. Eventually, I hope to transition into full-time life coaching and my second career. As a side benefit, both my sponsorship and recovery ministry service has stepped up to a new level. Cool.

Family recovery is an arduous process, and it is so helpful to have a guide that can demystify the recovery process, point out the pitfalls, and end the overwhelming sense of loneliness. You can choose to suffer in silence, secrecy, and shame, but we BALMers really hope you don't.

You don't have to walk alone.

To download Chris's chapter on Christianity, go to page 326 for the link to the free BALM online appendix.

SHARING BALM'S AMAZING APPROACH TO LIFE WITH OTHERS

Jill Prevas, RN, CBC
Certified **BALM** Family Recovery Life Coach
and **BALM** Parent
Pennsylvania/Maryland

Finding Beverly Buncher and the **BALM** Institute was such an answer to prayer. It all started in December 2014 when I hired a True Purpose® life coach to help me find my life purpose. I was already an entrepreneurial businesswoman. In 2008, I had left school nursing, became a certified health coach, and for three years had a health coaching practice. This was rewarding work; however, I felt like I was spinning my wheels, and something was missing. Through the True Purpose® work, God confirmed that my true passion was to come alongside families who had loved ones struggling with addiction.

This passion came about because in 2009, my husband and I discovered that our beautiful seventeen-year-old daughter was a full-blown heroin addict. At this time, the BALM program was not in existence. My husband and I followed the traditional route of attending Al-Anon meetings and working with a certified addiction therapist.

Fortunately, through participating in Al-Anon and therapy, and following the recommendations of the treatment professionals, our family obtained healing and recovery. Our daughter also received sobriety through a lot of hard work on her part. I am happy to say, she has multiple years of uninterrupted sobriety.

Unfortunately, our family story is not the norm. For whatever reason, most family members do not go to Al-Anon, they do not seek professional help for themselves — they jump right in and attempt to manage and fix their loved one's addiction. This does not typically bring positive lasting results to the family and definitely not for their loved one with substance use disorder.

Because of the process our family went through, and because our daughter had success with recovery, many people would reach out to my husband and me and ask for direction. We would share our experience, but many would still not heed our suggestions. That would soon change as I continued my True Purpose® work with my coach.

Fortunately, as my purpose was being revealed to me, my life coach happened to know Beverly Buncher and the wonderful work she was doing with families. I will always remember my coach saying to me, "Write this name and number down and call this lady ASAP." I followed direction and called Beverly that afternoon. We hit it off. I loved her mission of "helping all families blaze the trail to recovery." This absolutely fit in with my purpose. I signed up for the coach certification program and have never looked back. Because of my BALM coach training and the wonderful evidence-based curriculum, I have the opportunity to help hundreds of families "blaze the trail to recovery in their homes."

During the course of this work, I have referred many other coaching students to the **BALM** Institute, including my husband, Chris Prevas. He, too, has a God-given calling to help families navigate the family disease of addiction. His goal is to eventually leave corporate America and join me full-time in pursuing our joint mission. He is already coaching clients and attending networking events. It's just a matter of time for him to be coaching full-time.

In addition, many of the other coaches I have referred to Family Recovery Resources are local and within our community. We believe we need an army of **BALM** Family Recovery Life Coaches. This work is so important, it is lifesaving. With so many **BALM** coaches in our community, the word is beginning to get around. In fact, churches and therapists are beginning to tell families who come to them with addiction issues, "You need a **BALM** coach."

Additionally, in the treatment world, there is still not enough emphasis being put on the importance of the family getting healthy. Almost every treatment program focuses on the loved one with the addiction. This is great; we need this! But the family is just as important. As a result of not focusing on the family, the cycle of family addiction continues. The **BALM** Family Comprehensive changes all of that. A structure of change is provided. The family member receives education on the disease of addiction, plus new ways to communicate with their loved one.

They also become part of a community that provides support and encouragement. As a family member begins to implement the **BALM** 12 Principles, they realize a transformation is taking place. They receive the tools to mirror love, peace, and calm back to their family member, instead of fear, shame, and blame. They also learn how to "Be A Loving Mirror" to themselves.

As a Certified **BALM** Family Recovery Life Coach, I get to see firsthand these wonderful changes take place in my clients' lives! I am so grateful that I have the professional tools needed to coach family members through the trials and sometimes craziness of addiction. And the best part is, I get to use the **BALM** Principles in my own life as well. Being A Loving Mirror to myself and to others is an amazing way to approach life!

TAKING MY TRANSFORMATION TO A WHOLE NEW LEVEL

Jeff Spikes, CBC
Certified **BALM** Family Recovery Life Coach
Gallup-Certified Strengths Coach
Arizona

I found the **BALM** online while looking for a quick certificate in life coaching. When I called to get information about the coach training program, Bev quickly called me back (more than most of the schools I called did). Bev explained the value of engaging in a robust life coach training program rather than a paper mill or a quick certificate for learning basic skills and concepts.

After some deep conversation, including me learning what the **BALM** Institute and Family Recovery Resources offer and Bev learning about my passion and love for activating change in the world, Bev asked one question that has forever changed my life. She asked, "Have you considered what it would feel like to say, 'I'm in training to be a life coach at the **BALM** Institute' rather than 'I have a certificate'?" Wow, what a powerful question that was for me. That question stuck with me as a prominent consideration for a few days. I imagined what that would look and feel like and knew that being in training was the answer. A few days later, I took the plunge and joined the BALM community as a student.

I caught the vision of the program when she explained the mission of helping all families blaze the trail to recovery and became intrigued by the concept of going deep into both life coaching and family recovery. I felt connected to and inspired by the future of the program, the ICF accreditation, and the potential growth of additional programs.

As I look back, I realize everything Bev said was happening was, everything that was going to happen has, and what Bev explained as a vision has become the realization of a revolution against addiction, use disorders, co-occurring disorders, and codependency. Any and every person or program that stands for recovery is included and embraced. Real practices: calming, centering, and communicating, with myself and the world around me in a way that addresses codependency and delivers healing experientially on a core internal level.

As a person with over thirty years in long-term recovery, I had faced many challenges on the path to what I considered success. Fresh out of the Marines as a twenty-one-year-old, new in recovery for the second time, I followed the path of least resistance into a career, still somewhat a victim to my circumstances.

This led me down a road as a logistics/facility professional, and I climbed my way into the corporate world eventually to a position that embodied my idea of success. I was able to be a husband, father, son, brother, friend, mentor, and many other meaningful and joyous things.

My avocation along the way has always been about holistic recovery and self-improvement. I had worked both in the recovery field and in the corporate world as a person engaged in the business development and consulting end of things. I wrote and taught courses at church to raise awareness of codependency and how it affects our lives. I've challenged myself and others to evaluate personal effectiveness and find ways to increase our effectiveness in the world. I've been focused on new ideas and implementation, always on the lookout for great ideas making their way to the marketplace. I was always looking for more!

The year in BALM coach training gave me more than I could have imagined and is the "more" I had been searching for. It included exposure to global experts in the recovery field, substantial coach training written and delivered by experts in the fields of both recovery and life coaching, and a community of like-minded coach trainees all committed to changing the face of recovery by helping families.

Personally, I faced challenges head-on in the BALM way, using facts and love concurrently to help loved ones, recovery partners, business associates, and others, without losing my own integrity. I learned that I had been coaching (or what I thought was coaching) my entire life yet felt unappreciated for what I brought to the table. It was like I was hiding the best parts of myself from the world.

I got the opportunity to challenge myself on how I had shown up in the world and coined the personal phrase that I had been *coaching sideways* for as long as I could remember. I've been challenged to put intention toward ways of being I had for some reason locked up or controlled and shared sparingly when I thought it wouldn't be noticed and then wondered why people didn't notice the greatness.

Part of the work I engaged in over the course of the year in addition to coach training was having a life coach of my own. In that relationship, I worked through personal, business, and recovery challenges and found my own life purpose. I became a Gallup-Certified Strengths Coach, something I had practiced using for over fifteen years yet had refused to become certified in. I learned the value of investing in myself and have been able to gain an intimate understanding of what self-care is and does for me. I have lost close to one hundred pounds, maintained the loss, and addressed my relationship to food, exercise, and overall wellness. I engage today with the world around me in a more authentic way than ever before regardless of the environment.

When put together, the past eighteen months resulted in much more than just my BALM coach certification. I also got myself back-and in some ways, got to a whole new level of self-development in a powerful way. My understanding of change has been catapulted into a new dimension, and I've been able to sustain change where previously I had not found success. Everyone who knows me well has experienced the change and for the most part offers feedback that I am not attached to doing things the hard way and seem more at peace than ever. My relationships have improved tenfold, and I am no longer hiding my purpose and best self from the world.

The BALM is for families, individuals, and everyone. Actually, there are only two kinds of people when it comes to the BALM: those who work it and those who would greatly benefit by doing so.

THE GIFTS OF BALM® COACH TRAINING THUS FAR: DEEPER SELF AWARENESS AND MORE EFFECTIVE COMMUNICATION

Polly Stavrou
BALM Family Recovery Coach Trainee

I am finding the BALM Institute for Family Recovery Life Coach Training invaluable both to me personally and to my future coaching career.

When I came into the course had great apprehension as to whether I could learn the skills necessary to become an effective family recovery life coach. My doubts disappeared shortly into the course. I discovered who I really am including my strengths and core values, and I found the teachers and materials to be outstanding as they taught the amazing tools and concepts of the **BALM** Family Recovery Life Coaching.

Participating firsthand in how these tools work as well as witnessing the client "aha" moments that come as a result have been awe inspiring. Learning effective communication and coaching skills has not only helped in my ability to coach but also in my communication with my loved ones and others outside of the coaching environment.

The gift of deeper self-awareness and more effective communication skills which I have received through this course has been profound and life changing. I also feel that I have not only gained knowledge but also a family in my Cohort, teachers and **BALM** community, and am so grateful to God for bringing the **BALM** into my life. I am looking forward to learning even more as I proceed through the remainder of the Family Recovery Life Coach Training Course. I cannot wait to embrace the even deeper understanding of coaching, myself and life that will inevitably come as a result, and to utilize this amazing education to help families as a Certified **BALM** Family Recovery Life Coach.

BOOSTING MY SELF-CARE WITH THE BALM®

Jackie Stein
BALM Family Recovery Life Coach
Pennsylvania/Maryland

In the BALM family program, one of the things we are taught is that when it comes to addiction, there are no guarantees and that whether or not our loved ones can get and stay clean, we can still learn the tools to Be A Loving Mirror. I am here to tell you that it is true.

I first found the BALM community in the fall of 2015, as a family member of a loved one suffering from many years of alcoholism. He has many years of sobriety in the past, but for the last nine years, he has been unable to maintain long-term recovery. As a person in recovery myself, that has been a very difficult situation for me. At several stages in the relationship, before finding the BALM, the outcomes were painful and exhausting.

That being said, it has been so very different since I have been learning to use the BALM methods for transformation of my own life and learning the tools of self-care. There were many opportunities for me to grow mentally, emotionally, and spiritually. I was able to learn that there are Stages of Change for both the loved one and the family members, and I started to learn how to make those changes. I developed skills to keep the focus on myself and not on my loved one. I discovered ways to heal my relationships with my Higher Power, myself, and others. I heard important information about boundaries and how to set them.

My loved one's journey has had its twists and turns, and I have acquired tools to help me maintain my own. I am not perfect, and I am so much better than I was.

As a result of this journey, I chose to take the steps to become a life coach and BALM Family Recovery Life Coach so that I can share what I have learned with others. Being in recovery not only from substance use but also my current drug of choice (my loved one) and being able to guide others through their own tumultuous times is my passion. I am forever indebted to the BALM Method of Family Recovery and its creator, Bev Buncher, and the BALM Institute, for making this a reality for me.

BRINGING THE BALM® TO EUROPE

Lucy Tomkins, ACC, CBC
Certified BALM Family Recovery Life Coach
United Kingdom

In brief, I have a twenty-eight-year-old son who has been in recovery from drugs and alcohol for over five years, and in February 2015, I took the huge first step in looking after myself and asked my husband of thirty-two years to leave.

I had set a boundary after he came out of rehab eight years ago that I would support his recovery, but I would not support a relapse or his addiction if he chose not to reengage with his program and be honest with me. It was at this very scary time of my life, aged fifty-six, that I found the BALM on the internet and did the second huge step in my self-care and called Bev. A few weeks later, I enrolled in the coaching program and started my BALM education.

I had thought that I was just enrolling in a program to become a family recovery coach, to help the families of loved ones struggling with substance use disorder. I had no idea what an impact the BALM was going to have on *me*. I have learned more about myself in the last two years than I have in my entire lifetime. I have grown into the person I can love, trust, rely on, and believe in. I have finally started to grow up at age fifty-eight!! Well, perhaps not in everything, but it's a start.

In the beginning, everything I listened to, read, and was taught, I thought, "Oh, that would really help my son or my husband, never me." In my mind, I was not the screwed-up one in need of fixing. Now I hungrily digest everything for what it can do for me — how I can learn and grow from it. My job is to role model how I can live the most fulfilling, purposeful, happy, joyous life I can.

There is not enough room here to list everything I have learned through taking the BALM, but all I can say is that I am so grateful every day that I stumbled across it back in 2015. It has transformed my life. Is it a perfect life now? Absolutely not. Are there challenges'? Yes, most days. Do I feel I now have the tools, support, and education to deal with them? Absolutely yes. Thank you, the BALM, Bev, and my wonderful cohort — I owe you all.

LEARNING TO LET GO WITHOUT GIVING UP OR GIVING IN (AN INTERVIEW)

Tracy Ward
BALM Family Recovery Life Coach
Indiana/Kentucky
June 22, 2017

The BALM community welcomes a family member, recovering person, or expert in the field of recovery for scheduled live interviews related to their understanding of one of the BALM Principles.

At present, there are over 150 of these in the Family Recovery Academy archive for families to listen to.

One week, Bev interviewed Tracy Ward, a BALM coach from Indiana, for the Wednesday evening interview. Here is the transcript of part of that interview.

Bev: Good evening, everyone, and welcome to the Daily BALM! This evening our focus is on Principle 3: *It is important to let go without giving up or giving in.*

This principle is so pivotal in the BALM program as it turns tough love on its head. The BALM idea of love is actually the opposite of tough love. The idea is not to let go of the person you love, but to let go of your obsession with making things turn out the way you want them to.

Our guest this evening, Tracy Ward, is a BALM coach who has practiced this principle along with our other BALM Principles and Steps. Tracy Ward is our Lead Administrative Assistant and a Family Recovery Life Coach. She has been in the Twelve-Step recovery community for twenty-three years, has taken it upon herself to start a BALM Family Recovery Support Group in her community and to bring the BALM to as many families in her community as possible.

She is the proud mother of two wonderful children, and mentors other teens and young adult friends of her children. She came to Family Recovery Resources to find help for her son who struggles with a substance use disorder and has found hope and life beyond her wildest dreams. Her passion is to help families find the same hope she found, and get their lives back.

Good evening, Tracy!

Tracy: Good evening!

Bev: Tracy, I know this is one of your favorite principles. Could you share your journey with us, particularly as it relates to your growth in this principle?

Tracy: Yes. It is probably my favorite principle because I have found a way out of the fear and trying to control my son. I have learned to let go of the outcome or results, at the same time being able to keep my sanity by taking care of myself, setting and sticking to boundaries (not always so perfectly), using my support, and keeping a connection with my son.

Bev: How has your own recovery story contributed to your understanding of this principle?

Tracy: Being in recovery myself, and being a "real addict," meaning I know I cannot put any mood-altering substances in my body without the fear of becoming addicted, and setting off that phenomenon of craving, I was faced with the dilemma of my son practicing harm reduction with marijuana and alcohol after treatment.

To me, from what I knew of my own experience of an eighteen-month relapse after eighteen years of sobriety, that was a recipe for disaster that would lead him back to the horrific place we were before he went to treatment: of using any and all drugs he could get his hands on, including Xanax and IV heroin.

Bev: So when Sean decided to drink when he came home from treatment, what did you do and how did you ultimately decide to handle it?

Tracy: Well, I went to visit him in Arizona a couple of months before he came home, and on the last day I was there, we spent some time together, probably more quality time than we had spent in years. I really could see myself practicing what I had been learning over the past year in the BALM.

On that day, he was getting a bit antsy, and I had to be at the airport in a few hours, and he told me he was going to the restaurant across from his apartment to have a few beers with a friend. I didn't react, but inside I was struggling a bit. I said my goodbyes and headed towards the airport. Something inside me told me to go back and go to the restaurant, so I did, and I sat with them as they drank a pitcher of beer, and I continued just being present, and not judging, and I felt a new beginning for me and my son's relationship.

Bev: So how would this new behavior you have developed for yourself play out if he decided to start taking heroin again?

Tracy: That definitely would have been another story. I had set a boundary for myself, that I would not continue to support him if he chose to do anything illegal, and something that could ultimately kill him. Being that he is twenty-one, and I knew in my gut that we had made a transition in our relationship, that he had gotten to a place of being capable of making his own decisions, and that would be more meaningful for him than me trying to control the situation out of fear of him going back to using other drugs, and doing illegal or harmful behaviors.

Bev: What has it been like for you, watching your son practice harm reduction essentially with alcohol, when you know your history and that of his father?

Tracy: Honestly, it has not been easy. We have had a couple of incidents of his overusing alcohol, and me setting boundaries for myself, and how I want my home to be. I really have learned to let him have his own journey.

Bev: What I'm hearing from you, Tracy, is that you have striven to keep your relationship with your son alive in the most powerful way throughout. How have you done that?

Tracy: When I started really learning about motivational interviewing and the importance of keeping the connection with my son, I knew intuitively that this is what was missing in other ways I tried to deal with my son's substance abuse. For me, it was the next step after learning how to be calm, and have BALM conversations with him. It took it to another level.

Bev: Could you talk about how motivational interviewing and the 7 Steps to BALM have shifted your ability to help your son and your family?

Tracy: Like I said, I learned immediately coming into the BALM how to start communicating with him differently, by taking care of me, and learning to keep myself calm. Our relationship started changing then.

Then I took the 7 Steps to BALM and learned how to deepen my communication with him in a way that allowed him to keep his dignity. Then I learned about the motivational interviewing, and for the first time, instead of talking at my son with my agenda, I learned to allow him to think and process, and make choices for himself. This was so empowering for him; the control freak I had always been most of his life!

Bev: What would you say to a family member that is just not getting around to taking a 7 Steps to BALM course or showing up for group coaching, both of which are offered twice a week?

Tracy: I would say...the 7 Steps to BALM is transformational if you take it seriously, and put the effort into it. It is very simple, but so different than what I had been used to doing. I learned new behaviors that changed everything. The group coaching is very important to me because I want to be there to help other families that are where I was, and be there like someone was there for me! Plus, I am not perfect at it, and I want to continue to learn and get better at all the tools I have learned. Every time I go through the 7 Steps to BALM, I learn more deeply.

UPDATE BY TRACY 6-22-17:

Within fifteen minutes of doing the interview, my son came up to me and said "I am really struggling. I have smoked weed the last two days, and I don't know why I did it. I don't like the way it makes me feel. I am feeling really anxious and irritable. I am not doing it any more, plus I want the supervisor position

at work in a couple of months, and I was stupid for doing it."
I just stood there listening, and said, "Sounds like you have a
plan." I went to bed and slept well. To me, this is BALMing at
its finest!

PEACE IN THE MIDST OF GRIEVING

Maryann Williams, RN, CBC
Certified BALM Family Recovery Life Coach
Maryland

"Haven't you done enough, Maryann?," sarcastically stated my
middle child, Rob, as he started out of the driveway with a
large rolling duffel bag and his bicycle.

I was thinking, "Who is this person? It isn't my son. What
is wrong with him? Why is he calling me Maryann and not
Mom?" He had come back to the house after being kicked out
several weeks earlier, per our agreement, had called the police
when I refused to let him in the house without someone else
there, and collected as many of his belongings as he could carry
to go back down to the Baltimore City streets.

I was standing on the front porch with three police cars in
my driveway. Two of my friends had arrived during his visit. I
had called them, and they watched as I said, "I love you, Rob,"
when he was leaving.

I had been saying "I love you" as much as I could in the
last twenty-two years of his addiction, even through the angry,
cussword-laden, drug-infused conversations. I wanted him to
know I loved him in case anything ever happened when he
was out attending to his addiction. This time something did
happen. A week later, he was dead from an overdose of heroin
and fentanyl, found in an abandoned house in an undesirable
area of Baltimore City.

I was able to calmly tell him I loved him because of the BALM and my BALM coach, Bev, who was there to support me throughout that particular ordeal. I was so grateful that I had been able to tell him I loved him the last time I saw him rather than lashing out in anger as I had done years before when I had no tools to deal with an angry sick person.

Addiction is a disease, not a disgrace. I am grateful that I still have the BALM tools to deal with the other addicted loved ones in my life because our family has been as sick as Rob, and we are able to continue to learn a less dysfunctional way to behave together. We still have the behaviors of codependency, even if our addicted loved one is gone.

As of this writing, my thirty-six-year-old son died eight months ago, three months after my fifty-eight-year-old husband died of an eighteen-month fight with cancer. My heart is broken, and I am still deeply grieving with my other two children, but I am starting to be able to be grateful for so many things. I am very grateful that I was able to have my son in my home with me when my husband died and to have him for four months before he left. I was able to do that because of the BALM program. I knew it would be difficult, but with the tools of the BALM program, I have memories that I will cherish.

You see, I am also in recovery from alcoholism myself. I stopped drinking in 1987 when Rob was six years old. I used to take him to Twelve-Step meetings with me so I could learn how to live a life without being a throwing-up, falling-down, blacking-out drunk.

My three children do not know me as a drunk. I raised them as the best mother I could be. However, I began to realize along the way that I also had an additional issue, codependency. There is another program for people who are friends and family of alcoholics and addicts. A person like me knows a lot of people like that, many also in recovery. We are anonymous people, but we are everywhere. So, I was attending two different Twelve-Step programs while praying that Rob would get into recovery and stay there.

Over the years he had been in so many recovery programs and jails that I had lost count. I could not remember how many times I had kicked him out of the house, once on Christmas Eve, because of the stealing, lying, disrespect, and overall anxiety-producing behaviors that he exhibited. He had been homeless many times. My mother's heart suffered greatly for my child.

Codependency and the associated denial of the problem is such a multifaceted slippery slope. The definition that I understood of codependency the best was "being dependent with." My life was intertwined with Rob's in the earlier years. Then I learned detachment with love but had some of my family wanting to amputate Rob from our lives rather than giving him the love he, and so many other addicted loved ones, needed so desperately.

The thing with being in recovery myself is that I can so strongly identify with the feeling of being an unloved and worthless human being and truly believing that. We feel hopeless, helpless, and often want to die. Our addicted loved ones need our love so badly. Don't we all? Isn't that our primary mission in this life, to love God and each other? How are we all doing with that in the middle of this miserable opioid addiction problem scourging the United States? As far as the denial piece is concerned, how can we say this isn't our problem? The family of an addicted loved one is as sick as, or sicker than, the addicted person and needs help just as badly.

I was able to become an RN in 1996. I was going to further my nursing education around 2014 and discovered the **BALM** Institute. I thought that it would be great to be able to make a living in the recovery field since I just loved how it felt to be in recovery and to see the light come on in others' lives while they learned how to get into a new and better life.

Instead, I found a program for inner transformation. I had started my schooling in becoming a Certified BALM Family Recovery Life Coach by going through the yearlong BALM Comprehensive. My first week I entered into Principle 3 and was able to listen to the recorded lessons to catch up. Principle 3 was about getting and staying calm by providing the tools needed for the inner peace we need to reach our addicted or sick loved ones. Turns out that I was having trouble breathing that week because my husband and I had found out about his lung cancer.

As an RN, I knew the implications of this particular lung cancer. Despite the meditation routines and healthy lifestyle practices I had developed, I was still having trouble breathing. That is how I knew my being in BALM was a God thing: this first BALM lesson helped me breathe through a terrifying situation. The rest of my BALM education and the BALM community support helped me get through the rest of the story with grace and peace.

Addiction is a disease, just like congestive heart failure or diabetes. Why aren't we admitting our addicted loved ones to hospitals and treatment centers to help them? My son needed treatment for a longer period than just thirty days. The week he died, he made a feeble attempt to get into treatment without insurance, without success. We now have scientific evidence to show that we have neural pathways with addictions or habits.

The Surgeon General stated years ago that the addiction to nicotine is as strong as the one to heroin. How many people, like my husband, have died because they couldn't quit cigarette smoking? So how many of us know what it is like to try and quit heroin? Whoever has smoked knows what it is like. It takes a while, with a lot of support, to make new pathways in our brains that support a better lifestyle. Where are the medical facilities for the treatment?

I graduated November 2016 and am now a Certified **BALM** Family Recovery Life Coach. I have also been working as a hospice RN to finish out my nursing career. It is comforting somehow to know that I can still help other families that have addicted loved ones.

DO YOU WANT TO HELP FAMILIES TOO?

After reading the journeys of our coaches, you may be considering a career in Life Coaching and wondering how to proceed as a person who cares about those affected by their own or a loved one's substance use disorder.

Becoming a life coach is a powerful, purposeful career path. It entails learning how to meet clients where they are and help them access their own inner wisdom to reach their goals. Life coaching assumes that all clients are healthy and whole at their core, and on that basis, trained life coaches partner with their clients to move forward powerfully in the direction of the client's goals.

The ability of a life coach to ask powerful questions, listen deeply, and reflect what they are hearing to their client empowers the client to consider and move forward on a wide variety of options that previously may have been unavailable to them.

DO I NEED MORE THAN LIFE COACHING TO HELP LOVED ONES AND FAMILY MEMBERS?

Life coaching is an action-based process that works. But what if the client is a person struggling with substances or the relative of someone on drugs or alcohol? What if the situation of the client is more complex than a career change, career goals, or relationship issues?

Enter the specially trained Family Recovery Life Coach/ Recovery Life Coach.

These life coaches are trained in use disorders, recovery, and family recovery, as well as in life coaching. Family Recovery Life Coaches not only understand how to create powerful coaching relationships that help clients move their lives forward; they also have studied and practiced working with clients on the Stages of Change and motivational interviewing, both of which provide an even broader perspective from which to help a loved one or family member move forward from where they are to where they themselves want to be, more powerfully than life coaching alone could do.

WHAT MAKES THE BALM® INSTITUTE UNIQUE?

Different training venues may also focus on different specific methods of helping in addition to straight coaching. At the **BALM** Institute for Family Recovery Life Coach Training and Family Recovery Education, in addition to providing substantial life coach training, we train our coach trainees in the powerful Be A Loving Mirror Method of Family Recovery, through which the coaches become able to provide families with powerful communication tools to deeply reach and potentially influence their using loved ones to move in the direction of recovery.

The **BALM** Institute also offers courses to prepare you to directly coach the family member who is struggling with the use disorder, thus making it a full-service Family Recovery Life Coach training school!

In addition, the **BALM** Institute is an International Coach Federation Accredited Coach Training Program (**ICF-ACTP**). This means we have undergone a rigorous process to gain the top level of accreditation through the premier accrediting organization for life coaches in the world.

The trainees at the **BALM** Institute begin their studies with their prerequisites in the **BALM** Method of Family Recovery. This foundational work gives them the knowledge and practice they need to understand substance use disorder, recovery, and family recovery. With that background, they go on to study life coaching and **BALM** Family Recovery Coaching, the combination of which allows the coach to face the specific challenges families bring when they are facing a loved one's struggles, while the **ICF** core competencies and recovery focus provide the know-how **BALM** coaches need to work with anyone facing the issues of their own or someone else's recovery process.

Life coaching itself is a transformative process, but coaches who want to help families and loved ones accelerate their recovery need to know more and be more than a straight coaching school will allow. Specializing in **BALM** Family Recovery or **BALM** Recovery deepens their ability to serve in ways a life coach without a specialization in the **BALM** with Family Recovery and/or Recovery cannot.

See our FAQ on Life Coach Training in Appendix III on page 289.

Afterword

A SYNOPSIS OF THE LOVING PATH

The loving path is grounded in unconditional love for yourself and your loved one, as well as an understanding of the challenges and issues you face, so that you can most powerfully and effectively be there for them and give them their best chance at recovery.

Sometimes, we feel so desperate that all we can think about is survival. Keeping your child, your spouse, or your loved one alive is to be lauded in itself. Perhaps you have even had to bring them back from death with Naloxone. Who can argue that you don't care about keeping them alive? You do amazing work.

But the next step, once they step back from the brink or before they get there, is to empower your loved one to think more deeply about what's happening to them, so they can ultimately make better decisions. The loving path is designed to help you do that. It allows you to get your life back. You don't desert yourself anymore. But it's also thoughtful; you don't desert them, either. You're very much there with them. That's the two-pronged approach.

There is only today — that's all we have. If we focus all our energy and all our love and all our being on making this the best day possible, tomorrow has the best chance of evolving in a positive way. When we spend our time in regret for yesterday or fear for tomorrow, then we lose the power of this day. Tomorrow doesn't reflect the opportunities it opens up. You're creating a better tomorrow because you understand the power of this day. We introduced you to the first three of the 7 Steps to **BALM**: be the peace you wish to see in the world, objectively observe what your loved one says and does, and become aware of your inner emotional landscape without judgment. You may recall that these are the steps of self-transformation. Once on the BALM path, you will have them at your command again and again to help you help your loved one and with many other challenges in your life.

We discussed the promises of the loving path — which are many. It starts with living your life going forward with no regrets. The promise of the loving path is that you will have lived your life as best you could so that if in five years or ten years or only five minutes your loved one makes a decision to turn their life around, you will have lived a full life and not have been occupied and consumed with their life. The purpose of the Loving Path is fullness of life along the way. The promise of the Loving Path is the sense of doing all you can, to be their best chance.

As we turned outward to the transformation of your relationship with your loved one and others, we introduced you to the fourth step: document the facts so you can begin to unravel the behavior patterns emerging before your eyes.

Without documenting, the facts go back into the ether to be swallowed up by the natural denial that is part and parcel of this disorder. By documenting, you are able to build your ability to believe what you see and hear rather than the manipulations of someone whose brain is hijacked by a use disorder.

Be A Loving Mirror lights the way. The process of the Loving Path is the Be A Loving Mirror Method of Family Recovery. When one chooses to Be A Loving Mirror, they become the light in their family that everyone is drawn to. They're the beacon. They're the North Star.

Be A Loving Mirror creates a different relationship with those around you. You become wise. You had that wisdom in you the whole time, but it comes to the fore because you're not crazed or obsessed. You are at peace. You're able to see the facts and say them in a loving way. You light the path for others. But it's more than that. It's not you doing whatever they want. Be A Loving Mirror lights the way because you are being and generating love, but you are behaving toward others in a way that encourages rather than discourages.

Next, we covered steps five to seven of the BALM path: script a loving conversation, have a loving conservation at the right time and the right place with your loved one, and when necessary, set a boundary. Without these, all that you have learned stays inside you — making you want to explode. These three steps give you a nondefensive, offensive way to vent while providing you the means to help your loved one see past their blind side.

In this book, we also learned that at any time, a family is always contributing either to recovery or to the use disorder. The BALM Method teaches families how to continually contribute to recovery so that they can be their loved one's best chance. Five tips we specify: drop expectations, focus on yourself, Be A Loving Mirror, set boundaries, and get support. These are easier said than done, but the BALM program teaches you how to do these things powerfully, lovingly, and effectively.

We discussed that the way you create an attitudinal shift is through learning these ideas and then beginning to practice them. Creating your attitudinal shift is all about understanding your role as a contributor, studying and understanding the Stages of Change in yourself and in your loved one, and realizing that letting go is crucial.

Letting go does not mean separating or telling them to get lost. You are letting go of the attitude that is not allowing you to relate constructively to them. That attitude is one of such great upset that you can't function, that you can't speak calmly, that you can't think rationally. We teach families how to stop flooding and how to let go of the obsessive thinking about the future in order to be most wholly present, healthy, and effective today.

We also discussed strategies and tactics that people use to make the change we talk about in Chapter 6. There's Four-Four-Eight breathing, meditation, journaling, and techniques to battle flooding when you start to escalate.

If you have a habit or behaviors you want to change, take the following Stages of Change self-assessment so you can determine what stage you're in. Ask yourself pointed questions to determine what you really want and how you really want to live. Do whatever you can to be calm and to put yourself in a position where you're not reacting but responding healthfully.

THE SIX STAGES OF CHANGE SELF-ASSESSMENT

First, think about any number of changes you could or would like to make in your life or that someone has encouraged you to do so.

EXAMPLES OF CHANGES TO CONSIDER:

> › Stop drinking, drugging, smoking, gambling, overeating, etc.)
> › Stop enabling someone you love who is drinking, drugging, smoking, gambling, overeating, etc.
> › Eliminate clutter in your life
> › Find a new job
> › Find a new career path
> › Find your life purpose
> › Be A Loving Mirror toward yourself and others
> › Detach with love
> › Set healthy boundaries for your own benefit
> › Take better care of yourself
> › Get more support for your struggles with addictive substances and/or behaviors
> › Get more support for your own co-addiction

Second, choose only one at a time of any of the above or of any other change you want to make. Write your choice in the space provided below. You can save this form as a template and use it over and over again to get a sense of where you are with any change you wish to make.

THE CHANGE I WANT TO MAKE IS:

Third, think about where you are with this change and highlight or circle the statement below that applies to you.

WHERE I AM WITH THIS PARTICULAR CHANGE IS:

1. I solved my problem more than six months ago.
2. I have taken action on my problem in the past six months.
3. I am intending to take action in the next month.
4. I am intending to take action in the next six months.

Fourth, use this answer key to determine which stage you are in regarding the change you want to make and highlight or circle the statement that applies to you.

SELF-ASSESSMENT ANSWER KEY

› No to all 4 questions means you are in the precontemplation stage
› Yes to number 4 and no to all others puts you in the contemplation stage
› Yes to number 3 means you are in the preparation stage
› Yes to number 2 and no to number 1 means you are in the action stage
› A truthful yes to number 1 means you are in the maintenance stage!

Fifth, read or review the companion article to this self-assessment for more information on each stage. You can find the link to this on page 326.

Sixth, find the right strategies or processes of change for the right stage to help you move yourself forward. If you would like help deciding on your next steps, call us at (888) 998-BALM(2256) to set up a complimentary coaching consult with Family Recovery Resources. If we can't help you, we'll help you find someone who can!

Stages of Change Self-Assessment adapted from: Prochaska, James, John C. Norcross, and Carlo C. DiClemente. 1994. *Changing for Good: A Revolutionary Six-Stage Program for Overcoming Bad Habits and Moving Your Life Positively Forward.* New York: Harper.

Stages of Changes Strategies and Exercises can be found in Prochaska, James, and Janice Prochaska. 2016. *Changing to Thrive: Using the Stages of Change to Overcome the Top Threats to Your Health and Happiness.* Center City, MN: Hazelden.

A SYNOPSIS CONTINUED

Practical strategies like the Clear/Unclear chart, My Business, My Loved One's Business, God's/The Universe's Business, and more empower families to move from being a reactor who impulsively reacts to whatever comes their way into someone who has the presence of mind to receive information, absorb it in a peaceful way, and respond thoughtfully.

This is a very individual process. As you're reading this book, you may be the kind of person who can study what's in it, jot things down, make little note cards for yourself, start to practice it — and you'll just get it. You may be the person who needs to get on some calls or listen to some recordings. You may be a person who needs classes. You may be a person who needs Q&A. You may need group coaching. You may need private coaching. You may need all of it. It takes what it takes. The key is to not judge yourself, regardless of what it takes, and to be willing to do the work — regardless of what it takes.

"It takes what it takes" is about having the willingness to do whatever it takes to change your attitude and your life so you can have that shift, because the shift is what will allow you to live in a completely new, redemptive way.

My first **BALM** conversation was with my own husband. As you know, I am an individual with a food use disorder and I am married to an individual with a substance use disorder — my story is the foundation of the BALM story. As I learned how to love my husband, I developed the BALM.

When I eventually became a coach, my own clients and fellow coaches helped solidify the principles and expand on the teachings until I created what we have today: the BALM program. The early recoverers in BALM were people who didn't yet have access to the rich panoply of methods and resources that make up the BALM Comprehensive. The BALM was still in my head, so they needed an awful lot of coaching, more than today, because coaching was all they had.

The early recoverers helped me see that what I was doing wasn't enough, that I couldn't teach everything, that we needed classes and coaches who knew what I knew because there were so many more families than I could help by myself. All the work I did with the early BALMers led to the founding of the school, because the need was so much greater than any one person could fulfill.

The stories peppered throughout the book and in Chapters 10 and 11 are here to show you how this works. The BALM program is a practice, and these people each show how that practice can make a difference in *your* life — *and* in the life of your loved one. The names and identifying details have all been changed to protect the privacy of family members, but the events (and truths behind them) speak for themselves. The coaches have self-disclosed in Chapter 11.

When you have that attitudinal shift, you're no longer nagging your loved one. You're no longer begging them. You're no longer bugging them. You're no longer hovering over them. If they ask you a question, you answer it without blaming or shaming them. But you answer it honestly. If the answer is no, it's no. If you have something to tell them, you share the facts. You don't give them your opinion about how wrong they are. You've changed the way you speak with your loved one. You are at peace. You're not at blame. When they see that, it frees them up to look at themselves.

This shift can create a huge change in your loved one. It may happen rather quickly, or it may take a long time, which is why letting go is part of that shift. We encourage families, while they are learning how to do all this, to also be praying for their loved one, to be putting their loved one in God's hands or the Universe's hands, or if they believe in energy, to be sharing positive energy. All these things — your attitude, your spiritual demeanor, your speech and your behavior — contribute to your loved one's ability to get better.

Do we guarantee it? No. We don't guarantee a loved one's recovery. But even if recovery doesn't come, you can improve your relationships. Often, we see them greatly improve. There might be a long gap between the time you start doing BALM and the time a loved one attains recovery, but along the way, you can still have a loving relationship.

Love is the answer. Whether you're relating to a loved one struggling with a use disorder, a person at work who nobody likes, or someone who is a bully or bullied — whatever the issue, the answer is the same: love.

There are times when love feels painful because you're still watching your loved one do things that hurt. It's not this happy fluffy emotion at all times. But coming from love allows for less tension in the air, more peace, a bigger perspective. Sometimes it's painful, but ultimately it is peaceful and giving and whole. It's not tough love that we're talking about. It's gentle, ever-abiding love.

The other piece of it is to be a helper, not an enabler. We define an enabler as someone who makes it easier for their loved one to get their substance or behavior. Something that sets the tone for enabling is to not be present — to be too busy for your family, to be too busy to attend to your own life, to be so caught up in binge-watching or work or hobbies that you're really not present to the people around you.

While enabling is anything you do that helps them get their drug of choice, helping is anything you do that helps them move forward in their life and recovery.

Families are traumatized by a loved one's use disorder. That's why it's so important to have recovery in your life and to do whatever it takes to get that recovery. Often, families need a coach to help them manage their journey to recovery. Sometimes the trauma is so severe that they need therapy as well. Some families have to go in-patient. That's okay: it takes what it takes. The point is that pulling your family from the brink often requires that you become that first healing catalyst yourself. It takes what it takes.

Helping your loved one figure out where to go for treatment, setting everything up and being involved with the process, communicating, playing an active role in your loved one's recovery, not turning your back — you can do all this again and again without losing your sense of calm and patience if you are in a healthy place yourself. Just like diabetes, use disorder is relapsable. To be there again and again for your loved one in a healthy way requires a practice, a Loving Path to intentionally walk down.

Your family will go through traumas. They will go through large and small problems. If you are working the BALM Program, you will be able to walk with them.

THE IMPORTANCE OF AWARENESS

A lot of what we do, a lot of the practices and classes of the BALM Program, are really about getting out of denial and into awareness. Denial says, "This isn't really happening. It's not as bad as you think it is. Everything's okay." No. Everything's not okay.

But awareness knows that with love, everything *is* okay. There's a key difference: it's not *pretending* everything's okay and ignoring the very real challenges and traumas you face. It's the awareness and peace in your own self that knows that, despite those challenges, all is well when love is in charge.

Awareness is not ignoring the facts. Awareness is observing the facts without judgment. That's what the documenting notebook is for. You see something that's just a little bit odd, jot it down. You may never see anything odd again. If that's the case, it's nothing.

Tomorrow, if there's something weird, write that down. If there are patterns, they will become apparent. Those patterns are most easily detected when you're willing to be aware — not hovering, not hypervigilant, just aware. That comes from the peaceful path, the Loving Path. When you have a practice, you become more aware of thoughts. You become more able to objectively observe. You become more aware of your emotions.

YOUR PEACE = YOUR AWARENESS

How can you tell if a loved one is using? Are you overthinking it — are you just crazy? Those are the questions we ask ourselves. But remember: if you start feeling crazy or out of sorts, and there's no explanation, find out where it's coming from. See what's going on with your loved one. Sometimes your inner chaos is a reflection of theirs. That's why it's so important to stay in recovery, to continue to practice the first three steps and use four through seven as needed, because if you stay calm and they start to get chaotic, you are aware and able to respond in a powerful way. Without your own inner peace and awareness, you can't provide that.

My husband and I both had great self-awareness for ourselves and each other for many years. Then I got really busy at work; self-awareness was the last thing that mattered to me. I just wanted to make money and be successful. I wanted to help the kids and teachers I was working with. I wanted to advance. I was ambitious in my career. So my recovery fell to the wayside, and I didn't notice the first stages of my husband's relapse.

If your internal waters are stormy or choppy, you're not going to notice when your loved one throws stones. If your internal waters are calm and something ruffles the surface, you'll notice right away. Being your loved one's best chance is about nurturing your own recovery so that your awareness is calm and powerful.

Of course, this is a disease that tells a person they don't have a problem. It can be very difficult to work with. But that's exactly why your own internal shift is so important. When you are healthy and at peace, you can be there for your loved one during those critical times when they're in bad shape. It doesn't overtake you. You can be there for each other and for others in the family.

We BALM coaches spend a lot time with our families, helping them script their BALM conversations, build their recovery teams, and partner with their loved ones' professionals to develop a comprehensive treatment plan for their loved ones. Having a coach can accelerate a family's progress in helping their loved one.

But in the long run, it's the attitudinal shift of the BALM families we coach that allows us and them to become most powerfully effective. So we invite you to recall that this is a program about going deep within to create tremendous change within yourself and, like a beautiful domino effect, restore hope to your loved one and your family. Be A Loving Mirror!

QUESTIONS TO PONDER:

1. What are your next steps on your recovery journey?

APPENDICES, GLOSSARY, REFERENCES & INDEX

Appendix I

SUMMARY OF THE 12 BALM PRINCIPLES

Developed and Taught by
Beverly Buncher, MA, PCC, CTPC
Family Recovery Life Coach
Family Recovery Resources, LLC

While the **BALM** 12 Principles of Family Recovery may seem familiar, they are all infused with our special concept of Be A Loving Mirror. Everything we do, everything we suggest, and everything we teach is based on this concept. We do this because we see the changes in families that use the Be A Loving Mirror approach.

PRINCIPLE ONE
THE FAMILY HAS A CRUCIAL ROLE TO PLAY IN EARLY RECOVERY

The family has a powerful role in a loved one's recovery. Research shows when the family gets well, the addict has a better chance of getting well. This lesson maps out how the family can most effectively help a loved one choose to recover emphasizing 5 tips and the **BALM** 7 C's.

PRINCIPLE TWO
CHANGE HAPPENS IN STAGES

Change happens in stages. This is important for families to understand. Often, we have a substance-using loved one and all we want is for the use to stop. We 'put them in treatment', expecting everything to be all better. If only it were that simple. This week, we will look at how change happens in a person struggling with substances. We will also learn ways to communicate that can help you help your loved one move from one stage to the next. As we do so, we will look at the importance of being patient with yourself.

PRINCIPLE THREE
IT IS IMPORTANT TO LET GO WITHOUT GIVING UP OR GIVING IN

In this lesson, the focus will be on how to develop a sense of persistent inner calm in the middle of the storms that your loved one's addiction will inevitably bring into your life. To many people, letting go means 'standing back and doing nothing'. Using the Be A Loving Mirror approach, we will teach you to stay involved without holding on too tightly. Learn what kind of interaction with your struggling loved one is and is not beneficial. This is the work before you as a student of family recovery.

PRINCIPLE FOUR
YOU CAN BE YOUR LOVED ONE'S BEST CHANGE AT RECOVERY

A family member can either contribute to a loved one's addiction or their recovery. You will learn about enabling their addiction vs. helping their recovery; how to stay out of denial; the importance of setting and sticking to boundaries; making conscious decisions about your own behavior; and when to get outside help. With case histories, examples and guidelines, you will learn what it takes to become your loved one's best chance at getting and staying sober!

PRINCIPLE FIVE
KEEPING YOUR FOCUS ON YOURSELF AND OFF OF YOUR LOVED ONE WILL HELP YOU BOTH!

The importance of self-care is almost a truism. Yet, how does one justify taking their eyes off of a suffering loved one and putting their attention on themselves? This is the focus of week five. Replete with charts, lists and tables, this week's work book will give you many ideas to help you put self-care high on your list. In addition, you will learn about how dependency develops and how the phenomenon of Addiction Switching affects addicts *and* family members.

PRINCIPLE SIX
YOUR PRIMARY TASK IS TO BE A LOVING PERSON

"All you need is love." When the Beatles sang that line so many decades ago, a whole generation fell into an understanding of love both romantic and passive. BALM Family Recovery turns this definition on its head. There is a difference between being loving and being 'nice'; between doing things for others and encouraging them to take responsibility for themselves. We will look at the power of love to help you help your loved one get well.

PRINCIPLE SEVEN
DON'T SET A BOUNDARY UNLESS YOU ARE DETERMINED TO STICK TO IT!

If you ask any family member what is most difficult about dealing with a loved one's addiction, most will say setting boundaries and not giving in to manipulation. This lesson discusses what it means to set healthy boundaries, how to set them, the obstacles standing in the way of setting boundaries, and how to stick to the boundaries you set. If you have ever had to say no to a demanding addict, you will appreciate this lesson.

PRINCIPLE EIGHT
GETTING SUPPORT WILL GREATLY ENHANCE YOUR RECOVERY

One of the hardest things for a family member to accept is the fact that they need help as much, if not more, than their addicted loved one. Yet it is true. And there are two reasons for this: one, the family member witnessed and remembers all that their loved one did while the addict himself may not. Two, when the family gets help, the user has a much better chance for recovery. We will also look at resistance and how to get through it; the types of help and support available; and how to pick the help that's best for you.

PRINCIPLE NINE
YOU CAN EXPLORE AND/OR HEAL YOUR RELATIONSHIP WITH SPIRITUALITY

Figuring out what spirituality means to you and developing a relationship with that deeper reality, can offer a meaningful addition to your recovery journey. Yet, people whose lives have been touched by addiction, often experience anger and disappointment in relationship to that which is sacred or holy. If, however, you are open to finding or renewing an ongoing relationship with spirituality that works for you, this lesson can help.

PRINCIPLE TEN
YOU CAN HEAL YOUR RELATIONSHIP WITH YOURSELF

In this lesson, you will have the chance to better see your strengths and the potential for growth, as you discover a path to inner development. This powerful lesson gives you ideas to consider and explore which helps you develop a stronger, more positive relationship with yourself. The stronger and more self-aware you are, the more you will be able to help your loved one.

PRINCIPLE ELEVEN
YOU CAN HEAL YOUR RELATIONSHIPS WITH OTHERS

Being in relationship with a struggling loved one can be very painful. This lesson is about how to keep that pain from turning into suffering. The five ideas explored and developed in this lesson are: we are all connected; actions and reactions have an impact; it only takes one person to heal a relationship; moving from reacting to responding can change a relationship from toxic to healthy; and the value of working on yourself.

PRINCIPLE TWELVE
BE A LOVING MIRROR IS THE JOURNEY AND THE DESTINATION

This culminating lesson brings together the other eleven lessons and shows how **Being A Loving Mirror** can and does change the face of family life for the better. This simple concept has the power to change the way you relate to yourself and others in the long run. It can give you the power to live a more fulfilling life.

Appendix II

The following two articles introduce self-inquiry, one of several possible approaches to Step 1 of the 7 Steps to **BALM**. These are written by lead 7 Steps to **BALM** teacher Michael DeForbes. Try them and see if either one fits. If not, no worries. Find one that does.

SELF-INQUIRY AND THE 7 STEPS TO BALM

Michael DeForbes, MFA, LCDP, ACC, CBC
Certified BALM Family Recovery Life Coach

WHAT IS SELF-INQUIRY?

Self-inquiry is the use of simple open-ended questions on oneself when feeling anxious, flooded, irritated, frustrated, victimized, angry, or upset about something. When used effectively, it does two powerful things simultaneously: it exposes the true source of suffering, which is believing whatever your mind tells you about the situation, and it points toward an inner peace that is available immediately, in this moment.

Different self-inquiry instructors such as Byron Katie, Bob Adamson, Lester Levenson, Paul Hedderman, and Scott Kiloby use different self-inquiry questions to help their clients achieve long-lasting peace, especially when the clients are experiencing severe anxiety-inducing problems.

HOW CAN SELF-INQUIRY BE HELPFUL WITH THE BALM?

Simply put, one of the main "side effects" of self-inquiry is the feeling of ongoing peace and stability that never waivers. And Step 1 of the 7 Steps to BALM is be the peace you wish to see in the world.

AN EXAMPLE OF A SELF-INQUIRY QUESTION

As Family Recovery Life Coaches, we see many clients with severe hardship: addiction in the household, loss of loved ones, ending of relationships, financial ruin, and incarceration. Needless to say, many of them are in a state of extreme suffering. No matter what their situation, I tell all of them: Your stress does not come from the situation itself. It never does. Your stress and suffering come from identifying with what your mind tells you about the situation:

"My loved one is going to die."

"I will lose everything I hold dear."

"I'm not enough."

"I'm going to be alone for the rest of my life."

Self-inquiry facilitator Bob Adamson asks his students one question to show them where all their suffering and problems come from: *What is the problem with life, here and now, when you're not focused on your thinking?*

The mind may scream the answer, "The problem is my loved one is using drugs!" But that is still thinking. Remember, words are thoughts, whether aloud or in your head.

So, ask this question again, and let it sink in. Don't just say the answer, let the answer reveal itself: *What is the problem with life, here and now, when you're not focused on your thinking?*

Let your mind fade to the background because of the present moment and you'll see: there is no problem. There never was a problem. In the absence of problems, there is always this peace. The suffering comes from focusing too much on what your mind is telling you. And the more this peace reveals itself, the more the anxious thought energy fades, leaving the peace itself.

Notice now that your thoughts are gone, but the peace remains. This is what we really are at our core: peace and love.

SEEING THE NATURE OF STRESSFUL THOUGHTS

Bring up a stressful thought right now until you begin to actually feel some stress. Simply fade back into your conscious awareness and notice that the stressful thought contains these four elements:

› an image
› spoken words the mind repeats
› feelings or bodily sensations
› a backstory

One of my clients summed up this process very well. She said, "It's like a movie clip that loops over and over in my head."

Please take the time now and check this for yourself. Notice how a stressful thought is simply like a looping movie clip that plays over and over in your head. This is the nature of all stressful thoughts. Now, pretend you are a therapist trying to talk some sense into this movie clip. Play it again in your head and ask yourself: Where is the intelligence in this movie clip to talk some sense into?

Check for yourself and ask again: Where is the intelligence in this movie clip to reason with? The answer is: *there is no intelligent being behind a stressful thought* — it's just a movie clip coming up in your mind. This is the nature of the mind.

Have you ever noticed when you argue with an addicted loved one that both of you repeat things over and over? That repetition is the movie clip looping. As many teachers have said, Thought is not intelligence. There is only one higher intelligence, and thought is not it.

POINTING TO THE PEACE THAT IS ALWAYS THERE: THE PROMISE OF STEP ONE

Michael DeForbes, MFA, LCDP, ACC, CBC
Certified BALM Family Recovery Life Coach

In addition to teaching how to interact with your loved one affected by addiction, the 7 Steps to BALM also provides a transformative process of realizing that at your core, you are this peace and love that never waivers, no matter what is happening, no matter what thoughts and feelings you are having. This transformative realization can happen over a period of time by working the steps and engaging in a regular centering regimen, or it can be immediate. This "pointing to the peace" is to show how it can be immediate, but it involves being totally open to what is at your base level of consciousness.

This realization or seeing of this peace has been called "having a spiritual awakening" or "being enlightened," but remember, these are only words or labels. When they are given too much importance, it can make achieving this realization seem impossible. But this peace and love is something that every human being experiences every single day; it is just overlooked by the mind. Experiencing this peace actually occurs every morning when a person wakes up. The first realization that a person has is in knowing *that I am, that I exist.* It occurs before your eyes open, before the mind even thinks the words. But then the mind's thoughts quickly rush in with all of its errands, worries, and to-do lists; the body gets out of bed and goes about its day; and this awareness that you really *are* is forgotten.

As we begin this pointing, remember that we are using words, and words are only tools. They point to what's at your core, but they are not the real thing. It is like trying to use words to give a person the experience of tasting an orange — they can only describe it, but the description can never be the real experience of tasting an orange. Also, as the words are internalized, they must first go through your mind. But realization of this peace and love is not for the mind, because the mind can only understand things intellectually. It can only understand the meaning of the words and nothing more. The truth behind this peace is actually so mind-numbingly simple that the mind misses it every single time. But it won't stop the mind from trying to interpret these words. That's just what the mind does. Do your best to put your mind's thinking to the side for the duration of this pointing. Let the words sink past the mind into a deeper place of knowing and understanding until they resonate within you.

So, be here now and settle into a relaxed space physically and mentally the best you can, and take a relaxing cleansing breath:

› Go back to this morning when you first woke up. Again, the peace is in that initial knowing when you awaken that I am, that I exist. Be there now.

› If you are straining, having a difficult time going back to this knowing of I am, it is because the mind is trying do to it, and it can't. So try this: try *not* knowing that you exist. Do this now. You will find that you cannot know that you exist. No one can; it is impossible to *not* know that you exist. And trying to do so only causes the knowing of your existence to come forward. Be there now.

> Let us take a moment to explore this knowing of your existence, this "I am"-ness. Notice that it has two parts: it is aware, and it senses. This awareness hears, and the mind interprets, "That is a bird outside my window," or "That is my dog barking." This awareness sees, and the mind interprets, "That's a houseplant that needs watering," or "That is a souvenir I bought during my last summer vacation." Confirm this for your experience, the awareness sensing, and the mind's interpretations.

> Up to this point, I have asked you to focus your senses on your outer surroundings, but now I am asking you to turn your focus inward, to the awareness itself. So you will be this still, silent awareness being aware of awareness; awareness being aware of itself. Do this now.

> Some people (not all) report some kind of shift in experience when this is done. One lady said, "I feel that something else is there." Another person said, "I feel that my consciousness has expanded beyond my physical body." And another pushed his chair backward and said, "I feel something in my chest; what just happened?" It is the realization that something else beyond the mind's thinking was always there, this palpable sense of peace. Confirm this for your experience.

> If this is not your experience, try bringing up a memory of when you were extremely happy, a moment in your life when you didn't have a care or desire in the world. Let this memory bring up the feeling as well. Once you have that feeling of peace, joy, and relief, drop the image and focus on the feeling, and remain there with it. That is this awareness being aware of itself as well. It is also realized when all desire falls away.

Being here now with this awareness, let us explore it. Ask
yourself these questions with regard to this awareness:

› What is the age of this awareness: Is it young or old? This
  question doesn't seem to apply. It just is.

› What gender is this awareness? Is it male or female? If
  you're thinking, "The awareness is female," that is your
  mind trying to answer. But this awareness really doesn't
  have a gender, does it? It's not male, female, or both.
  Again, this question does not seem to apply; it just is.

› What religion is this awareness? Is it Catholic? Jewish?
  Muslim? Buddhist? Again, this question does not seem
  to apply for it just is.

› Doesn't it seem that this awareness was just always
  there? That it wasn't even born, that it had no date of
  conception? Your body was born and your body will die,
  but the awareness is not affected by this fact. It always
  just is. So if it was never born, then it can never die. It is
  eternal. Time does not even seem to apply.

› Confirm these answers as your experience. This awareness
  that you are does not seem to conform to any labeling,
  but it is there. It is alive and it is real.

› It is silent, but if it could speak, it would only say one
  thing: "I am." It is the knowing of its own existence: "I
  am." Confirm this for your experience.

› Remaining in this knowing of this "I am"-ness of
  awareness, slowly look around the room and focus on
  a single object. Notice how your consciousness, this
  awareness, seems to be interacting with it. It is as if this
  inanimate object in the room is looking back at you, as
  if it too is alive, that it is part of this awareness. As the
  awareness is seeing this object, it still only says, "I am,"
  as in, "I too am this." Confirm this for your experience.

› Now slowly scan your surroundings, and notice that whatever is seen, the awareness continues to communicate "I am," as in, "I too am this," "I too am this," and "I too am this."

This awareness, this consciousness, this aliveness, this "I am"-ness can be called many things, but all words fail to describe it. This is when you realize that words are only tools, and not very good tools for describing it.

Whatever this awareness comes in contact with, it only senses itself; that's why it only ever says the same thing in relation to whatever it experiences: "I am." It only ever senses and experiences itself, and because of this, it is unconditional love, unconditionally loving whatever it comes in contact with. Therefore, it always emanates this peace and love.

In the Old Testament of the Bible, "I Am" was also the word "Yahweh," which is also the first name of God: "I Am Who I Am." This awareness that you've been feeling, this consciousness at its base level, beyond the thinking of the mind, is the consciousness of God, only knowing itself, being what it is, and loving itself. And because of this, it emanates this peace that is always there.

Beyond the confines of this physical body and beyond the mind's thoughts, this awareness and the peace that emanates from it is what you really are. It always was, it always will be. This is the promise of Step 1 of the 7 Steps to **BALM**: at your core, you are this peace and love.

Appendix III

Thinking of Life Coach Training in the **BALM** Institute? Here are some answers to some of the questions we have heard from past applicants. If you still have questions after reading this FAQ, give the **BALM** Institute a call at 1888-998-**BALM** and we will give you a call. If you already know you want to apply, call to set up an admissions interview.

FAQ

WHAT IS LIFE COACHING?

Many people have goals. Not everyone achieves them. Over the past few decades, a career path has emerged which helps people powerfully reach the goals they set. Namely: Life Coaching. The history of this field has roots in the modalities of sports coaching, humanistic psychology, and personal growth, among other helping modalities. And yet it is none of these things. In and of itself, it is unique and powerful.

Life Coaching is an interactive partnership in which the client's goals and agenda form the foundation of a powerful professional relationship. Clients engage a coach in order to reach the goals that have thus far eluded them, and those goals guide the relationship unless and until the client becomes complete in achieving them or decides to shift focus to new ones.

The most important thing to understand about the life coaching partnership is that it is client driven. Coaches do not diagnose or prescribe medication for their clients. Instead, they offer them a different sort of expertise: that of asking powerful questions, listening deeply to their client's answers and using those answers to help the client go deeper into the client's deepest wisdom through further questions or specifically chosen activities or exercises designed to help the client move powerfully toward their goals and dreams.

WHAT TYPE OF EDUCATION IS NEEDED TO PREPARE A POWERFUL LIFE COACH?

This delicate powerful work is, at its best, carefully prepared for through substantive education and training. It requires very specific training to insure the client is well served, though ironically, many people call themselves life coaches regardless of their training or background.

Life coach training has a variety of components, all of which prepare the coach to be optimally present with their clients. These include an understanding of the underlying philosophy and process of life coaching, exposure to the wide variety of skills and tools a life coach needs to communicate deeply with a client, demos by competent coach trainers, and many rounds of practice with each other over the course of the educational training course.

And there is something more: An accredited program, with a highly reputable accrediting agency, is a critical factor behind powerful life coach training.

WHO ACCREDITS THE BALM INSTITUTE AND WHAT DOES THAT ACCREDITATION ADD TO THE TRAINING OUR STUDENTS RECEIVE?

The **BALM** Institute is an **ICF-ACTP** (International Coach Federation — Accredited Coach Training Program).

The International Coach Federation (**ICF**) is the premier global accrediting organization for life coaches. Born early in the coaching movement, The ICF has been both the source and the guide of the development of the core competencies and ethical standards and guidelines for life coaches.

To become **ICF**-Accredited, a life coaching school must go through a rigorous accrediting process that includes inclusion of specific didactic and experiential aspects. This work, of both imparting knowledge and experience must be done planfully to insure value to the students. ICF requires well-planned, substantial training of this type in its accredited schools.

In order to become an **ICF** Accredited Coach Training Program, a school must have an **ICF** Master Certified Coach (**MCC**) as its Training Director to oversee its educational curriculum to insure its compliance with all requirements. Then, the school must operate with all requirements of an ACTP for one full cycle before even applying for Accreditation.

Fully accredited programs include at least 125 hours of live instruction (ours includes mostly live online programming plus a 24 hour in person Practicum weekend for a total of 162 credits all together. Additionally, we offer our students over 140 available classes and recordings on a variety of use disorder and recovery topics at no additional charge as part of their program.

The classes cover Life Coach Training and Family Recovery Life Coach Training, Mentor Coaching Groups, One-on-One Coaching and the Live In-Person Practicum mentioned above to insure mastery of the **ICF** Core Competencies, student to student coaching designed to give students practice with each other as they grow as coaches, and business development in order to help them create both a coaching practice and business as they complete their studies.

To graduate and become a Certified **BALM** Family Recovery Life Coach, students must attend all classes and activities and the Practicum and must hand in two transcripts of their own coaching sessions that demonstrate the ICF Core Competencies. The rigorous process includes regular practice, demonstrations and help along the way to ensure that each student has their best chance of passing and operating on the high level a BALM endorsement and accreditation requires.

The courses are all taught by ICF-Certified Coaches and once a student has successfully completed their studies and oral exams, they become eligible to apply for ICF certification by handing in their **BALM** Graduation Certificate and coaching for at least 100 hours. Most of our graduates have the opportunity to complete their hours within their first year as a result of the many coaching opportunities the school gives them and encourages them to take.

The last hurdle remaining is the **CKA** (Coach Knowledge Assessment), an online exam that all applicants must take to become ICF certified. Due to the ongoing instruction, demos, reinforcement and practice provided in our ICF-ACTP, this assessment is not a hurdle for our graduates. Rather, it is just another steppingstone to their becoming a fully certified ICF Coach.

Once ICF-certified, students become qualified to teach in an **ICF**-Accredited Coach Training Program and open the door to many more opportunities in their coaching careers both in and out of the recovery field.

WHY DO I NEED THIS CERTIFICATION OR EVEN AN ACCREDITED SCHOOL OR EVEN LIFE COACH TRAINING? I JUST WANT TO WORK WITH FAMILIES...

When I started the **BALM** Institute, it was an advanced CCE (continuing education credits) program. I only accepted trained coaches. Unfortunately, many of the students who wanted to work with families (trained by a variety of coaching programs and schools from a weekend to 6 months long), simply lacked the firm foundational footing to work deeply and powerfully with families impacted by a loved one's addictive struggles. Additionally, when personal issues came up within the person, the coaches often appeared lost as to how to meet their clients' needs.

So, I contacted Fran Fisher, our Director of Training, and asked her to help us become fully accredited so that we could ensure that the Coaches we graduated were powerfully grounded in the **ICF** Core Competencies as well as in **BALM** Family Recovery. The result of this marriage of the two, the **BALM** and the **ICF** approaches, has been the creation of coaches able to help families and loved ones move powerfully forward in their lives.

Schools of course evolve. At first we taught these two approaches separately. Today, we provide a merging of two powerful helping modalities in a way that allows coaches to switch seamlessly between recovery work and coaching work, of course with the client's permission.

The **ICF-ACTP** Accreditation has allowed us to develop coaches of a high caliber. The **BALM** has allowed us to provide coaches with a deep understanding of addiction and recovery and the ability to be there powerfully for each family in the moment.

Our curriculum works for the benefit of our students and their clients. And the fact that our coach trainees come back for our advanced courses, and bring their own clients to enroll in our family programs speaks volumes to its value and effectiveness.

To become a Certified **BALM** Coach is to take your education seriously and treat yourself as a professional. To become a Certified **ICF** Coach after completing our program is to see the value in the profession itself and to take your place as a leader in the Family Recovery Life Coaching field.

At the **BALM** Intitute, we are committed to flexibility as well as high standards and excellence in training. Our admissions coaches work closely with our students to help them find the best combination of courses and the proper timing for each trainee while maintaining the integrity of our mission. To learn more about this visit our website at familyrecoveryresources.com or call us at 1888-998-**BALM** for more information.

Thousands of Recovery Coaches have been trained around the world, with more being trained every day. These coaches, also known as recovery support specialists, peer specialists, or peer coaches, are often people in recovery with a real heart for the work they are doing. They offer vital support for people both in and out of treatment, using a variety of models they have learned to support recovery. And yet, they often lack two components in their training that could greatly increase the positive impact of their work on clients. We already discussed the first component above: **ICF** Life Coach Training. Now let's look at the 2nd missing component in most coach training programs: The BALM (Be A Loving Mirror) Method of Family Recovery and the BALM Method of Recovery.

WHAT IS THE BALM METHOD?

The **BALM** Method is the loving path to family recovery.

WHY DO YOU CALL BALM THE LOVING PATH TO FAMILY RECOVERY?

BALM programs provide family members and their struggling loved ones with a path to peace and loving kindness that leads to freedom for the family and the user. BALM family members make the conscious choice to **be** peaceful, non-judgmental, observers in their loved one's life. On that basis, they share the facts of what they are seeing and are able to give their loved one the opportunity to hear those facts without getting defensive.

This approach changes the atmosphere in the home from one of fighting and conflict to one of peaceful acceptance of the reality facing the family. Rather than becoming a doormat, the family member has become someone their loved one can rely on to be real with them.

When they hear reality being shared without the anger, bitterness and judgment they have so often had to endure from those who witness their life choices, it is easier for the struggling loved one to digest it.

With this new approach established, family members give the person they love the chance to listen and learn and to potentially choose a new way of living.

DOES MY BALM BEHAVIOR GUARANTEE MY LOVED ONE WILL GET WELL?

This way does not guarantee a loved one will choose recovery, though it does increase the chances that they will. In addition, it allows the family members to 'be there' for their struggling loved one in a way that leaves a loving space open for their loved one to make healthier choices sooner than they otherwise would.

Often, people who practice BALM find that their relationships with their loved one and other family members improve, even when the loved one does not choose recovery.

WHAT DOES THIS BE A LOVING MIRROR PATH INVOLVE?

To Be A Loving Mirror, it involves:
> Getting oneself in a calm place
> Dropping all judgments, anger, and resentment
> Being a reporter and observer — stick with the facts of what happened
> Sharing what one sees objectively, lovingly, and calmly
> Always treating the struggling loved one with dignity and respect
> Regardless of their response or reaction, letting it go and going on with one's life
> Beginning to understand, absorb and apply the BALM 12 Principles and 7 Steps to BALM

WHAT DOES THIS LOVING PATH REQUIRE?

A Loving Mirror response requires that one:
> Change one's expectations of their suffering loved one. Trust them to continue to struggle unless and until they have actively committed to recovery. This helps take away the shock when they use or drink.
> Go about living life regardless of the loved one's behavior, and respect their right to live their life as well.
> Plan how one will *respond, **not** react*, to them when they arrive home drunk or high.
> When they do show up drunk or high, do ***not*** attempt to have a rational conversation with them at that moment.

› Observe their behavior non-judgmentally and lovingly.
› Do not clean up after them or clean up the consequences of their behavior, even if they throw up all over the house. That is *thier* responsibility.
› When they wake up and wonder what happened, give them an objective report of the facts of what happened, sharing unconditional love and respect for them along with the concerns for their health, safety and well-being.

HOW WILL I KNOW IF I AM A BALMER (BEHAVING IN A BALM FASHION)?

A person knows they have become a Loving Mirror when they see that they:
› Operate from love rather than anger or fear
› Observe rather than judge
› Respond rather than react
› Allow others to handle the consequences of their own behavior
› Handle their own emotions without assigning blame to others for how they think, feel, speak, or behave.

HOW DOES THIS RELATE TO COACH TRAINING?

Every coach trainee prepares for their work in the **BALM** Institute with a study of the Information component of the **BALM** program: the **BALM** 12 Principles. These principles, which every **BALM** family studies in the **BALM** Comprehensive Family Program as well, provide the foundation to understanding the loving path known as Be A Loving Mirror.

Divided into three categories, the **BALM** Principles open the door to a full understanding of addiction/use disorders, recovery, and family recovery. An understanding of the field is critical for coaches who will be working with families and loved ones and the **BALM** 12 Principles is where it all begins. Information is a good start, but not enough.

The second component of the **BALM** Method is that of transformation and is embodied in the 7 Steps to **BALM**. In this powerful 8 week class, families and coaches learn how to Be the Peace They Wish to See in the World. This inner work of the first 3 steps includes mindfulness, objective observation of the struggling loved one and inner e motional awareness.

Inner transformation is the work of a lifetime, yet in this course, coaches and families get a powerful start that lays the foundation for a lifetime of peaceful relationships with loved ones.

The last four steps of the seven are all about learning to communicate with your loved one (or any other challenging person in your life) in a way that opens the door to potential change on their part. We like to say it gives you a way to inoffensively vent while also sharing important information about their behavior in a way that makes it easier for them to hear it.

As the building blocks of the **BALM** the **BALM** 12 principles and 7 steps to **BALM** are critical to our coaches. Again and again new coach trainees come in planning to learn whatever they can to help others and before they know it they are reporting the big impact that learning and practicing the **BALM** is having on themselves and their families!

Many coaches retake these two courses many times over the course of their year in coach training and find themselves practicing their coaching on **BALM** families who they are assigned to take through the 7 Steps to **BALM**. Plus, they can use these hours toward certification, so it is a win-win for them and their intern clients.

IS THAT ALL?

Of course, there is so much more to the BALM for coach trainees to explore! They are only required to take the BALM 12 Principles and 7 Steps to BALM courses, yet many of them can be found in Coaching Groups, Journaling Workshops, and other offerings of the BALM Institute while they are in the coach training, and interning and teaching many courses for families upon graduation.

Once certified and experienced as coaches, they can also be found teaching coach training courses and guiding the newbies along on the path to being BALM coaches and fulfilling the BALM mission of helping *all* families blaze the trail to recovery in their homes!

When potential coaches choose the BALM Institute, they are choosing a school with the highest standards of coach training and of recovery, a school that respects each individual's approach to family recovery and recovery, encouraging families to become educated in the many opportunities for recovery and learning how to help families and loved ones along the recovery path as a result of their coach training and their own inner work to Be A Loving Mirror.

To learn more about the BALM Institute and how to become a BALM Coach, call us at 888-998-BALM or go to TheBALMInstitute.com

Glossary

A

Addiction Switching — Switching between use disorders (also known as addictions) occurs often. For instance, a person may stop using drugs and start using cigarettes. Or stop gambling and start using food or sex.

Al-Anon — the original family 12 step program which today focuses mainly on helping family members with their own self-care rather than providing a step by step way of helping them help their loved one. There are currently many other 12 step support programs for families including Naranon (for the families of narcotics addicts), Gamanon (for the families of gamblers), S-anon (for the families of sex addicts). The BALM finds its roots in the loving approach.

Attitudinal Shift — The change in attitude that occurs in a family member when they begin to learn and practice the skills and tools of BALM recovery.

B

BALM (Be A Loving Mirror) — Be A Loving Mirror is a method to help families and loved ones recover from the impact of a use disorder. For many who utilize it, it becomes a way of being that sets one's standard for relating to self, loved ones and the world in general. The expression Be A

Loving Mirror (abbreviated as BALM) describes an approach to communication that is fact-based, non-judgmental, and peaceful.

In life coaching, a coach can be a mirror to their client by reflecting back what the client says word for word so the client can hear herself or himself think. In recovery, a family member who is practicing BALM has a BALM conversation (see below) with a loved one in which they give the struggling loved one a mirror of facts through which the loved one is invited to see their own (the loved one's) words and behaviors.

BALM 7 C's — Seven statements all of which have an important word beginning with the letter C. The first 4 have their roots in Al-Anon, although the 4th has been changed from *you don't have to contribute to it* to the BALM's *you **can** contribute to their recovery.* The entire BALM program teaches families how to contribute to a loved one's (and their own) recovery. Additionally, the 5th, 6th and 7th C further define the BALM's unique approach, recognizing the family's deep connection to their loved one, the ability to learn to communicate effectively with someone involved in the struggle, and the understanding that the family member is always at choice.

BALM 12 Principles — BALM 12 Principles that provide the information families need to help themselves and their families to recover. See Appendix I for a summary of each principle.

BALM Conversation — Developed by Beverly Buncher, author of the BALM Family Recovery Method. A brief mini-intervention which is loving and factual that a family member can have with their loved one to share what the family member is seeing and hearing the loved one say and do.

A BALM conversation, though originated to help a loved one who is struggling with a use disorder, can occur in any situation where one person shares the facts of what another person is saying or doing or experiencing, especially when what is being seen or heard is dangerous, difficult, or otherwise of concern to the person initiating the conversation.

Interventionists have referred to BALM Conversations as 'daily mini-interventions' that families provide for their loved one to help their loved one wake up to the facts of their usage and the trouble it is causing. It is said that when families hold BALM conversations regularly, their loved one can gets a clear picture of the consequences of their behavior without judgment or malice.

These conversations help the loved one to put the pieces together of their own use and draw conclusions that could lead them to make changes in their own life. Often used in concert with Motivational Interviewing and the Six Stages of Change model, families can reach their loved one powerfully and make a difference earlier than they could without these tools.

The BALM Program — BALM 12 Principles and 7 Steps to BALM that outline all a family must know about how to help themselves and potentially their loved one. It is what this book is about. To learn more, visit our website at:

http://familyrecoveryresources.com.

Boundaries — what you will and won't live with. What you choose to have in your life and what you don't. Based on what is best for the person setting the boundary. Boundaries allow you to feel safe, to be in your loved one's life without their completely taking over your life. Don't set a boundary until you are determined to stick with it.

C

Calendar — The BALM invites new family members in the program to consider spending time working the BALM program before simply walking away from their struggling loved one. One method of making this more tenable is to get out a calendar, count forward three months and write "How are things now?" Then look forward six, nine and 12 months forward from now and write the same question. Once you have done so, know that though you can walk away, you are going to give family recovery a chance to make a difference and get to work using whatever help you need to make it work in your family. (See It Takes What It Takes below)

Calm — Another way of saying *Be The Peace*, being calm is both the goal and the starting point of the Be A Loving Mirror method. On the basis of calm perspective, a family member can potentially have a powerful positive impact on their loved one and on their family's recovery.

Clear/Unclear Process — A process of looking at a situation that is troubling and dividing everything about it into those things you know for sure and those you just think you know and those you are completely unclear about. BALM Coaches teach their clients how to move through this process and most clients find themselves increasing their level of sanity as a result of fewer things rattling around in the unknown category unconsciously. See the Clear/Unclear Chart in this book on page 41–42

Connection — The BALM 5th C is: *You are* **connected** *to your loved one on a level that transcends their struggles.* Recognizing this deep connection is a powerful way to fight the effect of stigma on your state of mind and your family. It can also help you remember the good memories of your loved one from before their use disorder took hold and brought chaos to your family.

D

Denial — In the language of the Prochaska method of the 6 Stages of Change, this is referred to as precontemplation, the state of believing everything is fine and there is no problem. Denial often persists until a negative consequence occurs, but often that is not enough to break the spell of "I got this!" Many times it also takes others in the person's sphere of influence intervening either with powerful questions or a loving rendition of the facts of what the person is saying or doing (a BALM conversation or other brief intervention) in order to wake them up.

Denial Is the Glue of the Addictive System — The family of a using loved one is often referred to as an addictive system when the addiction is ignored, accommodated, or handled in a way that does not consistently, lovingly, insist on change and do the follow through to be the loved one's best chance of making that change.

For that reason, we have the BALM saying that 'Denial is the glue of the addictive system.' This means that when everyone is in denial, the addiction or brain disorder is supported in the using loved one's life. As each person in the system (whether one at a time or together) faces the situation and stops believing the untruths that are holding the system in place, it starts to crumble.

For instance, if a family member says, "I notice you have drug paraphernalia in your bathroom." And the loved one says, "so what? That isn't mine." A family member can say, "Okay, thanks for clearing that up" and the system stays in place. OR they can say, "I also noticed the tracks on your arms and I am aware that the needle and syringe belong to you." When the loved one says, "What? Are you crazy? I told you I don't use anymore. You are making this up." A family member in denial or not wanting to confront or make a scene may say, "Ok. Thought I'd check."

Whereas a BALMer who has made a commitment to eradicating the addictive system in their family will say, "Sweetheart. I love you so much. And, I no longer believe your words. Instead, I believe my eyes and my ears." When this is said lovingly, without malice, accusation, anger, or fear, it can go under the radar of the loved one's denial directly from the heart of the family member to the heart of the loved one.

Detach — While this has historically mean to move away from the person physically or at least emotionally, the BALM defines detachment as moving away from one's own obsession with controlling the outcome. BALMers are invited to let go (or emotionally detach from) the result they so desperately desire for their loved one, while continuing to work toward its achievement in the calm, logical and evidence-based manner recommended by the BALM program and its coaches.

Detox — The process of detoxifying from one's drug of choice. Also refers to place a person detoxing goes to during the process of detoxification prior to treatment. The amount of time a person spends in detox depends on their level of toxicity based on the substances used, how much they used and for how long. This is a clinical decision. Not every drug requires a stay in a detox for detoxification. Alcohol, opioids and benzodiazepines do but cocaine, crystal meth, and marijuana do not. For more information on this and other topics of concern, call the SAMHSA (Substance Abuse and Mental Health Services Administration) National Help Hotline at 1800-662-HELP.

E

Enabling — anything you do that makes it easier for your loved one to use their substance or other disordered process. This can include getting them their drug, giving them money for their drug, giving them a ride to get to their substance, giving them free rent or other needs when they have income they could be using, providing ease at a time when a stretch in taking personal responsibility would make it easier to attain or stay in recovery than it would be to use.

Enabling vs. Helping — Not enabling is about discouraging use. Helping is about encouraging recovery. Our approach to enabling and helping requires a compassionate heart, the approach that respects encouraging personal responsibility with a clear understanding of what the particular individual in recovery needs and can and cannot do. This is not about pushing a person beyond their limits in areas where they may have educational gaps or developmental gaps. There can be a fine line here. If you are not sure where the thing you want to help with is enabling or helping, we recommend you speak with a BALM coach.

F

Flooding — A phenomenon that occurs when upset. A person who is flooding experiences their blood rushing to their feet, rapid heartbeat and, often, confusion and lack of logic and physical balance. Family members often flood when upset by a using loved one's behavior. There are things you can do to avoid or reverse flooding. See page 121 to learn more. Originally developed by Marriage and Family Therapist John Gottman, flooding has been further developed and explained by Andra Madea in her book *Conflict Unraveled: Solving Problems at Work and Home.*

H

Harm Reduction — We all reduce harm from various risky behaviors in our lives. Everytime you use a seat belt, you are reducing the harm of driving in a car. Everytime you skip dessert or control portions, you are reducing harm that extra sugar or larger portions could bring.

When it comes to substance use disorder, reducing harm can come in the form of structured moderation or total abstinence, or in the form of MAT (medically assisted treatment) where a doctor, treatment center or medical team determine an alternative medication to treat the drug the patient is currently using.

While Harm Reduction has been very controversial in the US, it has been implemented in Europe for years and in light of the epidemic of opioid overdose deaths (64,000 in 2017), this method is being recommended more often in mainstream addiction medicine. For more on harm reduction, see references below for Denning's *Over the Influence: The Harm Reduction Guide to Managing Drugs and Alcohol Use.*

Helping — anything you do that supports your loved one in their recovery journey toward health and wholeness. If your loved one has challenges, especially in early recovery, in organizing their brains and need assistance in things like: transitioning from treatment to outpatient, figuring out how to get to meetings without a car, resume writing, job search, etc., these could easily be things appropriate to help them with. Early recovery is often such a maze for new recoverers that it becomes an impediment to sustained recovery rather than a help.

Hitting Rock Bottom — Though this used to be a goal for struggling loved ones in order to help them wake up to the need to get clean and sober, this is a no longer tenable goal now that overdose is so prevalent. Today, we work with families to raise their bottom so that they begin implementing the tools and practices that will help raise their loved one's bottom with the goal of ending active use as soon as possible.

I

International Coach Federation — the premier accrediting organization for Professional Life Coaches and Life Coach Training Schools. The **BALM** Institute for Family Recovery

Life Coach Training is the first **ICF**-Accredited Coach Training Program to focus on the family recovery field.

Intervention — a planned and structured process of conversation with family and loved one, often led by a professional Interventionist for the purpose of helping the family convince their loved one to take positive steps toward recovery. **BALM** Conversations have been called daily mini-interventions. (See **BALM** Conversations above).

L

Learn to Cope — a support network located throughout the state of Massachusetts with satellites located in Florida and other places around the US. Started by Joanne Peterson, Learn to Cope provides in-person support and a crisis website for families affected by the opioid epidemic.

Letting Go without Giving Up or Giving In — This pivotal **BALM** concept (Principle 3) guides family members to let go not of their loved one, but with their obsession with getting their loved one to do what they want them to do. By letting go of obsessive thinking, family members then focus their attention on what the most effective actions are to help their loved one and do them, without giving into their using loved one's manipulations.

Leverage — A form of negotiation that a family can utilize with their loved one. To apply it well, have an idea of what will be most helpful for your loved one's recovery (your loved one's **BALM** coach and/or treatment center can help you with determining this and implementation. Basically you are encouraging your loved one to do what is best for their recovery in order to get what they want.

Anyone who has something the loved one wants, needs, depends on or values, can use leverage to encourage the individual to move forward in their recovery. Leverage is often used to help a loved one decide to go to treatment, to stay in treatment, or to move into recovery residence after treatment. Many family members do not realize how much leverage they truly have.

There is an exercise in this book to help you determine that and a large part of lesson one of the **BALM** 12 Principles Course is about how to figure out what your leverage may be.

Caveat: Use leverage sparingly and often in collaboration with your loved one's professionals. It is best applied in a calm tone without judgment, anger, or malice, as is everything you do with your loved one and everyone in your life.

Life Coaching — What It Is and What It Is Not — Life Coaching is a non-clinical helping modality guided by the client's goals and agenda. The coach is an interactive partner with their client, well trained to ask powerful questions, listen deeply and deeply reflect in order to help the client to go deeply within themselves in order to move forward powerfully in their lives.

Life Coaches begin with the premise that the client is healthy and whole and sees the client as their best self, and use their substantial skill set to help the client achieve the goals they came to coaching for.

Life Coaching is not therapy, mentoring, or consulting, though many life coaches may have dual certifications/ specialties in any of these other modalities. See FAQ on Life Coaching in Appendix III.

BALM Life Coaching, which offers substantive **ICF** Life Coach Training along with our special understanding of the **BALM** Programs, provides those who work with those impacted by their own or a loved one's use disorder, with powerful insight, education and skill to do so. To see an FAQ on how the **BALM** makes family recovery life coaching powerful, see Appendix III.

Limits — Limits are rules with consequences. Parents have legal obligations to care for and have authority over their minor children up to the age of majority. Thus, limits are most appropriate when dealing with a loved one who is a minor as they are based on an understanding that the adult has the final say.

Once the individual with an SUD has reached the age of majority (which varies from state to state) leverage becomes the more appropriate approach to encourage the loved one to move in the direction of recovery.

BALM conversations, motivational conversations and understanding of the stages of change can all help a family to reach through to their loved one where yelling, screaming and begging have failed. Often, it is helpful to bring professionals into the mix to help you determine the best approach and next steps.

Loved one — the loved one is what we in the BALM say when referring to the person struggling with or recovered from struggling with a use disorder or other addictive process.

M

Mindfulness — Also known as *Be the Peace You Wish to See in the World* (Step One of the 7 Steps to BALM) is defined as being aware of oneself and one's surroundings in each moment without fear or upset about the past or future. It is a peaceful state of being that is the result of daily practice of inner work as defined by the **BALM** Program.

Motivational Interviewing — developed by Robert Miller (Miller, et. al) to help counselors have conversations that encourage recovery through a loving approach and a loving relationship. Though not the same as a BALM conversation, a motivational conversation is designed to help the loved one go deep within to move themselves toward the change they wish to achieve.

This is not a trick method to 'get one to do what you want them to do.' Rather, it is a way of interacting that allows the person being interviewed to uncover and move in the direction of their own best outcomes. See page 123 for more information

My Business, His/Her Business, God's Business — This activity is designed to help the family member understand that they are not responsible for everything in their loved one's life, that in fact, their most important job is to determine what they are and are not responsible for and to, as one of our BALM Coaches Jackie says time and again, "Stay In your own hoola hoop!" *(go to page 326 to get the link to download this chart).*

N

Naloxone — medicine that reverses opioid overdose. Can be administered by trained family members, EMT's or ER staff. Also known by its brand name NarCan.

O

Opioid Overdose Epidemic — this epidemic killed over 64,000 people in 2017, making it one of the deadliest epidemics in US history.

P

The Power of One — While BALM or any family recovery program is optimal when done by the entire family, BALM believes in the Power of One, meaning, if only one family member begins to practice the Be A Loving Mirror Program, the results can greatly impact the person practicing BALM, along with other family members and the struggling loved one. Often, we will see one person practicing BALM and then another joins and another and another. For that reason, the BALM membership is a full family membership so that everyone can join in if and when they are ready.

Prevention is Early Intervention — No matter if you are reading this book when your loved one is 15 and just starting to use or 60 and relapsing again, you have the potential to possibly prevent worse problems by getting involved now in your BALM recovery process and learning how to do whatever you can to prevent further use. You can shorten the timeline by getting help *now*!

R

Raising the Bottom — At BALM we are all about raising your, and thus your loved one's, bottom, making life in the family illness or the SUD more difficult to sustain. As we teach you about SUD, enabling, denial, and how your dysfunctional responses can contribute to your loved one's malady and potentially to their demise, you become more open to finding new ways to relate and begin to move toward recovery. Then, as you relate to your loved one with leverage, boundaries, loving communication, helping and *not* enabling, you make it easier for them to choose recovery and more difficult for them to continue active use. Thus, their bottom has been raised, making it less likely that they will keep falling toward that rock bottom from which, more and more today, there seems to be less and less chance of return. Our goal is to raise your bottom so that you will have a better chance of being able to raise theirs.

Recovery — healing and moving away from active use or behavior. BALM Recovery for a family comes when the family begins to get their lives back and as they learn new ways to interact with each other and their struggling loved ones.

Recovery Residence — a place recovering persons can go in order to live in a drug-free, safe environment with some structure and supervision and usually a requirement that the residents support themselves through outside work while also attending recovery meetings and, sometimes, aftercare services.

Due to the challenges that some traditional halfway houses and sober living environments have had with continually providing a safe drug free environment, both national and state certification boards emerged to ensure safe environments for the newly recovering.

These certified recovery residences follow national or state standards, and are accredited and followed by those accrediting them. A listing of certified recovery residences can be found at narronline.org, the National Alliance of Recovery Residences site. This is a relatively new alliance and the website has a map showing which states have certified recovery residences, which don't and where some are in the process.

Relapse — A lapse in one's consistent recovery. Can occur in the person using the substance as well as in the family member in BALM recovery.

Recycling — Prochaska's term for a person who finds him or herself starting over in their recovery process (relapsing).

S

Self Inquiry — a form of self-questioning designed to help one point to where the stress is coming from (one's thinking process) and where peace is (being present to this moment).

Seven Steps to BALM — The core process of the BALM Method of Family Recovery. The first three steps create a self-transformation within the BALMer which makes way for the transformation in communication and relationship with the loved one and others outlined in steps four through seven. This process is also known as the pearl of the BALM program as it is something both beautiful and hidden within the challenge of being in relationship with someone with a use disorder. The result of working these seven steps is that the family member becomes a BALMer and in the process becomes their loved one's **best** chance at recovery.

Smart Recovery — An educational support network for those with SUD that emphasizes Cognitive Behavioral techniques and tools along with the support of others in recovery. Meetings are held locally around the country and can be found online at smartrecovery.org

Six Stages of Change Model of Change — Developed by James Prochaska and DiClemente, this transtheoretical model of change focuses on when specific interventions, called catalysts for change, will help a person move from one stage to the next on their change journey. See pages 88 for more information.

Stay in Present Time — An Al-Anon slogan designed to remind the family member to let go of obsessive thinking and stay in the present moment.

Substance Use Disorder — the current nomenclature used to describe the brain disorder previously known as substance abuse or addiction. This name is designed to reduce stigma and recognize that it is not the person's fault they have this challenge, rather it is a result of something that happens to some people's brains as a result of use of substances.

T

Transformation — a change within a BALMer that happens as a result of working the BALM program, particularly the Seven Steps to Be A Loving Mirror which are known as the transformation piece of the BALM program.

Treatment — the term used to describe the help that is recommended for a person struggling with use disorder or the family malady. Can be inpatient, outpatient, clinical, behavioral, or non-clinical. Can include aftercare, recovery life coaching, and be online or in person. The longer the entire treatment process from inpatient through outpatient aftercare and non clinical coaching is provided, the greater chance the person has of sustaining their recovery. A year minimum is recommended though early recovery can last between two and five years.

True Purpose® — Created by Tim Kelley and laid out in this book True Purpose (see reference list), this program is designed to coach participants to find the purpose they are meant to live in this life. The entire BALM program arose out of Bev's True Purpose® work over a several year period under the tutelage of Tim Kelley and his team of coaches and trainers at the True Purpose Institute. Bev's own work as a Certified True Purpose Coach (**CTPC**) led her to develop the Life Purpose in Recovery Program™ which is simply True Purpose® work for people in recovery.

Twelve Step Anonymous Programs — originally developed by Bill W., Dr. Bob and the original 100 recovering alcoholics, this abstinence based program was designed to provide alcoholics with a 3 prong approach to a psychic change through spiritual surrender, self-inventory/cleaning house, and helping others. Over the years the 12 steps have been applied to every use disorder/addiction under the sun. Many BALM ideas arose from the author's experience as a 12 step sponsee and sponsor, as well as from evidence-based practice, mindfulness, personal study and coaching.

Tough Love — an approach to helping addicts based on a concept of applying negative consequences with the loved one in order to encourage them to change. The BALM does *not* utilize or support a tough love approach. To learn more about the loving approach of the BALM, read this book.

Two Prong Approach — The BALM Program has a two-prong approach to family recovery: 1) get your life back and 2) help your loved one get their life back.

Three Components of BALM — The three components of BALM are Information, Transformation, and Support. *Information* consists of online conferences that have resulted in 400 recordings and 400 handouts designed to teach families about the 12 BALM Principles from the perspective of BALM lessons, expert interviews with professionals in the field of SUD treatment, family members and persons in long term recovery. *Transformation* is the inner change that people who study and practice the 7 Steps to BALM. *Support* is the one on one and group coaching available to members of the BALM community as they grow in their understanding of BALM recovery and BALM Family Recovery.

U

Use Disorders — Previously known as addictions, use disorders come in many forms: Alcohol Use Disorder, Substance Use Disorder, Gambling Use Disorder, Food Use Disorder, Sex Use Disorder, etc. "The Diagnostic and Statistical Manual of Mental Disorders, Fifth Edition (DSM-5), no longer uses the terms substance abuse and substance dependence, rather it refers to substance use disorders, which are defined as mild, moderate, or severe to indicate the level of severity, which is determined by the number of diagnostic criteria met by an individual." (https://www.samhsa.gov/disorders/substance-use)

Resources

Al-Anon Family Group Headquarters, Inc. 1971. *The Dilemma of the Alcoholic Marriage.* Virginia Beach, VA: Al-Anon Family Group Headquarters, Inc.

Al-Anon Family Group Headquarters, Inc. 1992. *Courage to Change: One Day at a Time in Al-Anon II.* Virginia Beach, VA: Al-Anon Family Group Headquarters, Inc.

Alcoholics Anonymous World Services, Inc. 2001. *Alcoholics Anonymous: The Story of How Many Thousands of Men and Women Have Recovered from Alcoholism.* Fourth ed. New York: World Services, Inc.

Alter, A. 2017. *Irresistible: The Rise of Addictive Technology and the Business of Keeping Us Hooked.* New York: Penguin Press.

American Psychiatric Association. (2013). *Diagnostic and statistical manual of mental disorders (5th ed.).* Arlington, VA: American Psychiatric Publishing.

Bassett, L. 1995. *From Panic to Power: Proven Techniques to Calm Your Anxieties, Conquer Your Fears, and Put You in Control of Your Life.* New York: HarperCollins Publishers.

Beattie, M. 1990. *Codependents' Guide to the Twelve Steps: How to Find the Right Program for You and Apply Each of the Twelve Steps to Your Own Issues.* New York: Fireside.

Beattie, M. 1990. *The Language of Letting Go: Daily Meditations on Codependency.* Center City, MN: Hazelden Publishing.

Brown, S., and V. Lewis. 1999. *The Alcoholic Family in Recovery: A Developmental Model.* New York: The Guilford Press.

Brown, S., V. Lewis, and A. Liotta. 2000. *The Family Recovery Guide: A Map for Healthy Growth.* Oakland, CA: New Harbinger Publications, Inc.

Chapman, G. 2008. *Love as a Way of Life: Seven Keys to Transforming Every Aspect of Your Life.* Colorado Springs, CO: WaterBrook Press.

Denning, P., J. Little, and A. Glickman. 2004. *Over the Influence: The Harm Reduction Guide for Managing Drugs and Alcohol.* New York: The Guilford Press.

Fletcher, A. 2013. *Inside Rehab: The Surprising Truth About Addiction Treatment — and How to Get Help That Works.* New York: Penguin Group.

Grant, A., and S. Sandberg. 2017. *Option B: Facing Adversity, Building Resilience, and Finding Joy.* New York: Alfred A. Knopf.

Izzo, J. 2008. *The Five Secrets You Must Discover Before You Die.* San Francisco: Berrett-Koehler Publishers, Inc.

Johnson, A. 2016. *The Little Book of Big Change: The No-Willpower Approach to Breaking Any Habit.* New Harbinger Publications, Inc.

Katherine, A. 2000. *Where to Draw the Line: How to Set Healthy Boundaries Every Day.* New York: Fireside.

Kelley, T. 2009. *True Purpose: 12 Strategies for Discovering the Difference You Are Meant to Make.* Berkeley, CA: Transcendent Solutions Press.

Kelly, J. F. 2013. *The Science of Addiction Recovery Mutual Aid: An Interview with John F. Kelly, PhD.* By W. White. Selected Papers of William L. White. http://www.williamwhitepapers.com/pr/Dr.%20John%20Kelly.pdf.

Kiloby, Scott.2017. *Natural Rest for Addiction: A Radical Approach to Recovery Through Mindfulness and Awareness.* Oakland, CA: Non-Duality Press.

MacLeod, A. 2007. *The Instruction: Living the Life Your Soul Intended.* Boulder, CO: Sounds True.

Medea, A. 2005. *Conflict Unraveled: Fixing Problems at Work and in Families.* Chicago: Pivot Point Press.

Miller, W. R., and S. Rollnick. 2012. *Motivational Interviewing: Helping People Change.* Third ed. New York: The Guilford Press.

Nepo, M. 2012. *Seven Thousand Ways to Listen: Staying Close to What Is Sacred.* New York: Free Press.

Neufeld, G., and G. Mate. 2014. *Hold On to Your Kids: Why Parents Need to Matter More Than Peers.* New York: Ballantine Books Trade Paperback.

Orloff, J. 2017. *The Empath's Survival Guide: Life Strategies for Sensitive People.* Boulder, CO: Sounds True.

Patent, A. M. 1995. *You Can Have It All: A Simple Guide to a Joyful and Abundant Life.* Hillsboro, OR: Beyond Words Publishing, Inc.

Pliskin, Zelig. *Gateway to Happiness.* Bnai Yakov. 1983

Prochaska, J., J. C. Norcross, and C. C. DiClemente. 2006. *Changing for Good: A Revolutionary Six-Stage Program for Overcoming Bad Habits and Moving Your Life Positively Forward.* New York: Harper.

Prochaska, James, and Janice Prochaska. 2016. *Changing to Thrive: Using the Stages of Change to Overcome the Top Threats to Your Health and Happiness.* Center City, MN: Hazelden.

Progoff, I. 1992. *At a Journal Workshop: Writing to Access the Power of the Unconscious and Evoke Creative Ability.* New York: Putnam.

Rubin, G. 2015. *Better Than Before: Mastering the Habits of Our Everyday Lives.* New York: Crown Publishers.

Sandella, D. 2016. *Goodbye, Hurt & Pain: 7 Simple Steps for Health, Love, and Success.* Newburyport, MA: Conari Press.

Tsilimparis, J., and D. D. Schwartz. 2014. *Retrain Your Anxious Brain: Practical and Effective Tools to Conquer Anxiety.* Don Mills, Ontario: Harlequin.

Index

C

H

Harm Reduction 48, 90, 95, 247, 248, 303, 315
Helping 5, 8, 11, 26, 28, 36, 39, 43, 44, 56, 59, 69, 77, 81, 88, 104–108, 114, 141, 146, 147, 150, 151, 153, 161, 162, 165, 177, 185, 199, 204, 208, 215, 219, 225, 234, 236, 239, 240, 255, 266, 268, 274, 286, 290, 296, 297, 302–305, 309, 312, 313, 316
Hitting Rock Bottom 304

I

Information 26, 75–77, 158, 163, 174, 179, 199, 231, 294, 295, 313
International Coach Federation 256, 288, 304
Intervention 68, 124, 129, 213, 225, 298, 300, 304, 308, 321
It Takes What It Takes 127, 128, 129, 140, 185, 263, 266, 299

J

Journal Your Way to BALM Recovery 125, 148

L

Learn to Cope 43, 193, 304
Letting Go 6, 27, 30, 34, 40, 93, 109, 156, 250, 260, 265, 273, 305, 315
Leverage 70, 78–81, 176, 206, 305, 306, 309
Life Coaching 1112, 147, 206, 216, 223, 234, 235, 238–240, 242, 254–256, 286–288, 291, 298, 305, 306, 312
Life Purpose in Recovery 149, 150, 217
Limits 71, 73, 81, 153, 302, 306
Loved One 115, 116, 173–186, 187–194, 263, 273, 274
Loving Path i, v, 19, 21-66, 128, 188, 257, 258, 259, 266, 267, 291, 291, 293, 294

M

Mindfulness 307
Motivational Interviewing xxiv, 123, 124, 248, 249, 255, 298, 307, 316
My Business, His/Her Business, God's Business 115, 263, 307

O

P

R

S

`T

U

This book is written by Beverly Buncher, Founder and CEO of Family Recovery Resources and the BALM Institute.

To learn more about our programs, visit our website at familyrecoveryresources.com or call us at 1888-998-BALM.

The BALM team will be more than willing to help you find the educational and/or coaching help that will empower you to move to the next level of your recovery and/or your recovery career.

Bev is also available to keynote at your next in-person event or online presentation. If you would like to speak with her personally, give her a call at 786 859 4050 or email her at bbuncher@familyrecoveryresources.com.

Our gift to you for purchasing this book, is to offer several of the charts and articles in and beyond the book to you for free. To download these, go to our thank you page at: https://goo.gl/Fn36Ax

Until we meet again, remember: Be A Loving Mirror!

ABOUT THE AUTHOR

Beverly Buncher, MA, PCC, CBC, CTPC, often referred to as the Foremost Family Recovery Life Coach in the Nation, is the Founder, Director, and CEO of the BALM Institute for Family Recovery Education and Coach Training. Utilizing techniques developed as a professional coach, teacher, educational administrator, and person with 30 years of personal family recovery experience, Bev developed the Be A Loving Mirror Family Recovery Method. The BALM Program is designed to make the tools of family recovery accessible to all whose lives are affected by a loved one's struggles with substance and other use disorders. A former teacher and school principal, Bev is married to Alan and has a step son, a daughter, and a two-year-old granddaughter who she loves building castles with and singing to sleep at night.

Made in the USA
Columbia, SC
04 October 2020